StoptheCar!

DISCOVERING CENTRAL ALBERTA

Stop the Car!

Judy Larmour & Henry Saley

BlueCOUCHBooks

National Library of Canada Cataloguing in Publication
Larmour, Judy, 1957-
Stop the car! : discovering central Alberta / Judy Larmour and Henry Saley.

Includes bibliographical references and index.
ISBN 1-894739-03-5

1. Alberta—Guidebooks. 2. Alberta—History, Local. 3. Historic sites—Alberta—Guidebooks.
4. Automobile travel—Alberta—Guidebooks. I. Saley, Henry, 1953- II. Title.

FC3657.L37 2004   917.123'3044   C2004-901519-2

Cover and interior photos by the authors unless otherwise indicated
Authors' photo: APN Photo
Maps: Robert Nichols

Authors' acknowledgments:
This project was a cooperative venture between the authors and Olds College.

The project was partially funded by the Alberta Historical Resources Foundation,
Buck for Wildlife, Ducks Unlimited, Watchable Wildlife Program, Shell Environmental Fund
and Alberta Sport, Recreation, Parks and Wildlife Foundation.

Every effort was made to ensure that the information contained in this book was accurate
at the time of printing. The publishers and the authors shall not be held liable for
the use or misuse of information contained in this book.

Blue Couch Books
an imprint of Brindle & Glass Publishing
www.brindleandglass.com

1   2   3   4   5   08   07   06   05   04

PRINTED AND BOUND IN CANADA ON ANCIENT-FOREST-FRIENDLY PAPER

We dedicate this book to Les and Darlene, our spouses.
They supported us with endless patience as we racked up the miles touring the region,
covered the kitchen table with county maps, and subjected them to endless
discussions of how to piece together this guidebook.

Table of Contents

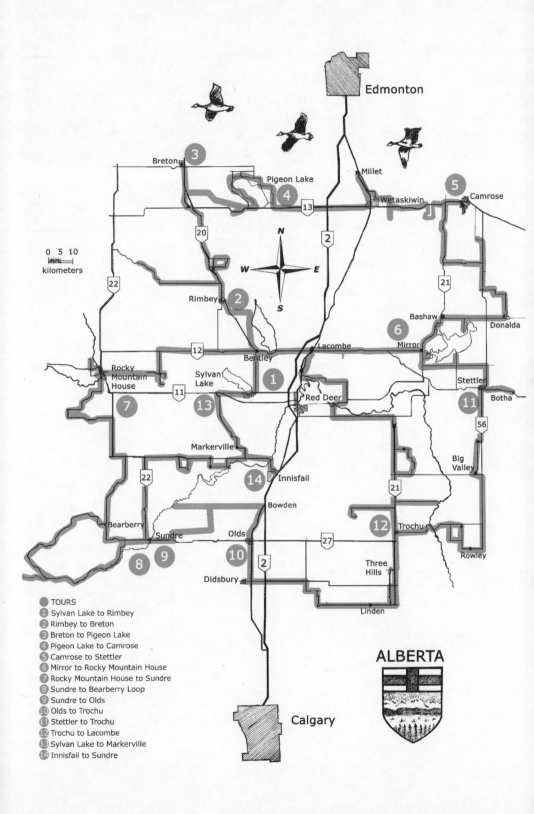

Edmonton

Breton ③

Pigeon Lake

Millet

④

Wetaskiwin

13

⑤ Camrose

0 5 10
kilometers

20

N

22

W   E

S

Rimbey ②

21

Bashaw

Donalda

⑥

Mirror

12

Lacombe

Bentley

Rocky
Mountain
House

Sylvan
Lake

①

Red Deer

Stettler

Botha

⑦

11

⑬

⑪

56

Markerville

Big
Valley

⑭ Innisfail

Bowden

22

21

Bearberry

Sundre

⑧   ⑨

Olds

⑫ Trochu

Rowley

⑩

27

2

Three
Hills

Didsbury

Linden

● TOURS
① Sylvan Lake to Rimbey
② Rimbey to Breton
③ Breton to Pigeon Lake
④ Pigeon Lake to Camrose
⑤ Camrose to Stettler
⑥ Mirror to Rocky Mountain House
⑦ Rocky Mountain House to Sundre
⑧ Sundre to Bearberry Loop
⑨ Sundre to Olds
⑩ Olds to Trochu
⑪ Stettler to Trochu
⑫ Trochu to Lacombe
⑬ Sylvan Lake to Markerville
⑭ Innisfail to Sundre

ALBERTA

Calgary

About this book

Stop the Car! will introduce you to the central Alberta landscape—both natural and human-made. When travelling, we often become focussed on destinations rather than what lies in between. We hope that these routes combine the pleasures of the journey with the satisfaction of a destination.

We take you to the best spots to experience nature, explore our historical roots, observe agriculture, and witness other aspects of the rural economy. We hope to pique your curiosity along the way and lure you to linger for a while.

The text of *Stop the Car!* includes:
- **Stops**: the best spots to stop with things to do, watch, learn, buy, and eat!
- **Along the Way**: descriptions of what may be seen from the car window
- **Digging Deeper**: background explanations of history, nature, agriculture, and industry
- **Featured Wildlife**: descriptions of the unique features of selected animals
- **Featured Plants**: descriptions of the unique features of selected plants
- **I Spy**: specific items to spot from the car window
- **Directions and Maps**: that show all routes with locations of stops

The driving tours described in this guidebook are organized as excursions and loops, which begin and end on major highways. We provide you with detailed directions and maps to take you off the beaten track with confidence.

Road patterns in rural Alberta reflect the original survey of the province on the township system that was calculated in miles (1 mile equals 1.6 km). Township roads run east–west every two miles, and range roads run north–south every mile—think of them as avenues and streets. Counties in central Alberta place signs at most intersections: Township Roads are marked as TWP and the first pair of numbers will get larger the further north you are. Range Roads are marked as RR and generally the first number will get higher as you go west. For areas in this book the range road sequence will repeat itself when you cross the Fifth Meridian that runs north–south extending through the middle of Gull Lake.

Simple? We thought so! But in fact each county has decided to number its roads signs on a slightly different system. It is possible to see RR 2–4 or RR 2.4 or RR 24! Similarly you may encounter signs that show township roads marked TWP 480 or TWP 48.0 or TWP 48–0. Natural obstacles often interrupt the grid system, some road allowances were never developed, and a few roads follow old trails that do not fit the grid. Do not worry—our directions match what you find on the signposts as you drive. We have given you distances in kilometres that allow you to set your odometer at will.

Start your adventure from anywhere you wish and combine the tours to suit your time and interests. Using a road map, you may link tour routes with other travel destinations you have in mind.

Although we have designed these tours to be taken in one direction, you may decide to drive a tour in reverse order. If you do, please skim through the entire tour first. You will then have a much easier time following the tours.

It is impossible to indicate how long any tour segment will take. Please judge for yourself by calculating the mileage involved and estimating the length of time to be spent at the various stops. Be prepared to find yourself wishing you had more time than allotted—as we did!

Every effort was made to ensure that the information contained in this book was accurate at the time of printing; however, as history tells us, everything is subject to change! When choosing a destination, please call ahead when possible to avoid disappointment, and use this book in conjunction with the latest official road maps.

Tips on Rural Driving

Rural roads are generally quiet but we would like to share basic things to make your trip more pleasant and safe.

- Wide loads and slow moving farm machinery are commonly encountered. Remember that farm machinery, such as a combine, moves very slowly and that you will overtake it almost as quickly as a stationary object. These vehicles have limited rearward vision so be sure that the driver has seen you before you pull out to pass.

- Cattle and other domestic animals sometimes stray onto the road. Always slow down when passing them as they may unexpectedly move in front of your vehicle. If you are lucky enough to see a cattle drive on the road, pull to the side and come to a complete stop until all the cattle have passed.

- Some of the tours include stretches of gravel road. Dry gravel roads are not slippery, but stopping distances are much longer than on pavement. Drive and brake accordingly.

- Take care when cresting hills or entering curves where vision is limited since a vehicle travelling in the middle of the road may be approaching.

- Take care when approaching all crossroads, especially those with equal right of way and more particularly where vision is poor because of trees.

- Most railway crossings are uncontrolled in rural areas and there is often poor vision to the track. It is safest to stop completely and check for trains before proceeding.

- Rural roads in central Alberta are generally maintained in good condition but it is always possible, especially in spring, to encounter a rutted or muddy section. Please pay attention to the road conditions ahead of you.

- The speed limit on secondary roads is generally eighty kilometres per hour unless otherwise marked.

- Avoid dawdling, sudden stops or unpredictable behavior while driving. Trucks with long stopping distances may be close behind.

- Watch out for crossing wildlife! Speeding vehicles frequently kill coyotes, skunks and porcupines. Larger animals such as moose and deer are a major hazard. Pay close attention at dusk when animals are more likely to be encountered.

The Country Code

Rural driving can be a relaxing, rewarding experience with none of the pressures or urgency of major highway or urban driving. Nevertheless, vigilance and care are necessary to make your trip safe.

- Vehicles other than cars use rural roads and you are expected to give way to most of them. Most rural drivers attempt to make it as easy as possible for farmers to move machinery or conduct cattle drives. Stop and enjoy the scenery until such obstacles no longer present a problem. It is considered unseemly to appear in a hurry at such times and rural residents seldom sound their horn or attempt to proceed before it is clear to do so.

- When parking off a rural road try to choose a spot that will not block access to a field or farmyard, or block the road for oversize machinery traffic. Be sure to park in a level area where your vehicle can be clearly seen for some distance from both directions. It is best not to park on the shoulder as many are narrow or steep; if possible, move your vehicle completely off the road.

- Be courteous when passing pedestrians or other cars, especially on gravel roads. Flying gravel and dust from high-speed traffic is unpleasant and dangerous. If you are the one at the side of the road, be cautious and watch children carefully to keep them from harm's way.

• None of the activities or sights in this book suggests that you walk on private property. Please remember that farmers do not want you to walk across pasture for a good reason. It results in uneven grazing patterns, since cattle avoid places where people walk. Climbing fences results in weakened or broken wire. Remember never to leave a gate open.

• If you drive into a farmyard, park on the worn ground and walk to the house. You would not want someone driving on your lawn! You will find that rural people will be very helpful in getting you back on track if you should become lost.

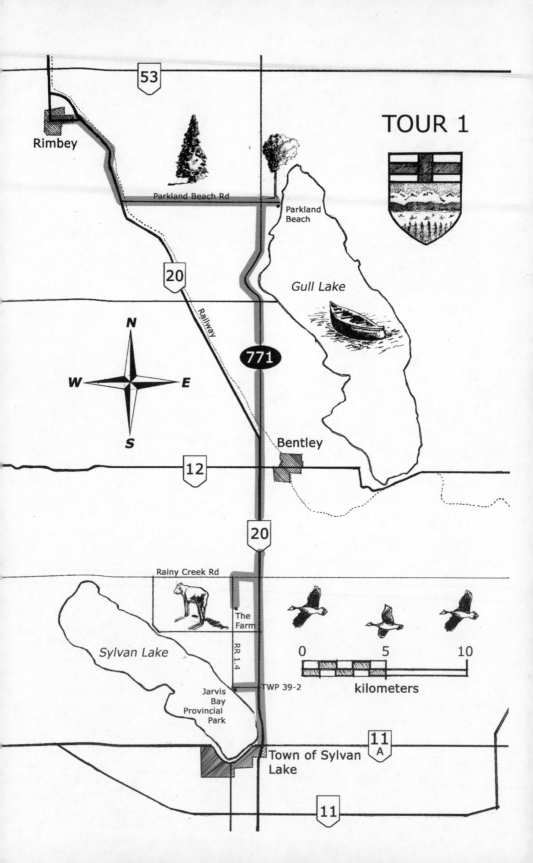

Sylvan Lake to Rimbey

DIRECTIONS: Take HWY 20 north from the junction with HWY 11A just before you come to Sylvan Lake town (for Sylvan Lake itself see page 201) and follow the signs for Jarvis Bay Provincial Park (west on TWP 39-2).

STOP: Jarvis Bay Provincial Park

Jarvis Bay is the best place to view Sylvan Lake in a natural setting. Sylvan Lake is deemed shallow, but that description does not hold true in comparison to most Alberta lakes. It reaches a maximum of about eighteen metres, whereas nearby Gull Lake has a depth of less than eight metres. Although incoming and outgoing streams flow only intermittently, springs with high concentrations of sodium and magnesium from the surrounding watershed feed the lake. These minerals help to inhibit green algae blooms, which torment swimming enthusiasts at many other lakes during hot summer spells.

Pick up a map at the permit booth when you enter the park. Take the first right and park at the shower building. To the left of the building a hiking trail leads past the amphitheatre and onto the North Gorge Trail. This

The red squirrel stays active during every month of the year.
PETER LLEWELLYN / SPLIT SECONDS

1

aspen forest has very dense undergrowth, dominated by hazelnut shrubs. Look for the jagged edges of its leaves and the nuts, which grow in pairs. They are covered with fuzzy green skins ending in "beaks." Hence the name: beaked hazelnut.

The nuts of this shrub are so popular with wildlife, especially squirrels and deer, that you may have a difficult time finding them. Challenge your family or travelling partners to see who can find one first! When you do, pick and skin it to see how closely it resembles a store-bought hazelnut. Yes, they are edible, although they taste much better roasted over a campfire.

The trail is an orchard of nuts and berries. You will find saskatoon, chokecherry, pincherry, and cranberry. Look also for the brilliant orange flower of the western wood lily, which blooms from June to July along the woodland edges of the trail.

The trail soon reaches the lakeside cliffs of Sylvan Lake, where a viewing deck overhangs the precipice. This is an excellent vantage point to watch people and wildlife.

DIRECTIONS: Retrace your route to HWY 20 and continue north.

ALONG THE WAY: Draped Moraine

Heading north on Highway 20, the road begins to climb the slopes of a draped moraine. An apt name, since just as a decorative throw is draped over a couch, glaciers left a thin layer of till (approximately three metres) over the landscape. That still doesn't explain the large size of the hill. For that explanation, we must go back in history long before the glaciers. These hills contain rock from as far back as 65 million years ago, when massive rivers and inland seas deposited thick layers of sand and gravel into the province. During that time the Rocky Mountains were being thrust upward, and they provided much of the loose gravel being washed in by water. Essentially, you are driving over scraps from the Rocky Mountains, left here as great mounds of debris.

After the Aspelund Road turnoff at the crest of the hill, the terrain flattens into the valley of the Blindman River, where you may enjoy views of several spectacular river meanders on the east side of the highway.

DIRECTIONS: West on Rainy Creek Road for 1.6 KM, and then south for 2 KM on RR 1-4.

STOP: "The Farm"

"The Farm" is home to Pat Matheson's ceramic studio and gallery, where he produces raku-fired ceramics with metallic-like glazes. Imagine pulling white-hot clay pieces out of a kiln and plunging them into smoking news-paper—that's part of the magic of raku, which has Japanese origins. "Each piece is unique and the unexpected happens," Matheson explains. On sum-mer weekends Matheson often has his Mum's watercolours, his Dad's old barnwood creations, and his sister's bent willow furniture on display. If he has time, Matheson loves to give tours of his family homestead, complete with a blacksmith shop and 1902 barn, and which boasts the best outhouse in western Canada. Judge for yourself!

Open by appointment.

Tel: (403) 748-2557

I *SPY*: Meander in the Blindman River

Rivers meander or "snake" their way through flat terrain. The slow-moving water winds back and forth as it takes the easiest route by cutting its way through the softest soils and bedrock.

As the illustration shows, the future path of the river will eventually be shifted downstream. That is because the faster-flowing water on the outside edge of each curve cuts away at the banks while sand and silt is deposited by the slower-moving waters at the inside edge of each curve.

During a flood, the river may take a shortcut between the loops, cut-ting off a portion of the river. That abandoned river loop becomes known as an oxbow lake.

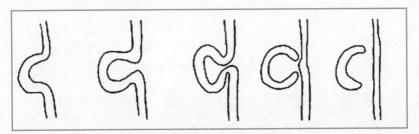

Meandering river and oxbow lake.

DIRECTIONS: Continue north past Bentley through the junction with HWY 12. After 3 KM, take HWY 771 to the northeast, following the shoreline of Gull Lake.

ALONG THE WAY: Gull Lake

You will enjoy scenic views of Gull Lake on the east side of the highway, and the rolling farmland of the Blindman River Valley on the west side.

Gull Lake is the remnant of a much larger lake formed by the melting of glacial ice. Glacial rivers flowed around or cut down through the ice, forming meltwater channels. The Blindman River occupies one of these ancient channels.

There was never a permanent inlet to the lake; it is fed by runoff and by underground springs. At one time water did exit from the south, draining to the Red Deer River, but that stream dried up long ago due to a serious drop in water levels. Between 1924 and 1975, the lake dropped 2.6 metres!

Today, Gull Lake may be categorized as a very large slough that seems to be maintaining an acceptable level of water quality. The lake is well-used for recreation with five campgrounds, numerous cottages, and camps distributed all along the shoreline, except for the extreme north end. There, dense populations of weeds, cattails, and bulrushes create ideal habitat for waterfowl, gulls, and other birds. Gull Lake is a major stopping area for migrating birds, many of them staying to nest.

The highway takes you past several lakeside communities: Birch Bay, Sunnyside, Poulson's Pasture, and Parkland Beach.

HISTORIC *POINT* OF INTEREST: Logging on Gull Lake

What did the good ship *Kangaroo* do on this lake? Stop at the historic point of interest pullout, where the road curves at Birch Bay, to find out.

DIRECTIONS: Turn east on TWP 422 (Parkland Beach Road) and follow it to the end.

STOP: Parkland Beach

Parkland Beach is one of the recreational hot spots on Gull Lake, offering many services for those wishing to enjoy lake activities for the day or longer. Campgrounds are located on both sides of the road and concessions offer summer treats.

When the road reaches the lake, turn right into the Provincial Recreation Area. Park your vehicle and walk south along the shore until

Camp, walk, and swim along the shores of Gull Lake.

you reach a fence with an opening for pedestrians. You will soon encounter a red shale trail that leads you to the public beach, complete with playground equipment, pit toilets, and sand.

FEATURED WILDLIFE: Gulls

At Gull Lake, you will see gulls that migrate from California and Mexico to nest at the lake. They are particularly obvious when they try to steal the sandwiches from your picnic table! The gull is a scavenger that eats just

about anything classified as food, providing it fits into its mouth: duck eggs, mice, insects, garbage, roadkill, worms, small shorebirds, and even clams. Owing to their omnivorous eating habits, they are important as "cleaner-uppers" of the lakeshore.

Ring-billed gulls are the most frequently seen birds of the summer.
PETER LLEWELLYN / SPLIT SECONDS

The most common gulls in the area are the white-headed ring-billed gull, the herring gull and the California gull. Black-headed gulls include Bonaparte's gull and Franklin's gull. Do not mistake them for terns, which have a different way of flying and a forked tail. Always on the lookout for fish and insects, the tern keeps its bill pointed downward as it scans the water.

Gulls that have brown speckles all over their feathers are not a different species. They are the young born earlier in the year. They do not grow those beautiful pure white feathers until their second year.

DIRECTIONS: Take Parkland Beach Road (TWP 422) west 9 KM to cross the railway line, once known as the "Peanut line," and rejoin HWY 20. After a short distance north, turn west into Rimbey at the sign.

DIGGING DEEPER: The Peanut Line

The "Peanut Line" replaced the stage wagon from Lacombe to Rimbey. Whatever its reputation, it was better than the sickening lurching over the muddy potholed trail, which often saw wagons bogged down to their axles. The Lacombe and Blindman Valley Electric Railway was incorporated in

1909, sponsored by merchants and farmers of Bentley and Rimbey, who petitioned and lobbied for a rail line. War delayed the construction schedule, but by 1917 the tracks had been laid as far as Bentley.

The first locomotive on the line was an oil turbine trolley car from England. This was replaced by a gasoline outfit, then an electric car nicknamed ".22 short" and later "The Peanut," before the introduction of more conventional rolling stock. The Lacombe and North Western Railway, as it was renamed in 1919, finally reached Rimbey in 1921. A station and two grain elevators to serve the town soon followed.

By 1929 the rail line had been extended through Hoadley, Winfield, and Breton. The Canadian Pacific Railway then bought it and completed the line to Leduc. The train was famous for its speed (averaging ten to twelve miles per hour), lack of adherence to a schedule, delays en route while the crew went hunting prairie chickens, and more tragically, derailments. Today the rail line only runs as far as Rimbey, onto a branch line serving the Rimbey Gas Plant.

The electric "Peanut" in 1919.
FRED SCHUTZ

STOP: Rimbey

"Rimbey—the Friendly International Town," reads the welcoming sign. There are indeed people from around the world living in Rimbey, but here "international" in fact refers to the International Truck collection at the Smithson Truck Museum at Pas-Ka-Poo Historical Park.

Kansas Ridge was the first name given to this fledgling community, as many of the settlers came from Kansas. Among them were the three Rimbey brothers, Sam, Ben, and Jim, for whom the town was soon named. A 1909 brochure declared Rimbey to "have every prospect of becoming a good town. It now has two stores, a large hotel, grist mill, saw mill, government creamery, school, Methodist Church, and Church of England."

THE GRAND HOTEL

Hardly grand, but strategically placed at a four-way stop, the coffee shop is the ideal spot to watch the comings and goings of small-town life and catch up on local gossip over coffee or a meal. This hotel is typical of many in central Alberta—farmers rub shoulders with business people and the local newspaper editor is always on the lookout for a story. Have yourself an old-fashioned milk shake.

Joe Morrisroe, affectionately known as "high-collar Joe" for the foam he left on the beer, opened the hotel as the Ben Franklin in 1947. In the 1950s when beer was king, and Alberta's liquor laws did not allow for hard liquor sales, the hotel was a busy place on a Saturday night. Waiters

The main street of Rimbey is sadly lacking its early buildings, due to fires and modernization. Many have even disappeared since town photographer Michael Jarmoluk took this photograph on the occasion of the Rimbey parade in 1954.
MICHAEL'S STUDIO ARCHIVES

with ties and white jackets served customers. Today the tubular 1950s-style chairs are gone, as is the separate "Ladies and Escorts" entrance, but the bar retains its attraction.

THE BEATTY HOUSE

Jack Beatty had a well-established hardware business by the time the railroad brought a minor economic boom and an influx of settlers. When his store, with living quarters above, burned to the ground in 1923, he built this house, set on the edge of town. In the 1920s this was the architectural design of the minute—California bungalow. The Beatty Heritage House Society has worked hard to bring the house back to its early appearance, even replicating the fine fieldstone wall, which was buried below the present grade of the sidewalk. Today the community uses the house for a variety of functions and at Christmas it is spectacularly lit up. You are welcome to sit in the summer shade of the garden and use the picnic tables.

PAS-KA-POO HISTORICAL PARK (0.7 KM north of four-way stop on HWY 20)

Have a picnic and visit the museum. Pick up a walking tour guide to the Park's historic buildings. Among them are five of Rimbey's early buildings

The Beatty House as it was in the late 1920s.
BEATTY HERITAGE HOUSE SOCIETY

that have been moved to the Park, including the 1902 school, the town office, Mowbray's butcher shop, and Spink's barber shop. Look for the Anglican Church of the Epiphany that once sat on Rimbey's Main Street. According to the specific wishes of the benefactor in far-off Britain who sent money for the church, Carpenter Ben Rimbey saw to its construction from vertical logs in 1908. A range of machinery is on view in two open machine sheds, and two museum display buildings hold a host of belongings from early settlers in the Rimbey area.

Open daily May 1–September 15 10:00 AM–6:00 PM

Tel: (403) 843-2004

Pas-Ka-Poo Historical Park.
APN PHOTO

The Park also hosts the Smithson Truck Museum, which boasts a complete collection of half-ton International trucks. You can compare the changing models over a forty-year span. The International truck collection is in a separate building, which also serves as a visitor centre for the town.

Open year-round daily 9:00 AM–5:00 PM

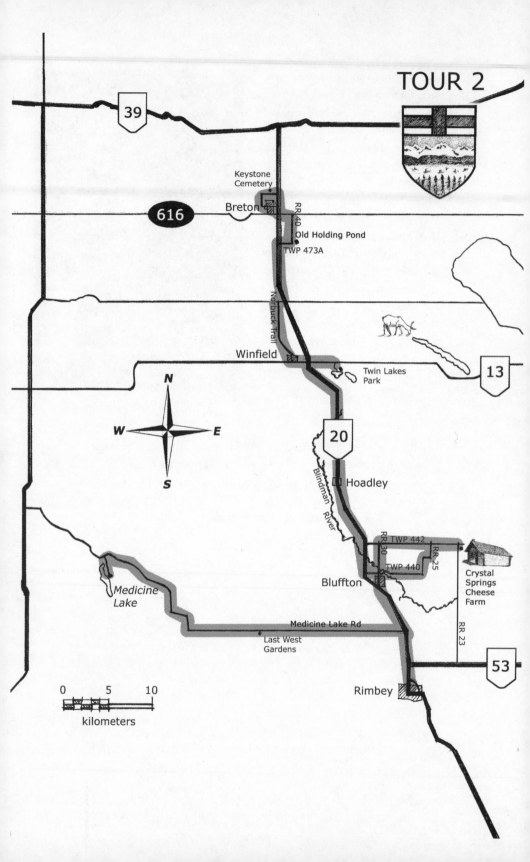

TOUR 2

39

Keystone
Cemetery

Breton

616

Old Holding Pond

RR 40

TWP 473A

Norbuck Trail

Winfield

13

Twin Lakes
Park

N
W   E
S

20

Blindman River

Hoadley

TWP 442

RR 30

RR 25

TWP 440

Bluffton

Crystal
Springs
Cheese
Farm

RR 23

Medicine
Lake

Medicine Lake Rd

Last West
Gardens

0   5   10
kilometers

Rimbey

53

Rimbey to Breton via Winfield

DIRECTIONS: Take HWY 20 north from Rimbey. After 6.6 KM, turn west at the sign onto Medicine Lake Road.

ALONG THE WAY: Roadside flora

On major highways, the roadsides are mowed regularly, keeping the highways tidy but bare. Along roads such as this, colourful blooms decorate the ditches with purples, yellows, blues, and white. When you see a particularly showy spot, park at the nearest pull-off and explore.

FEATURED *PLANT*: Goldenrod

The bright yellow blooms of goldenrod decorate the fields for many weeks in late summer. The goldenrod is a plant favoured by countless insects, including bees and butterflies, for its abundant supply of nectar. Insects carry pollen on their legs and bodies, unknowingly fertilizing other plants as they travel from one flower to another.

FEATURED *PLANT*: Prickly Rose

The prickly rose is seen everywhere in Alberta. It thrives in the open sun of roadside ditches but also favours growing at the margins of thick woods. The showy pink flowers are so typical of Alberta that it was named as Alberta's floral emblem. In winter, the bright red rosehips stand out in striking contrast to white drifts of snow. Wildlife such as squirrels and mice derive much-needed winter nutrition from the seeds of the rosehip fruit, and they can be steeped for a flavourful tea that contains high levels of vitamin C.

DIRECTIONS: 17.3 KM from HWY 20, look for the little bridge before the entrance with a red mailbox marked "Rallison," on the south side of the road.

STOP: Last West Gardens

Carolyn Rallison, well-known in Alberta gardening circles, has a passion for plants and nature. Twenty-nine years ago when her family moved their house into an undeveloped valley, Carolyn started creating flowerbeds around the house. Today her five-acre garden is a showcase with hundreds

Look for these common plants that thrive in the sunny, dry, and dusty conditions of a roadside ditch: sweet clover, purple aster, common yarrow, Canada thistle, prairie sage, fireweed, harebell, Kentucky bluegrass, lamb's quarters, goldenrod, red clover, prickly rose, and foxtail barley.

of varieties of flowers, trees, shrubs, and roses, interspersed with rocks, bird feeders, and baths, woven crafts, and willow furniture—all made by Carolyn.

A large pond, created from a spring-fed slough, has increased the population of colourful birds, dragonflies, frogs, and toads, which limit the number of pesky mosquitoes.

Carolyn proves her gardening expertise by successfully growing specimens normally found much farther south: Zone 5 perennials and Zone 4 roses, trees, and shrubs. Her Explorer Rose Garden features a series of roses named for Canada's explorers—including Alberta's David Thompson. You are welcome to visit but it is necessary to call ahead. Allow an hour or two to smell the roses. You can picnic at one of Carolyn's tables, sit back, and listen to the birds.

Open by appointment.
Tel: (403) 843-6703

Admission is by donation to help feed the birds!

A showy corner at Last West Gardens.
JAN BOYARZIN

DIRECTIONS: Retrace your route to HWY 20.

OPTION: Medicine Lake excursion: This excursion will take you to Medicine Lake (another 25 KM west from Last West Gardens on Medicine Lake Road). This is a gravel road and is sometimes in poor condition—but is rewarding.

STOP: Medicine Lake

This is a picturesque, long, and slender lake in an area of hummocky topography that gives rise to a mixed forest of aspen poplar, white spruce, lodgepole pine, and birch. Medicine Lake is the headwater of the

View of Medicine Lake with water lilies in the foreground.

Medicine River, the primary river draining this area as it flows southward past Eckville and Markerville and joins up with the Red Deer River just west of Innisfail.

Facilities: camping, picnicking, boat launch, informal hiking trails, fishing.

FEATURED PLANT: Cow Parsnip

As you hike the trails around the lake, notice this big-leaved plant which may reach eight feet in height! The name suggests otherwise, but cows are not fond of this obnoxious-tasting plant, which grows in moist soil. The huge, white flowers bloom from June to July on the tips of hollow cardboard-like stems.

The loon is a bird of the wilderness. Though Medicine Lake is very popular for recreation, there are marshy, secluded bays in which the loon finds peace. Since its feet are placed far back on its body, it finds walking on land very difficult, making it virtually impossible to get up the speed to take flight. However, on the water that adaptation serves it very well, adding power to every leg stroke when diving for fish or speeding along the surface for takeoff.

DIRECTIONS: Retrace your route to HWY 20.

DIRECTIONS: Head north on HWY 20. Take RR 30 1 KM east into Bluffton at the sign. At the stop sign at the school (0.7 KM past Bluffton), turn right onto TWP 440. Follow the winding road east 0.4 KM to the bridge.

STOP: Blindman River Erosion

Park by the bridge over the Blindman River—this is a good place to have a look at the erosion caused by the river.

Think of central Alberta as being covered by a blanket—a blanket of dirt! Receding glaciers originally deposited that blanket, filling in the river valleys and other cracks in the earth much the same way as we apply plaster to holes and cracks in a wall.

In this spot where the river has carved its way deep into the soil, you can see where the water has cut into more than just the blanket of glacial sand, gravel, and clay. The sandstone bedrock, which dates back millions of years, is also exposed.

The Bluffton General Store is the hub of the community year-round.

This hay bale would certainly be a challenge for any weightlifter! In fact, a special mechanized pick-up system is required on the trucks used today to transport bales—each bale weighs approximately 700 kilograms (1,540 pounds).

DIRECTIONS: Continue up the hill above the river. From the bridge it is 1.5 KM to the first intersection. Turn north onto RR 25. At the T junction (3.3 KM) turn east onto TWP 442 and follow the road uphill. Turn south onto RR 23 for 0.8 KM to Crystal Springs Cheese Farm.

STOP: Crystal Springs Cheese Farm

Cheesemaker Johan Broere works with milk, pasteurized on-site, at Crystal Springs Cheese Farm. Bacterial culture added to the pasteurized milk determines the flavour. A rennet enzyme helps the milk to coagulate. Next the milk is separated into curds and whey. The curds are scooped into moulds and pressed for a number of hours. Once removed from the mould the cheese is soaked in salt brine, waxed around the outside, and left to age.

The strength of a cheese depends on how long it has been aged. You will not be able to resist sampling the excellent range of Gouda in traditional rounds, along with fetas and other favourites, available at the "Renegade Milkmaid" retail outlet on the farm at unbeatable prices. Also available are locally produced Mennonite sausage, buffalo meat, yogourt, and honey.

Open Monday–Saturday 10:00 AM–6:00 PM

Tel: (403) 843-4553

Crystal Springs Cheese Farm can also be reached from HWY 53 (east of Rimbey) onto RR 23 travelling 12.4 KM north.

DIRECTIONS: Retrace your route to TWP 442 and continue west for 4.9 KM. Turn south at RR 30 and follow over the bridge into Bluffton. At the four-way stop at Bluffton school turn west on TWP 440 to rejoin HWY 20.

I *SPY*: The Bluffton Rock

At the intersection of TWP 440 and HWY 20 is a local oddity that has its own place-name story. In 1967, the people of Bluffton placed this glacial erratic in this spot as a centennial project! On the anniversary of Confederation, western Canada was losing the generation that held the living memory of the settlement of the land. Nostalgia for "pioneer history" was apparent as more and more Albertans left farms and moved to urban centres. At the same time, the old school districts shown here on the rock were becoming obsolete. Today only those people who live in such localities retain the use of these names.

DIRECTIONS: Continue north on HWY 20.

ALONG THE WAY: Hoadley

Hoadley was another hamlet on the Lacombe and North Western Railway. Little remains today. One of Hoadley's most famous sons was Leroy Brownlee, who arrived from Missouri in 1911 to homestead. By the 1920s Brownlee was running a sawmill and feed-grinding outfit, and in the 1930s he operated a saw and shingle mill. He turned his skills in another direction in 1940 when he built a printing press, and went into the publication business under the name *The Star Press*. He wrote and published four do-it-yourself books on farm blacksmithing, building a farm lumber sawmill and shingle mill, as well as circular saw hammering. Flyers, posters, and handbills for the community rolled off his press. The press is now preserved at Heritage Park in Calgary. Brownlee finally became a newspaperman on a one-sheet monthly, the *North Country Times*, that carried local news and advertisements. Brownlee, who remained a bachelor, had a romantic streak. From 1949 to at least 1958, he published a "lonely hearts," or personal ads, newsletter. It had the rather strange title of *National Hobby and Trader*, and reached the lovelorn across Canada.

ALONG THE WAY: Muskeg

Look for low areas of muskeg, marked by the growth of black spruce and tamarack. Muskeg develops where water is trapped. Cold air accumulates in low areas, where the ground stays frozen longer in the spring and continuous moisture causes soil to cool as water evaporates. The stagnant, cool water tends to be low in oxygen and becomes acidic. All of this causes plants to decompose very slowly.

Over the years, mosses and other plants build up, and "pickle" in the acid waters. On this layer of partly decomposed plants, called peat or muskeg, only certain species are able to grow: sedges, tamarack, black spruce, willows, and dwarf birch. (See also page 111.)

DIRECTIONS: At HWY 13 turn east for 3 KM. At the sign for Twin Lakes Park, follow the road south into the valley.

STOP: Twin Lakes Park

Visit this small park to experience a secluded, miniature world of boreal forest in the midst of aspen parkland country. As you drive down into the

Looking for wildlife at Twin Lakes Park.

park, you meet with an unexpected scene of white spruce, lodgepole pine, black spruce, paper birch, and tamarack, mixed in with the ever-present trembling aspen. Such vegetation is normally only found farther east or north, but a microclimate was created by the steep terrain of this crater, produced from a large chunk of ice that broke loose from a glacier. When it melted, a deep pool of water was left behind, which now drains northwest from the lake, eventually entering the North Saskatchewan River.

West Twin Lake is thirty-five metres deep—an impressive depth for such a small body of water. It has become quite popular with scuba divers. Just 700 metres to the east lies a much shallower lake called East Twin Lake. You can drive to its shore and enjoy the pristine view.

Twin Lakes is a popular facility for camping, picnicking, and fishing, operated by the County of Wetaskiwin. The lake is stocked with rainbow trout, which share the waters with native northern pike, turbot, and yellow perch.

DIRECTIONS: Retrace your route west on HWY 13, cross HWY 20, and continue west on HWY 13. Turn north at the sign for Winfield and head up the main street.

I SPY: Abandoned Rail Bed

Opposite the turn into Winfield look south—here you get a first glimpse of the abandoned rail bed of the Lacombe and Northwestern Railway that ran north through the logging camps.

ALONG THE WAY: Winfield

The town of Winfield is now a quiet shadow of its former glory days as the only town serving numerous logging camps in the area. Saturday night was loggers' night in town, as the men came in from the bush in all directions ready to party, but today the Winfield Hotel is boarded up. As you leave town heading north, look for the tiny St. George's Anglican Church, located among trees on the east side of the road.

DIRECTIONS: You are now travelling on the Norbuck Trail, which curves as it follows the old trail that once served the logging camps. The abandoned railway bed is clearly visible at intervals on the west side of the road. After 8.2 KM on the Norbuck Trail you come to a T junction. Turn east for 0.6 KM, and at HWY 20, turn north for Breton.

This was once logging country. Imagine this entire area north to the Saskatchewan River covered by spruce as far as the eye can see. Today's farms are the result of immense change in land use over the past sixty years. At the turn of the century, it was dense forest. It was then logged, and the stumps eventually obscured by second-growth forest. By the 1950s the trees had been cleared through two successive waves of the logging industry, and the timber berths had given way to tracts of farmland.

Edmonton lumbermen John Walter and Donald R. Fraser worked timber berths in the gently rolling country around Breton and north to the Saskatchewan River, from about 1907 until World War I. A series of trails for wagons or sleighs cut through the woods linking the main lumber camps to burgeoning areas of settlement, which provided much of the seasonal labour. In fall before the ice set in, Walter's steamer brought supplies upstream that had to be hauled into the camps.

The huge loss of logs during the great flood of 1915 on the North Saskatchewan River ended the days of the river drive. The extension of the Lacombe and Northwestern Railway to the Breton area in 1926 once again saw the area thrive as the logging industry revived. By 1929, there

Loading a sleigh with logs to be hauled to a dump on Poplar Creek.
PROVINCIAL ARCHIVES OF ALBERTA, A.5085.

were fifteen sawmills employing over 1000 men in the Breton area. Unlike during the earlier logging boom, the sawmills were right on site rather than in Edmonton, and the finished lumber was shipped out by rail.

DIGGING *DEEPER*: The Logger's Job

The logging business required dedicated teamwork and men with different skills. The operation was carried out in four main phases. The first was felling the trees with axes and bucking them—cutting them with buck saws—into saw logs. Felling gangs worked in groups of two or three men.

Next the logs were skidded from the stump area out to skidways on logging roads. A chain was wrapped around one big log or several smaller ones, attached to a skid hook, and hitched to a horse, which hauled it out on a skidding trail through the bush. An alternative to the chain was skidding tongs: as the horse moved forward the tongs tightened on the log.

A skidway was essentially a large storage pile of logs. Men called rollers built them at intervals, to facilitate the "scaling" or measuring of the logs, and to serve as a pick-up point for the teamsters who hauled the logs to the water.

Hauling was done after Christmas when snow conditions were optimal for teams of horses to haul the loads of logs on sleighs. These sleighs comprised two bobsleds with nine-foot runners shod with iron, coupled one behind the other, with timber bunks, on which the logs were piled. Logging roads that had been cleared earlier in the fall were rutted for the sleighs and sprinkled with water each night, using a water tank mounted on a sleigh, to produce a glassy surface for the sleds to run on. Once the sleigh was loaded, the team took off at a pace for the dump. Dumps or decks were built along the banks of creeks and rivers, ready for the drive.

DIRECTIONS: Turn east at TWP 473A, and follow for 1.6 KM to the T junction. Turn north onto RR 40. Drive down towards the bridge that spans Poplar Creek, where it opens out from an area of high cliffs and flows more slowly. Park your vehicle on the far side of the bridge.

STOP: Old Holding Pond

The log drive downstream to the sawmills of Edmonton was a tricky operation. Beginning in April, it involved getting the logs from the timber berths along very small creeks into the water successfully, and driving them into the Saskatchewan River and downstream to Edmonton with the least possible number of jams and breakage.

The loggers piled logs in ponds of backed-up water that were formed by constructing dams and sluice gates in autumn to control the water flow on the creek. Then in spring, the sluice gates were opened when the ice went out to increase the water volume. You can see the remains of earthworks on the west side of the road.

On the east side of the road here on the south bank of Poplar Creek you can see an old holding pond for logs.

ALONG THE WAY: Flesher farm

Continuing north through this sloping valley, you pass the Flesher farm. This was once the main camp for the logging operation run by David Ricker, a legendary character and one of the contractors who worked

Bunk houses at David Ricker's camp. George Fink was an itinerant photographer who travelled from camp to camp on horseback with his camera, capturing scenes such as this one. He developed the glass plates in a root cellar on his property and sold them as postcards on his return trip to the woods.

PROVINCIAL ARCHIVES OF ALBERTA, A.5091

Walter's timber berths. Known as Ricker's Ranch, this camp, like all others, was a dangerous place. The work was tough, conditions rough, the pay low. The men lived in bunkhouses and ate at the cookhouse. Over-fond of the bottle, Ricker apparently met his end sometime after 1911 by falling out of an upstairs window of an Edmonton hotel!

I SPY: Breton Plots

Immediately past the Flesher farm entrance, you will notice a chain link fence and cairn. This marks the Breton Plots set up by the University of Alberta on the Flesher farm for agricultural research in 1930. Since then research undertaken here has had far-reaching results, most recently in looking at the relationship between soil management and climate change.

ALONG THE WAY: Grey Wooded Soils

Much of the farmland west of the fifth meridian in central Alberta is classified as Luvisolic or grey wooded soil. These soils are found under coniferous forests that once covered the region. Grey wooded soils present a special challenge to farmers, as they tend to be acidic and low in organic matter. Plant nutrients and minerals leach badly out of the topsoil and many crops do poorly in the acidic environment. Research at the Breton Plots found that the addition of sulphur as a fertilizer and a five-year rather than a two-year crop rotation improves crop quality and yield on grey wooded soils.

DIRECTIONS: Head west on HWY 616, crossing HWY 20. At the sign for Breton turn north and follow 51st street into Breton.

STOP: Breton and District Museum

Located in an old school house, this is well worth a visit to learn more about the early black settlement of Keystone and the logging industry. You can locate the logging trails on a map, view a collection of logging tools and see historic photographs. Relive the classroom atmosphere of the 1940s in this unique Alberta community. Join the celebrations at the museum the fourth Sunday in February, during Black History Month each year.

Open daily July 1–Labour Day 11:00 AM–5:00 PM

Admission by donation.

DIRECTIONS: Continue north on 51st Avenue to the four-way stop. Turn west over the abandoned railway line onto TWP 480A.

I *SPY*: Timber piling yard

Look for a pile of red bricks in the field on the north side of the road, immediately past the rail line. This corner wall is all that remains of the safe that sat in the office on Bill Fraser's timber piling yard. The yard, complete with planer mill and offices, was built at Breton in 1941, next to the rail line, for shipping finished lumber. "Big Bill" Fraser, who according to one source weighed in at 233 pounds and stood six-feet-two inches high, was the son of Donald R. Fraser. In the 1920s he continued the operation of his father's company with a saw and planer mill at Fraspur, southwest of Breton. During WWII there was a huge increase in demand for lumber and in 1942 Fraser relocated his sawmill to a site on Buck Creek and built a new planer mill at Breton.

Linda (Jackson) Campbell entertains a crowd during Black History Month in 2003.
BRETON AND DISTRICT MUSEUM

DIRECTIONS: Continue west to the T junction and turn north onto RR 42 (Funnell Road). Turn east onto TWP 482.

DIGGING *DEEPER*: Oklahoma immigrants

The black settlers who cleared land here at Keystone were among a larger group of immigrants from Oklahoma who came by train to Alberta in 1910. Despite vocal public opposition in 1911, most of the Oklahoma settlers decided to stay in Alberta. Some families settled in Edmonton and Calgary while others formed rural communities. The Hook family was among those who sought a rural life rather than an urban one. Along with the Baileys and the Robinsons, they joined families who had already taken up land at Keystone, the first of whom had been William and Mattie Allen.

The woody land at Keystone was more like the Mississippi land where

Fraser's timber piling yard in 1952. Note the planer mill on the right, and the timber piled in the backyard, behind the office yard.

BRETON AND DISTRICT MUSEUM

their people originated than the dry Oklahoma they had recently left. Soon there were fifty-two families at Keystone. The settlers bought basic supplies at the general store at Yeoford, kept chickens, and canned their own vegetables and copious amounts of wild berries that grew around them. At the centre of community life was the Good Hope Baptist Church built in 1911, and the Funnell School, a frame building heated by a big potbellied stove, that still functions as a community hall north of town. When the railway came in 1926, the settlement changed. Its name was changed to Breton, after D. C. Breton, MLA for Leduc 1926–1930, and a largely white population, employed mostly in the logging trade, once again moved in.

STOP: Keystone Cemetery

This cemetery was established in 1910 when the Henry Allen family, the first to have a death at Keystone, donated a plot. The graves are unmarked but the names of those at rest are inscribed on the plaque on the commemorative rock. Why broken glass shards once covered many of the graves has remained an unsolved mystery. Today you can tread across a carpet of violets to the grave of Charlie and Emma King, the last two Keystone settlers to be buried here before the cemetery was declared inactive in 1983.

I *SPY*: Homestead

Watch for the log building in the field to the north as you approach HWY 20—part of the homestead of the William Allen family.

DIRECTIONS: Continue east on TWP 482 to HWY 20. Turn south on HWY 20 to bring you back to the turnoff for the town of Breton. From here you can join Tour 3, Breton to Pigeon Lake.

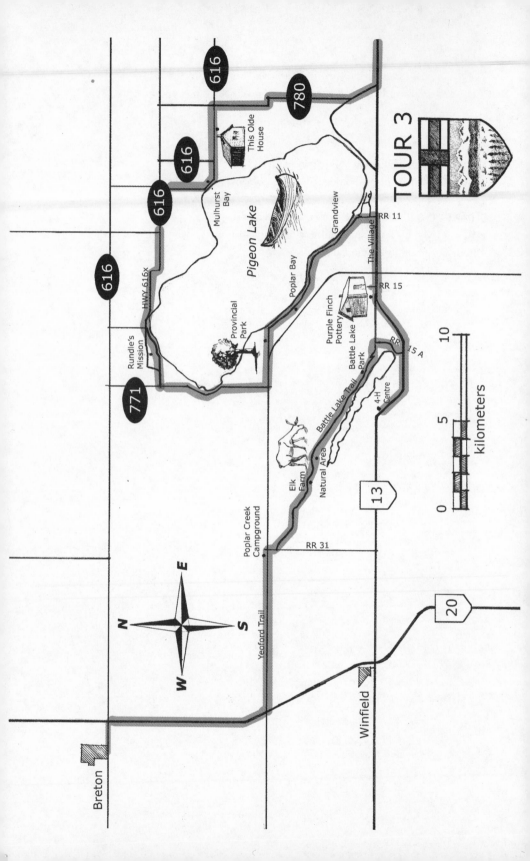

Breton to Pigeon Lake via Battle Lake

DIRECTIONS: From Breton take HWY 20 south for 10 KM and turn east on the Yeoford Trail (TWP 470).

ALONG THE WAY: Yeoford Logging Trail

You are now travelling through muskeg (see page 17) on the Yeoford logging trail that linked the Breton area with Battle Lake and Pigeon Lake. Early settlers used this route to reach the Calgary–Edmonton Railway at Wetaskiwin.

STOP: Poplar Creek Campground

At 7.8 KM along the Yeoford Trail a small campground offers the cool shelter of a spruce forest. It has a cookhouse, firewood, and pit toilets, but no water. Walk 0.5 KM east of the campsite down the hill to an excellent bird-watching area at the ponds on either side of the road.

FEATURED BIRD: Tree Swallow

Watch for long lines of glossy-blue tree swallows resting on overhead wires. At other times, they are swooping back and forth over the water, snatching up mayflies, moths, and other insects. If there are downed trees around the pond, the swallows have likely excavated nests in the soft wood.

Tree swallow.
FRED SCHUTZ

DIRECTIONS: Turn south at the sign for Battle Lake Park onto RR 31, passing Yeoford Hall on the west side of the road. Then immediately turn east onto TWP 465A. You are now on the Battle Lake Trail, a winding gravel road.

A proud elk in the wild.

ALONG THE WAY: Elk Farming

Are you wondering why some farmers are erecting such tall fences? Look closely and you will see herds of elk. The fences serve the dual purpose of keeping domestic elk in and wild elk out to prevent interbreeding and the transmission of disease.

Alberta Game Farm Regulations do not allow the hunting of domestic elk. The product of elk farms is antler velvet. Each fall the velvet is stripped from the emerging antlers on the bucks and exported, mainly to the People's Republic of China, where it used to produce medicines and aphrodisiacs. The female elk give birth each spring to twins, kept as new members of the herd or sold as breeding stock to other farms. Elk farms are an example of diversified agriculture in central Alberta.

I *SPY*: Mount Butte Natural Area

Watch for the signed "Natural Area" along the south side of the road where the vegetation opens up, giving a view of a small lake that drains south into Battle Lake. Here William and Asta Loov, reminded of their native Sweden, settled in 1933. There is no formal access to the site.

DIGGING *DEEPER*: Alberta's Natural Areas

Natural Areas are lands set aside by the provincial government to protect landscapes of significance. They restrict commercial use while at the same time allowing for low-intensity recreation. There are over a hundred Natural Areas in the province but only a few have formal trails. The rest, such as the Mount Butte site, serve the needs of wildlife more than people.

ALONG THE WAY: Battle Lake

The Battle Lake Trail winds along the north side of this long, narrow lake. The lake was named for the frequent battles waged between the Blackfoot and Cree in the vicinity. The steep slopes of the valley produce vegetation more typical of the boreal forest north of Edmonton. Some of the spruce still standing along the lake are close to 200 years old. The County of Wetaskiwin recognizes the significance of wildlife at this lake, which is home to nesting bald eagles, moose and the common loon. Landowners are restricted in how they use the land and in their ability to subdivide it, with a goal to preserve as much of the original vegetation as possible.

STOP: Battle Lake Park

The County of Wetaskiwin operates this popular campground, a pleasant place for swimming and canoeing. Drive in to the day use/beach area and enjoy the view as you look up from the bottom of the Battle River valley. The steep valley walls provide a natural shield from the outside world. To minimize disturbance to wildlife, boaters are restricted to twelve kilometres per hour.

DIGGING *DEEPER*: The Battle River System

Battle Lake is the headwater of the Battle River, which drains water from the surrounding watershed, collects water from Pigeon Lake via Pigeon Lake Creek, turns northeast at the town of Ponoka, collects water from Coal Lake, passes into Driedmeat Lake, then flows east to Saskatchewan where it meets up with the North Saskatchewan River near North Battleford. Eventually, the Saskatchewan River system joins the Nelson River system, which flows into Hudson Bay.

DIGGING *DEEPER*: The Formation of Battle Lake

Battle Lake is a long narrow lake that looks more like a wide river. In fact, its life most likely began as a river. Geologists surmise that a colossal glacier once sat on the north side of the valley. As it melted, a torrent of water raged along its edge, gouging over 100 feet into the earth.

FEATURED *PLANT*: Water Lilies

A crop of water lilies adorns the waters just offshore from the day use area. The floating heart-shaped leaves are attached to long, air-filled stems, which are rooted in the mud and can easily support the weight of a frog. Each produces a single, brilliant-yellow flower on a short stalk that blooms from summer to fall. You may find pieces of the rootstalk, about three inches in diameter, washed up on shore, bearing large scars where the stems were attached.

DIRECTIONS: Continuing on the Battle Trail, take the right fork downhill, keeping right as you join TWP 462. Turn south at the Baptist Church onto RR 15A and follow downhill along the lake to HWY 13. Turn west uphill for the Alberta 4-H Battle Lake Centre on the north side of the road.

STOP: Alberta 4-H Centre—Battle Lake

Before hiking down to the lake, study the trail map located in the gazebo beside the parking lot. Allow about 1.5 hours for hiking the Fern Valley and the Porcupine Trail. Cavernous ravines lead from the aspen forest on the valley top into the cool streams and forests of the valley floor. An impressive fern glade flourishes in the fertile soil of the stream banks. As you walk along the lakeshore, grebes give a laughing call and dive underwater to catch a meal. In the depths of the valley, rock formed 65 million years ago is exposed in a narrow gorge along the lake. The Alberta 4-H Centre offers an Environmental Appreciation Program for schools and youth groups, who explore the habitats, wildlife and plants of the Battle Lake valley while canoeing, hiking, and learning outdoor skills.

Tel: (780) 682-2153

FEATURED WILDLIFE: Porcupine

As you walk into the spruce forest on the Porcupine Trail, notice how many trees have been stripped of their bark by hungry porcupines. The porcupine seems to have a distinct preference for balsam fir. That dubious honour has been the death of countless fir trees along the trail.

If you happen to get close to a porcupine, you can rest assured that they do not shoot their quills. However, do not get too close, because a swish of the tail can implant those painful weapons in your hide!

Each quill has tiny barbs pointing outward, which anchor them into their victim. If you squeeze on the quill to pull it out, the hollow shaft bulges, planting the quill even more firmly into the skin.

FEATURED *PLANT*: Ostrich Fern

By midsummer, the ostrich ferns in this glade reach up to five feet in height. The fiddleheads or not-yet-unfurled leaves make a very tasty green salad. The dense growth of ferns in this glade is the result of two methods of reproduction: new plants arising from underground stems and by spores. Ferns, like mushrooms, produce spores rather than seeds. Short, dark stems grow from the middle of the plant, bearing spherical spore cases which split when mature to release a yellow powder, made up of billions of spores. The spore-bearing stems are stiff and woody, and remain erect after all the other leaves have died off.

DIRECTIONS: Retrace your route east on HWY 13.

ALONG THE WAY: Purple Finch Pottery

Just 1 KM north on RR 15 from HWY 13 look for local potter Donna Brunner, who works in her studio, built from straw bales. Her brightly painted free-form work is distinctive.

Open: Catch her if you can!

Tel: (780) 586-2466

DIRECTIONS: Continue on HWY 13, passing HWY 771, for the Village at Pigeon Lake on the north side of the Highway.

STOP: Eco Café at the Village at Pigeon Lake

This unique eating spot offers the best of central Alberta produce. Local dairy products, eggs, vegetables, and locally butchered bison, lamb, elk, and chicken are combined in wonderful and surprising recipes on a seasonal menu. An earth-centred philosophy and a belief in community relationships is evident in this popular sunny café run by well-known chef Tim Wood and his wife Deb. The Eco Pantry is a connected "picnic basket" deli. Takeout items include fresh pannini sandwiches, salads, and dips. The work of local craftspeople, including pottery and woven and carved items, is also for sale.

Open Monday–Thursday, Sunday 6:30 AM–8:00 PM; Friday, Saturday 6:30 AM–9:00 PM

Breakfast daily 6:30 AM–11:00 AM

Tel: (780) 586-2627

The Village at Pigeon Lake is a good place for travel supplies, gas, groceries, and other services, including accommodation.

ALONG THE WAY: Sustainable Agriculture

What does this term mean? It means that those who produce food on a small or specialized scale can find markets and realize reasonable prices for their produce. This area of Alberta is one of mixed farming and it attracts people who wish to raise animals or grow vegetables outside the mainstream agricultural infrastructure. Local purchase and consumption of locally grown food makes its production sustainable and strengthens the economic and social base of the community. Local producers of cheese, yogourt, meat, poultry, and garden produce are to be found throughout central Alberta. Keep an eye out for them along all of the tour routes.

DIRECTIONS: At the Village turn north from HWY 13 onto Norris Beach Road (RR 11). It curves and then follows the shoreline of Pigeon Lake through Crystal Springs, the first of several summer villages with homes on either side of Lakeview Drive. Please drive with care.

ALONG THE WAY: Pigeon Lake

The Stoney and Cree who frequented the area first knew Pigeon Lake as Woodpecker Lake. Aboriginal people found this region an important source of fish and game. Today, their descendents live on the Pigeon Lake Indian Reserve on the southeast shore of the lake.

At the turn of the twentieth century, Pigeon Lake bustled with new immigrants looking for ways to make a living. By December 1907, the Pigeon Lake Sawmills Company had ten teams hauling lumber to their planing mill in Millet. In the winter of 1912–13 there were over eighty-five teams hauling lumber on the trail.

A fish-packing plant was supplied with thousands of whitefish pulled out of the lake each year by commercial fishermen. During the 1920s some of the fish was exported to special markets in New York and Chicago by rail from Millet.

Pigeon Lake is a popular recreational getaway for Edmontonians, who have built cottages along the shore since the early 1900s. Today this large but shallow lake (nine metres maximum depth) has little natural shoreline left, as 2,300 cottages, ten summer villages, and various parks and campgrounds occupy most lakeside property.

DIRECTIONS: At the fork in the road keep left onto Snell Drive. At the T intersection, turn right for Grandview Village, and follow the shoreline road through Poplar Bay. Follow the curve until you see the sign for Pigeon Lake Provincial Park. The entrance sign may say "Pigeon Lake Family Park," as the park is now privately operated.

An extensive trail system at the park takes you through young and mature aspen parkland, along wooded shoreline and past the lush vegetation of marsh and swamp terrain.

STOP: Pigeon Lake Provincial Park

Park at the day-use area and walk toward the lake where the wide gravel trail begins. Pigeon Lake offers a prime example of aspen forest—the typical forest cover in central Alberta—and the variety of species that grow in the understory.

Along the trail, openings to the lake are supplied with benches where you can sit back and enjoy the view. If you walk down to the lakeshore, look for the green alder, which pops up along the edge of any pond, lake or stream. It resembles birch with its toothed leaves and tiny cones.

Soon the trail angles away from the lake and drops suddenly to low ground, where a stream flows into the lake. Here the vegetation changes dramatically. A dense growth of shrubby plants with beautiful, drooping yellow flowers adorns the right side of the trail. These are touch-me-nots. When the seedpods ripen, they fly open explosively with just a touch.

Facilities: camping, picnicking, playground, washrooms, concession, beach, boat launch, fishing, hiking trails, swimming.

FEATURED *PLANTS*: Aspen and Balsam Poplar

Balsam poplar grows close to the lake and on streamsides, since it prefers moist soil. It has oval leaves and heavily furrowed bark. During winter and spring the large, sticky buds make identification of this tree easy. Their pungent scent was used as an early form of aromatherapy for head colds.

The smooth, powdery bark of the aspen poplar tree.
FRED SCHUTZ

The aspen poplar prefers dry ground. The bark is not furrowed, except perhaps at the base of old trees, and has heart-shaped leaves. Take a close look at the leaf stalk. It is flat like a rubber band, causing the leaves to tremble in the breeze. Hence it has another common name: "trembling aspen."

DIRECTIONS: From the park, head west for HWY 771. Continue north on HWY 771 for 8.5 KM. Turn east onto HWY 616X. Take the right fork off HWY 616X downhill, following the sign for Rundle's Mission.

STOP: Rundle's Mission

Englishman Rev. Robert Rundle picked this spot in 1847 for the first Methodist mission to Aboriginal people west of Red River. Before departing for England in the summer of 1848 he noted in his journal that he had planted beans and potatoes at the mission—"May the Lord give the increase!" Missionaries Ben and Margaret Sinclair remained at Pigeon Lake to encourage the Nakoda people who lived in the area to grow grain and vegetable crops, and to go to their church. The mission at Pigeon Lake was not very successful in either aim, and unrest among Aboriginal people resulted in its closure in the early 1860s.

In 1865, John McDougall and his wife Abigail Steinhauer reopened Rundle's mission. By 1869 they had built a church and renamed the mission Woodville. Rev. Peter Campbell succeeded the McDougalls. Campbell described the mission building as a miserable bark-roofed hut, where he lived a life fraught with fear, as the country continued to be in a disturbed state. Conditions settled over the next twenty years as the treaties established reserves and the land was surveyed for settlement. These changes resulted in the Woodville Mission moving to Bear's Hill in 1883, then to Wolf Creek in 1884, before finally dispersing in 1892. Abandoned, the buildings at Pigeon Lake fell into ruins.

The Rundle mission site has since been revitalized. Rundle's Mission is now the site of a lodge and conference centre. The 1912 Telford Methodist Church, built by settlers in the valley of the Strawberry Creek north of Pigeon Lake, has been moved to the site. Behind the church is the Fisherton Cemetery and to the east lie older Aboriginal burial grounds.

To learn more about the mission site, which is a Provincial Historic Site and a National Historic Monument, take a walk along the interpretive board walk trail beginning just east of the Conference Centre.

Kiskayo Trail can be joined at Rundle's Mission. Kiskayo Trail, a multi-use trail around the lake, is part of the Alberta TrailNet, the local provincial coordinating body for the TransCanada Trail.

DIRECTIONS: Continue along the lakeside road 3 KM to three-way stop. Turn north. At the next intersection, turn right onto HWY 616x and follow east 10.7 KM.

ALONG THE WAY: Underlying Bedrock

As you drive along Highway 616X you drive over extremely hilly topography. You might think that glacial till (sand, gravel, and clay) was dumped unevenly in the area, but if you could check the depth of the till, you would find it to be less than three metres thick. That means the underlying bedrock was shaped this way before the last glaciers passed through. Obvious landforms that were deposited by the last glaciation are the linear ridges or flutes situated north of the highway and oriented in a northeasterly direction.

ALONG THE WAY: Flutes

As glaciers move, they sometimes come up against obstacles: hard, protruding bedrock or boulders. As the ice flows around the obstacle, a space develops on the lee side, which then gets filled in with a muddy paste of till, resulting in a long ridge called a flute.

DIRECTIONS: At the sign for Mulhurst Bay, turn south downhill for 3 KM to the lake.

STOP: Mulhurst Bay

Once a centre of logging and sawmill activities, this is a pleasant place to while away a summer evening or have supper as the sun goes down in the west.

DIRECTIONS: Follow the road along the lakeshore and then uphill away from the lake. At the four-way stop go straight ahead onto HWY 616.

STOP: Van Volkenburg Stopping House (This Olde House Country Restaurant)

This is one of the few remaining stopping houses that served early travellers in Alberta. Stopping houses were Alberta's first rough-and-ready Bed and Breakfast establishments.

Travel with horses required rest stops with feed and water for the horses. Stopping houses, always located near a water source, charged for horse feed as well as meals. Travellers sometimes stayed for supper and camped outside, or slept indoors—often on their bedroll thrown down on the floor. In the morning, all were up early for breakfast and off on the next leg of their journey on the trail.

The Van Volkenburg stopping house was established in 1912 on the lumber trail from Pigeon Lake to Millet. Mr. Von Volkenburg had the mail contract from Bonnie Glen to Millet for a year, and was a fire ranger from 1913–17. The Von Volkenburgs ran the house as a stopping place until 1921.

Once again the family has opened its doors to the travelling public. Ask Phyllis about her grandparents, whose lives are captured in photos on the walls. The house is has undergone extensive renovations, with a new wing on the west side. It is now a pleasant licensed restaurant with magnificent sunset views of the lake.

Open Victoria Day weekend–Labour Day weekend Tuesday–Sunday 10:00 AM–9:00 PM

Labour Day weekend–Victoria Day weekend Tuesday–Sunday 10:00AM–8:00 PM

Tel: (780) 389-2203

DIRECTIONS: Continue east on HWY 616. Turn south on HWY 780. At HWY 13A turn left to head east joining Tour 4 for Wetaskiwin, or right to return west to the Village at Pigeon Lake.

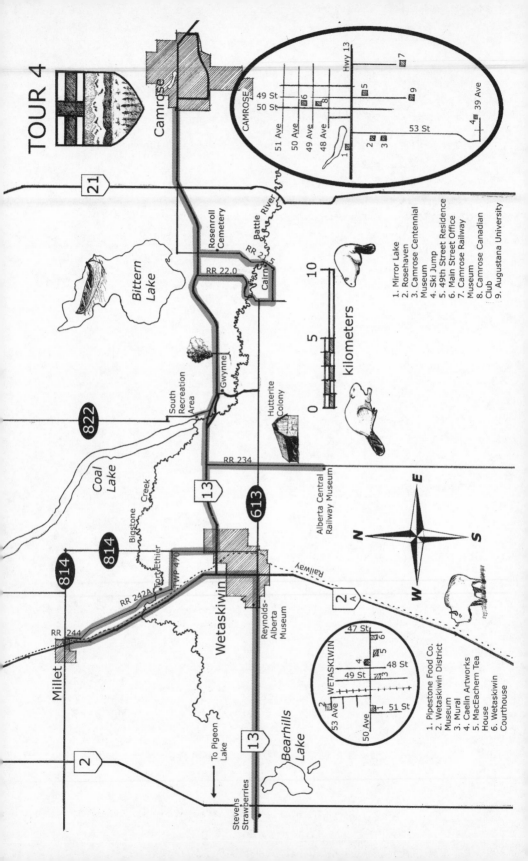

TOUR 4

Camrose

CAMROSE (inset map)
Hwy 13
49 St
50 St
51 Ave
50 Ave
49 Ave
48 Ave
53 St
39 Ave

1. Mirror Lake
2. Rosehaven
3. Camrose Centennial Museum
4. Ski Jump
5. 49th Street Residence
6. Main Street Office
7. Camrose Railway Museum
8. Camrose Canadian Club
9. Augustana University

21

Bittern Lake

Rosenroll Cemetery

RR 22.0

Battle River

RR 21.5
Cairn

Gwynne

Hutterite Colony

kilometers
0   5   10

822

Coal Lake

South Recreation Area

Bigstone Creek

RR 234

Alberta Central Railway Museum

13

613

N E W S

814

814

Fort Ethier

RR 242A

TWP 470

Wetaskiwin

Railway

2A

Reynolds-Alberta Museum

Millet

RR 244

To Pigeon Lake

Stevens Strawberries

13

2

Bearhills Lake

WETASKIWIN (inset map)
47 St
48 St
49 St
51 St
53 Ave
50 Ave

1. Pipestone Food Co.
2. Wetaskiwin District Museum
3. Mural
4. Caelin Artworks
5. MacEachern Tea House
6. Wetaskiwin Courthouse

Pigeon Lake to Camrose, via Wetaskiwin and Millet

DIRECTIONS: Begin this tour at The Village at Pigeon Lake or join at the junction of Hwy 780 and HWY 13. Travel east on HWY 13 for Wetaskiwin. The entrance for Stevens Strawberries is on the south side of HWY 13, less than 1 KM west of the HWY 2 overpass.

STOP: Stevens Strawberries

Delicious strawberries for U to pick! No sprays used here on this seven-acre patch. Kerry Stevens will give you a lesson in strawberry picking and set you out with a pail to fill.

Open mid-July–late September 9:00 AM–8:00 PM

To avoid disappointment call ahead for availability, as demand is high.

Tel: (780) 352-7278

I *SPY*: Brightview

Just as you come off the overpass across Highway 2 look southeast to the buildings in the trees at the northeast tip of Bearhills Lake. Here the old trail, and then road, to Wetaskiwin ran past Brightview.

DIGGING *DEEPER*: Brightview Stopping House, Store and Post Office

The Goodhand family ran Brightview from 1906–16. The store kept everything a settler might need, as Bessie Goodhand later recalled: "Dried apples, prunes, peaches, apricots, raisins and pears in wooden boxes . . . alongside onions, wooden boxes of tasteless white cookies with pink candy on them, and ginger snaps that often had a piece of wood in them. . . . There were wooden pails of hard mixed candy of various colours and shapes, chocolate drops and caramels in neat rows and a bucket of conversation lozenges with sentimental words on them that the young fellows bought for their girlfriends. Usually there was stick candy, striped peppermint or vivid pink cinnamon flavoured. . . . licorice sticks and horehound candy for colds."

The shelves behind the counter were full with goods such as "castor oil, pain killer, Epsom salts, vanilla and lemon extract, Brenard's linament,

The Goodhand Family at Brightview.
PROVINCIAL ARCHIVES OF ALBERTA, A.5269

Dr. Chase's Salve, and Vaseline. There was plug tobacco for chewing and smoking, snuff, and Casino Tobacco. . . . In large tin cans were green bean coffee and roasted bean coffee, and rice—25¢ a lb." The store also had "cotton print, overalls, gloves, mitts, men's socks, and a few pairs of shoes." Many of the travellers who stayed at Brightview were lumbermen hauling loads to Wetaskiwin, and in winter the men sat by the pot-bellied stove in the store.

DIGGING *DEEPER*: From Trail to Road

The earliest trails in what was to become Alberta developed as overland routes travelled by Aboriginal people and fur traders. By the late 1870s the North West Mounted Police patrolled trails for the Métis freighters with their Red River carts. The Calgary–Edmonton Trail became the most important trail, but from the 1890s new trails also led east and west to new settlements and connected with branch trails and local trails that crisscrossed central Alberta.

Mail, stage, and freight services all used the network of main trails, which had stopping houses at intervals. Post offices and stores were commonly located on or near a trail. Many of these trails were rendered obsolete by the Dominion Land Survey's subdivision of land into townships, with road allowances at intervals. Property owners soon began to fence their livestock, put up gates across the trails, and build "roads"—little more than trails with some grading work—on the road allowances.

By the early years of the twentieth century a system of old trails—some of which became public highways—newly opened road allowances, and "colonization" roads built in areas where the road allowances were not suitable for public travel, all connected to provide transportation routes for Albertans. The provision and maintenance of an adequate land transportation infrastructure, including ferries and bridges, was a major political issue as settlement progressed.

Commercial centres were growing much faster than transportation routes and crossings to serve them. "It is a well known fact," noted the *Ponoka Herald* on November 22, 1901, "that Ponoka is losing a large amount of trade and business in all lines which justly belongs to this place because of the condition of the road leading from here as far as Red Deer and Buffalo Lakes. There are as many as forty families east of us whose nearest town is Ponoka, yet owing to the condition of the road their patronage has gone to Wetaskiwin and Lacombe."

As more settlers arrived in central Alberta the number of trails and roads multiplied and so indeed did the difficulty of finding one's way. As "Elijah" in the Little Red Deer neighbourhood column of the *Innisfail Province*, May 17, 1906, noted: "Now that so many strangers are driving around land hunting and generally taking stock of the country, would it be not a wise move on the part of our Local Improvement Authorities to post up on the corner of the main roads notices showing where each road leads to, the distances etc. It might spare strangers much unnecessary driving and let them know where they were without having to enquire every mile or so."

In 1906 the province launched an ambitious program of expenditures on roads under W. H. Cushing as Minister of Public Works, but there was no dramatic improvement. Although the automobile heightened the demand for better roads, many of Alberta's roads remained seasonally impassable until well after WWII.

STOP: Wheels and Wings at Wetaskiwin

The Reynolds family is synonymous with wheels and wings in Wetaskiwin. Ted Reynolds and sons Stanley and Bert were well known to Albertans during the craze of racing stripped-down Model Ts that swept the province between 1941 and 1951. Stan Reynolds won the 1947 Canadian Model T Championship in Calgary. A mechanical wizard, Stan Reynolds has been an avid collector of cars, planes and agricultural machinery for over fifty years and his collection forms the basis of the collection at the Reynolds-Alberta museum.

REYNOLDS-ALBERTA MUSEUM (1 KM west of Wetaskiwin on HWY 13)

Not to be missed! Extensive displays, demonstrations, interactive exhibits, and AV shows tell the story of the development of transportation and agricultural technology at this slick state-of-the-art museum. Watch restoration work in progress at the restoration shop. Catch a special event or a

The Riley family stop for lunch by the roadside between Calgary and Sylvan Lake, 1921.
When auto tourism took off in central Alberta during the 1920s, driving was
still a challenge. Breakdowns, muddy, impassable, and badly graded
dirt roads and trails—not to mention bad drivers—were all hazards of any trip.
Drivers never went out without their toolbox and repair kit.
GLENBOW ARCHIVES, M-8375-4-39

ride in a restored vintage vehicle. The museum also has an extensive library where you can research any number of vehicles and farm equipment.

The museum is also home to Canada's Aviation Hall of Fame, located in a display hangar next to the Wetaskiwin Municipal Airport's runway. It houses the second-largest collection of airplanes in Canada. Meet those early heroes of the skies, men and women such as Wop May and Molly Reilly, who established airmail routes and worked as bush pilots.

Open daily Victoria Day weekend–Labour Day weekend 10:00 AM–5:00 PM; July, August 10:00 AM–6:00 PM

Winter hours: Tuesday–Sunday 10:00 AM–6:00 PM
Closed on Mondays except holiday Mondays.
Admission fee.
Tel: 1-800-661-4726 or (780) 361-1351

CENTRAL AVIATION INC. ANTIQUE AIRPLANE RIDES

Be brave! Don an old leather flying helmet and take to the skies in an open
cockpit antique bi-plane. Aviator Bryon Reynolds will take you up on a
barnstorm tour of Wetaskiwin—an experience you will never forget.

Operating from Reynolds-Alberta Museum.

May 15–July 1 weekends only

July, August from 1:00 PM—weather permitting. Other times and
points of departure by prior arrangement.

Telephone answering service: (780) 352-9689

For cost and further information: (780) 352-6201

Intrepid rookie aviators take to the sky with Bryon.

DIGGING *DEEPER*: Barnstorming

Airplane rides were a new way to get a thrill in the early 1920s! Aviators
eager to make a career of flying, some of whom had flown during World
War I, were quick to take advantage of the public fascination with human
flight. These "barnstormers," as they were known, travelled around the

province to perform stunts often during fairs and rodeos. Landing in bumpy fields, they offered rides—at a price—to anyone who wanted to go up.

DIRECTIONS: Continue east 2 KM and turn north on HWY 2A. Turn east at the water tower at 50th Avenue to bring you to historic downtown Wetaskiwin.

I *SPY*: Wetaskiwin Water Tower

You cannot miss it. The tower is 150 feet high and the steel tank, which has graced the skyline since around 1909–10, stores 200 thousand gallons of water. The Galt engineering firm of Winnipeg and Toronto drew the plans for the tower, pumping station, and power plant for the city. The tower takes the excess of available water from the mains; when it has reached its capacity limit, the pumps automatically shut off. The water level in the tower never drops below the volume required to deal with a major fire. When lightning struck the tower in the 1940s, a lineman climbed on to the roof, pried off the burning shingles and boards, and threw them to the ground. The water tower still serves Wetaskiwin after more than ninety years.

Take a rest on one of the city's shady benches while on the historic walking tour.

STOP: City of Wetaskiwin

First known simply as Siding 16, Wetaskiwin got its name on the suggestion of missionary Father Lacombe. Meaning "the hills where peace was made," it commemorates peace between the Cree and Blackfoot in the 1860s. Incorporated in 1906 as Canada's smallest city, Wetaskiwin remains a city in motion, well-known for its antique shops and its auto mile of car dealerships.

WALKING TOUR

The City of Wetaskiwin boasts a fine red brick commercial area and many buildings have a plaque revealing the story of their past. Pick up a map of the downtown walking tour from the Wetaskiwin and District Museum.

WETASKIWIN AND DISTRICT MUSEUM (5010 53rd Avenue)

When the lights went on in Wetaskiwin it was all because of this unimposing building—the Electric Light Station. Constructed in 1908, it now houses the museum—the place to go for any information on Wetaskiwin that is not related to automobiles! The health care and war years exhibits are highlights. The museum hosts travelling exhibits.

Open June 1–August 31 Tuesday–Saturday 9:00 AM–5:00 PM; Sunday 1:00 AM–5:00 PM

September–May Tuesday–Friday 9:00 AM–5:00 PM

Small admission charge.

Tel: (780) 352-0227

THE PIPESTONE FOOD CO. (4911 51st Street)

The restaurant where you can eat and then take the table with you! At the right price all the antiques are for sale. Located in the historic Burns Block built in 1911, restauranteur Brady Weiler offers a menu that changes daily. Relax for a leisurely lunch in the airy space that has a modern atmosphere while preserving the hardwood floors and pressed tin ceiling. Notice the eyebrow windows and original advertisement on the outside wall on 51st Avenue. At the corner of 51st Street on 50th Avenue is the entrance to Weiler's latest venture—The Iron Boar Pub. It's smoke-free, although the light pub fare includes smoked ribs and beef!

Open Tuesday–Saturday 11:00 AM–10:00 PM. The Iron Boar stays open until midnight.

Tel: (780) 352-9596

CAELIN ARTWORKS (4728 50th Avenue)

When artist Colleen McGinnis opened a gallery in this house in 1991 it felt like coming home. Here she took piano lessons for ten years from the much-loved Anna Condie, who lived her whole life in this house, built by her father in 1912. A piano still sits in the exact spot that Mrs. Condie's piano did—it always puts a smile on former students' faces. Colleen now writes her own music for piano and other instruments. Look for her CD, *Awakening*, at the gallery.

Colleen's painting studio is upstairs where the light is perfect—even and warm. She works in both watercolour and oil, and her realist images have a painterly quality.

Colleen shares the gallery space with photographer husband Leon Strembitsky, who specializes in black-and-white large-format fine-art work. When out capturing a suspended moment or detail of central Alberta's landscape or buildings, Leon is to be seen under a dark cloth with his big old-fashioned field camera with bellows extending from the front. Limited editions of both Colleen's and Leon's work are produced at the gallery.

Open Monday–Friday 9:00 AM–5:00 PM; Saturday 12:00 PM–4:00 PM
Tel: (780) 352-3519

A number of outdoor murals depict aspects of Wetaskiwin's history.
This one, by Colleen McGinnis, is located on the Moose Lodge building
on the corner of 50th Avenue and 49th Street.

THE MACEACHERN TEA HOUSE (4719 50th Avenue)

Donald MacEachern was a former mayor of Wetaskiwin and community stalwart. The house now welcomes visitors for breakfast and lunch, as well as afternoon teas. Specialty teas and coffees go well with their famous orange rolls if you work up an appetite on the walking tour!

Open year-round Monday–Friday 10:00 AM–3:00 PM; Summer Saturday opening 10:00 AM–3:00 PM is weather-dependent—call ahead.
Tel: (780) 352-8308

WETASKIWIN COURTHOUSE (4705 50th Avenue)

The courthouse is every bit as imposing from the sidewalk as Provincial

Architect A. M. Jeffers intended. Its construction in 1907 reflected the importance of the city of Wetaskiwin as the centre of a new judicial district following the move from territorial to provincial administration in 1905. Designed in the classical revival style of architecture, it is constructed in red brick with sandstone trim, and has a painted sheet metal cornice. The magnificent portico entrance with ionic capitals is reached by a flight of steps.

There are not many restaurants in Alberta in houses as old as the MacEachern Tea House; it has graced 50th Avenue for over a hundred years.

DIGGING *DEEPER*: Provincial Historical Designation—What does it mean?

Designation by the provincial government of Alberta provides important historical buildings and other sites with recognition and protection for the future. Owners of designated sites are eligible for assistance in restoring or maintaining their property. Examples of designated sites include tipi rings, fur-trading posts, railway stations, farmsteads, coalmines, churches, office and commercial blocks, and private residences, among others.

DIRECTIONS: Return to HWY 2A and continue north 15 KM to Millet.

Inactive as a court of law since 1983, the Wetaskiwin courthouse is now a designated Provincial Historic Resource.

STOP: Millet

Millet was at the end of a trail east from Pigeon Lake and served as that burgeoning community's link to the rest of the world (see page 33).

DIRECTIONS: To explore Millet, we suggest you park in the parking lot on the east side of HWY 2A opposite the museum at the north end of town.

MILLET & DISTRICT MUSEUM (5120 50th Street—Hwy 2A)

A Veterans' Wall at the museum honours Millet's veterans of two world wars with over 200 photographs of servicemen and -women, and a display of military uniforms. Several local businesses are featured in the exhibits, including the barbershop of well-known curler John Barth. Your interpretive guide will bring the characters and objects to life. Our favourite story is the one about the recipe book open on the kitchen table—its owner had written her recipes on her blinds and when she replaced the blinds she cut them up and sewed the pieces together as the pages of a book to preserve the recipes!

The original furniture from the Hillside School southwest of Millet has found a home here. A teaching certificate from Ireland complete with marvellous Celtic designs hangs on the wall. It belonged to Margaret Atkins from Ireland, who taught at the Hillside school in 1909. The writing on the blackboard is a lesson prepared by a former teacher at the school from textbooks used in the 1920s. You can relive stepping off the train in the 1920s when you check out the new gallery exhibit "From a Sign Post in a Slough."

The museum also serves as the tourist information centre. Pick up a map showing the location of the historic churches in Millet—each one has a plaque outlining its history.

Open May–August Monday–Saturday 8:30 AM–4:30 PM
September–April Tuesday, Thursday 1:30 PM–4:00 PM
Tel: (780) 387-5558

THE BURNS CREAMERY ROCK GARDEN (Immediately north of parking lot east side of HWY 2A)

Linger for a while in the garden that once was the pride of the creamery in Millet. The Millet and District Historical Society and Communities in Bloom have lovingly recreated it from historic photographs.

DIGGING *DEEPER*: Communities in Bloom

Communities in Bloom are what you see all over Alberta! In 2000 Alberta had the highest number of entrants in Canada in this largely volunteer competition, which thrives on community cooperation and partnerships. From provincial to national to international levels, each community is judged on a population basis in a number of categories that range from best landscaping to heritage preservation. Individual backyards as well as municipal parks play a role in making a community bloom. Alberta communities keep company with ones of similar size in England, Slovakia, and Ireland, and other European countries. Millet has won national honours, which gives it twinning status with Audley in England.

KILBORN'S ANTIQUE STORE (1.5 blocks off HWY 2A on 50th Ave)

Al and Louise Kilborn have been in the business for many years and their store is well known to Alberta collectors. A large range of quality furniture, china, and jewellery items is to be found, among other collectibles.

Open Wednesday–Saturday 11:00 AM–4:30 PM
Tel: (780) 387-4546

AMARANTH ART NEEDLEWORK (5011 50th Avenue—off HWY 2A)

Needlework teacher Barbara Lacroix was excited to find a home for her

The Mercantile Company building in a pre-Christmas mood.

gallery of original Alberta textile and needle art in the old Millet Mercantile Company building. This is an opportunity to see the work of well-known artists and one-of-a kind garments. Needlework supplies include a wide range of specialty items that include silk, linen, and cotton threads in exquisite colours. Hand-dyed silk threads and ribbons, patterns, kits, beads, and books—your creative urges will surge!

Open Tuesday–Saturday 9:30 AM–5:30 PM

Tel: (780) 387-5532

DIRECTIONS: Returning south on HWY 2A, before you leave Millet, turn east over the railway tracks at the Petro-Canada gas station, for 0.3 KM. Turn south onto RR 244 (the Calgary–Edmonton Trail) which runs parallel to HWY 2A.

ALONG THE WAY: Sand Dunes

As you drive through this area, look for signs of sandy soil. The large flat area between Wetaskiwin and Ponoka was once a massive lake left after continental glaciers melted. As the lake dried up, the sandy bottom was blown into the Millet area. You can see evidence of the sand in the form of dunes of up to seven metres thick.

A dune is simply a mound of fine-grained sand that has been shaped by the wind. Those dunes are now covered with vegetation, but look carefully to make out horseshoe shapes with the blunt, steep ends facing the direction of the wind. They were created when the wind pushed the sand along, creating a gentle slope, ending in a steep side where the sand grains tumbled down.

This sand is composed mostly of quartz, a very common component of rock that is quite resistant to erosion. While other minerals break down small enough to be dissolved in water, quartz remains as small particles. Vegetation that favours sandy soil, such as jackpine and juniper, are seen along the way.

DIRECTIONS: At fork in road (4.3 KM), stay right and continue straight on.

ALONG THE WAY: The Calgary–Edmonton Trail

You are travelling on the old Calgary–Edmonton trail. It was first known as the Wolf Trail because the first section south from Edmonton ran to the Wolf River, now known as the Blindman River. It was also referred to as the Bow River Trail. Prior to the establishment of Fort Calgary, the focus was first on a route west to Rocky Mountain House from Wolf Creek, and second on a southwest route to the Bow Valley. The orientation of travel and freighting was from north to south. Once the Canadian Pacific Railway arrived in southern Alberta, reaching Calgary by 1885, goods were unloaded and freighted north by the most direct route to Edmonton. The trail then became known as the Calgary–Edmonton Trail.

The development of the Calgary–Edmonton Trail was directly linked to the establishment of a new government weekly mail service between Calgary and Edmonton from July 1, 1883. Passenger traffic soon followed and early travellers on the Calgary–Edmonton stage included members of the North West Mounted Police, missionaries, travelling salesmen, and members of the Geological Survey of Canada. In 1885 the fare for passenger service one-way was twenty-five dollars. For this you got a bone-rattling ride that required five nights out on the trail, sleeping at crowded stopping houses, and suffering indifferent food and inclement weather!

In 1886, when the Calgary–Edmonton trail was surveyed, it largely followed the original cart trail for the 200 miles between the two settlements. As George Roy, the Dominion Land Surveyor responsible for the northern half of the route, stated: "In view of the great traffic and immense travel which some day may be done this way, my intention was to make the road as straight as the actual direction of the trail between the two extreme points, Red Deer and Edmonton, would allow, without neglecting the advantages of a hard bottom, easy grades, and good drainage."

DIRECTIONS: At the next fork in road, keep left onto the gravel. At the four-way stop, continue straight on. You are now on RR 242A.

I SPY: Bigstone creek

As you go down the hill, the road crosses Bigstone Creek, at what was known as Lucas Grove. If you look to the north you can see the old bridge abutment on the Calgary–Edmonton Trail, which ran south up along the trees to join the present road. Here on the south bank of Bigstone Creek was Government Supply Farm No. 18, set up by the Department of Indian Affairs and located at a central point between the reserves in the area. In 1879 Samuel Lucas came west from Ontario as the farm instructor. He travelled from reserve to reserve as a part of his duties. In 1883 a detachment of the NWMP was stationed at the farm. The Calgary–Edmonton telegraph line went across the farm, and the NWMP operated the telegraphic office located there. A grist and saw mill served the needs of the farm and the small number of settlers in the area. The Department of Indian Affairs moved the farm and instructors—including Samuel Lucas, who was appointed agent—to the Hobbema Reserve in 1889.

ALONG THE WAY: Fort Ethier

As you come up the hill from the creek look to the east for the Fort Ethier block house in the trees. The threat of rebellion in 1885 saw the

The Block House remained a landmark on the Calgary–Edmonton Trail after 1885. It has been restored and is seen here in the splendour of a winter evening.

Canadian Militia sent west to quell any possible uprising. In May 1885 detachment No. 8 of the 65th Mount Royal Rifles, under the command of Captain Ethier, took possession of the Government Supply Farm. After a party of Indians had been detected in the area, a decision to build a fortification was made. The fort took ten days to construct. According to observer Charles Daoust, "A blockhouse ten feet square and two stories high dominates the hill and the river . . . In front of this the road from Calgary to Edmonton is covered by a sentinels box. On the other side there is a large ditch and two sentry posts."

Please note that the Block House is on private property. It is clearly visible from the road. You are requested not to park on the property or to block access.

DIGGING *DEEPER*: The Lucas Stopping House

Travellers on the Calgary–Edmonton stagecoach were welcomed at the stopping house beside Fort Ethier, opened in 1889 by Frank Lucas (brother to Sam) and his wife Margaret. The house only had one spare room and bed, and, according to family recollections, "when the stage arrived there was a race to the house to determine who got the bed, first come first served. If the first to arrive was a minister he got his bed free, irrespective of his profession or faith." By 1891 business fell off as the Calgary–Edmonton railway passed only a short distance to the west. In 1898 the Klondike gold rush brought many prospectors north over the Calgary–Edmonton Trail. Samuel, son of Frank Lucas, later recalled that the trail was "jammed with fortune hunters heading for the Klondike. Some had pack trains, some had teams and wagons and ox carts, while others were walking with big packs on their backs."

The Calgary–Edmonton stagecoach sets out in fair weather.
GLENBOW ARCHIVES, NA-1902-5

DIRECTIONS: At the T intersection turn east on TWP 470. At HWY 814 (2.8 KM), turn south. After 3.2 KM turn east on HWY 13. Follow the signs for the Central Alberta Railway Museum. After 5.1 KM, turn south onto RR 234. Cross the railway line with caution—this is a main line. Continue south, crossing HWY 613. Watch for the silhouette of a grain elevator to the southwest—your first glimpse of the Alberta Central Railway Museum.

I SPY: **Hutterite Colony** (See page 188).

STOP: **Alberta Central Railway Museum**

Beyond the trees lies the world of the railroad that was once the main link between communities in central Alberta. Cross the tracks to buy your ticket at the station wicket for a guided tour. Ask the stationmaster what a train order hoop is to get him talking! You will soon be on your way to

see the rolling stock and cars under restoration. Restoration of the 1906 Alberta Grain Company grain elevator from Hobbema is also underway. The mail express exhibition car has been adapted to interpret CPR rail history in western Canada. You can have a short train ride on the restored track before you begin the next leg of your tour. Check out Railway Day on the third Sunday in August.

Open Victoria Day weekend–Labour Day weekend Wednesday–Sunday 10:00 ᴀᴍ –4:00 ᴘᴍ

Tel: (780) 352-2257

Alberta Central Railway Museum, one of Alberta's best-kept heritage secrets.
ALBERTA CENTRAL RAILWAY MUSEUM

OPTION: You can return to Wetaskiwin by turning west at HWY 613.

DIRECTIONS: Retrace your route to HWY 13 and turn east. The flat terrain suddenly drops away into a wide U-shaped valley.

DIGGING *DEEPER*: Gwynne Channel

This wide, scenic valley dwarfs the narrow lake—Coal Lake—at its base. Could the flow of water have once been large enough to gouge such a channel?

Over 10,000 years ago, a lake that stretched as far as the eye could see covered the Edmonton area. The climate was warming up, glaciers were melting, and the water we call glacial Lake Edmonton was held in place by a wall of ice. The ice was eventually breached on the southeast side, sending an incredible torrent of water, with icebergs as big as houses, in this direction. Before the ice broke, there was no valley; the land here was at the same level as the top of the valley is now.

In just a few days, that wall of water, with about one thousand times the flow of the North Saskatchewan River, scoured away thousands of tons of sand, gravel, and rock. It left this impressive valley, called a glacial meltwater channel. Further south, the Gwynne channel provides a path for the Battle River.

DIRECTIONS: After 5.6 KM, turn north on HWY 822 (RR 230A). Take the first left fork to enter Coal Lake South Recreation area.

STOP: Coal Lake South Recreation Area

The camping/day use area south of the dam offers a central water pump, picnic tables, fire pits, and pit toilets. This is a good spot for a picnic.

You are at the south end of Coal Lake, a narrow, eighteen-kilometre-long channel of water that lies forty-five metres below the top of the valley. This valley also holds Saunders and Ord lakes, and Driedmeat Lake, which joins with the Battle River. Coal Lake is named for the beds of coal along its northeast shore. Though it was never mined commercially, local farmers dug the fuel to heat their homes until the 1950s.

COAL LAKE

Coal Lake has long been used as a water supply for Wetaskiwin. When the lake depths dropped to below 2.5 metres, the water took on an unsavoury taste and colour. Alberta Environment subsequently built an earthen dam with a low-level riparian outlet and a concrete overflow spillway. The lake is now kept at a fairly steady mean depth of 3.5 metres, ensuring not only a good-quality water supply for Wetaskiwin but also a reservoir of water to keep the Battle River flowing in times of drought. The dam is also a boost to the fish population since winterkills are no longer a threat. Fishermen have good success here with white suckers, northern pike and yellow perch.

Being a hyper-eutrophic lake (one rich in nutrients), Coal Lake often presents tremendous blooms of algae. It may be unsightly, but simply shows the tremendous amount of nutrients available to higher forms of life.

FEATURED *PLANT*: Algae

Algae are the "grass" of the aquatic system, providing food to the insects, amphibians, and fish that in turn feed the next level of the food chain. Over

25,000 species of algae inhabit the earth, and they include everything from seaweeds such as kelp to the "pea soup" algae seen in Alberta lakes.

Algae have no true leaves, stems, or roots, since they live entirely submerged in water. To reproduce, the individual plants may produce spores, or multiply by fragmentation in which a piece breaks off the parent plant and grows into a new plant. Single-celled algae, such as our "pea soup" variety, simply divide into two. When the heat and sunlight of midsummer trigger each of the millions of microscopic organisms to split every twenty-four hours or so, it does not take long to amass high concentrations of algae that colour the water with a bright green hue.

DIRECTIONS: Return to HWY 13 and continue east, through the hamlet of Bittern Lake.

OPTION: Gwynne outlet loop: This 16-kilometre loop takes you on a scenic drive through the Battle River Valley. During wet weather conditions on this route can be muddy and slippery, but in dry conditions the gravel road presents no problems.

DIRECTIONS: Turn south off HWY 13 onto South Bittern Lake Road (RR 22.0). Follow the winding road into the valley, over the bridge, and out of the valley on the other side. At the top of the hill continue straight on through the first intersection. After 7.5 KM turn left, go through the next intersection following the sign for the bridge, and continue north on RR 21.5 down the hill onto the valley floor again.

ALONG **THE WAY: Valley Floor**

You can imagine the massive wall of meltwater that, if taking place right now, would pick you up like a tiny cork and sweep you off toward Camrose. Today, the scene is pastoral with only the slow-moving Battle River as a reminder of the former deluge.

The soil is very fertile on the valley floor where cattle graze and hay is harvested. The road crosses the river heading south and takes you up the south side of the valley. As you drop again into the valley you travel through stands of aspen poplar.

I SPY: **Peter Fidler Historic Cairn**

Just south of the second bridge, on the west side of the road. The legendary Peter Fidler, explorer and mapmaker for the Hudson's Bay Company, crossed the Battle River in 1792.

You will enjoy spectacular views of the Gwynne Channel as the road
winds down to the kilometre-wide valley floor.

FRED SCHUTZ

DIRECTIONS: Cross the bridge and follow the road north 15 KM out of the
valley.

I *SPY*: Rosenroll Cemetery

This is all that remains of Rosenroll, whose inhabitants were literally put
out when the Canadian Pacific Railway placed a station and new town
site at the south end of Bittern Lake on its branch line east from
Wetaskiwin in 1904. Rosenroll was a going concern just two miles away.
Nevertheless, Rosenroll continued to grow, riding on a promise from
the Canadian Northern Railway that a branch line would eventually be
built through the town, and soon had a creamery, store, two implement
dealers, church, school, livery and feed barn, blacksmith, and a telephone exchange. The hotel that had been built at Bittern Lake even
moved to Rosenroll! Hope that the Canadian Northern would run a
branch line through Rosenroll was finally dashed in 1909.

Amalgamation of Bittern Lake and Rosenroll took place July 1,
1910, as the post office took the name of Bittern Lake. Messrs. Olstad
and Murray placed their general store on bobsleigh skids pulled by
twenty teams of horses and moved to Bittern Lake. Other businessmen

and house-owners soon followed suit. Ironically, the last building to move to Bittern Lake was the hotel that had originally been built there.

DIRECTIONS: At HWY 13 turn east for Camrose.

DIRECTIONS: At the junction of HWY 21 (5.1 KM) you can join Tour 5: Camrose to Stettler (page 66) or continue to Camrose.

STOP: Camrose

Scandinavian immigrants originally settled this fast-growing community. There is plenty to do here—take your pick of nature or heritage walks, visit museums, or enjoy refreshments in an historic setting. You can browse for books, antiques, and art on the lively historic Main Street.

HISTORIC DOWNTOWN CAMROSE WALKING TOUR

Pick up a copy of the walking tour brochure at the Main Street Office at 4949 50th Street or at Pop'lar Books at 4952 50th Street. Find out the history behind the facades along 50th Street and the Sparling district on 49th Street north of HWY 13.

MIRROR LAKE PARK

The continuous paved trail around the lake is a pleasant thirty-minute walk in either direction. Look out for swans and ducks as you walk, or rest a while on one of the benches. Cross the lake by the bridge on Grand Avenue and then rejoin the trail.

There is a parking lot on north side of 48th Avenue, before 53rd Street.

BILL FOWLER CENTRE

The Bill Fowler Centre houses the Chamber of Commerce and Visitor Centre.

Open year-round Monday–Friday 8:30 AM–7:30 PM

Victoria Day weekend–Labour Day weekend Saturday, Sunday 9:00–5:00 PM

FEATURED WILDLIFE: Trumpeter Swans

The trumpeter swan is the largest swan in the world. By the early 1900s, it was nearly hunted to extinction for its beautiful feathers and tasty meat. Today, it is a protected species that is being reintroduced into its former breeding area. The Camrose swans are part of that program. Young from these swans have been relocated to Elk Island National Park east of

Edmonton, where adults are already nesting in the wild. The cygnets (young swans) are fostered with the wild adult birds. If they become well-accustomed to the location, they are likely to return there to breed.

Trumpeter swans, with the yellow teardrop in front of the eye, are similar in appearance to the tundra swan, a common species that passes through Alberta in large numbers during migration. The trumpeter has all-white feathers and a black bill with a red border on the lower mandible of its beak. Listen for its call: a low, bugling sound.

A few mute swans also make their home at Mirror Lake. They are a domesticated European variety and can be distinguished from the trumpeters by their orange bill and lack of a voice—except a hissing sound when threatened.

The Mirror Lake swans must have a small bone removed from their wings to prevent them from flying away. They are overwintered in a special facility of pens and water tanks, living up to thirty-five years in captivity.

CAMROSE NORMAL SCHOOL (4612 53rd Street)

Now the Rosehaven Care Centre, this impressive building was built to house the Camrose Normal School in 1915. Camrose Normal was the second Normal school established in Alberta to train the teachers so urgently needed in the legions of one- and two-roomed rural schools across Alberta. Student teachers as young as sixteen tackled myriad subjects, including penmanship. The average grade required to pass was 50 per cent. The eager graduates, women for the most part, then sallied forth to teach in challenging conditions, where knowledge of wood stoves and first aid was as essential as geometry.

Camrose Normal closed in 1938. The Department of National Defence used the building during WWII. Since 1947 the building has provided care for the elderly. You might want to have a snack at the Rosehaven Courtyard Cafe in the central atrium of the renovated building.

Open year-round Monday–Friday 8:30 AM–4:30 PM

Closed weekends and holidays. Entrance lower level.

CAMROSE & DISTRICT CENTENNIAL MUSEUM (46th Avenue and 53rd Street—access off 46th Avenue)

Over 10,000 artifacts, including early surveying instruments, are on display in the main building. Also on site are a number of restored buildings, including a log house, a church, and a school. The replica of the 1907 Camrose fire hall holds a wide array of firefighting equipment including the first fire trucks used in Camrose—here you can see a shiny well-polished red 1929 half-ton International automobile hose car with pump engine, along with its companion—a 1929 one-and-a-half-ton Ford Model AA chemical truck, used to carry two forty-five gallon soda-acid tanks. Soda-acid was the fastest line of defence in any fire; water came second. Both vehicles served Camrose until 1955.

Open May 15–Labour Day Tuesday–Sunday 10:00 PM–5:00 PM
Tel: (780) 672-3298

In summer, the ski jump is no less awe-inspiring.

CAMROSE SKI JUMP (End of 39th Avenue off Parkview Drive through Parkview Estates. Follow city campground signs to Stoney Creek Centre parking lot.)

The Norwegians who settled in the Camrose area were able to continue the love affair they had with their handcrafted wooden skis. Both ski jumping and cross-country were popular in Alberta after the turn of the century. At Camrose the Fram Ski Club began construction on a forty-foot tower in the fall of 1911 on the Thompson farm. Spectators were eager to pay the twenty-five cent entrance for the first ski jump tournament held in January 1912. Adolph Maland soared seventy-four feet through the air to be acclaimed the winner. The club then extended the scaffold another ten feet, so the next record of ninety-one feet was established in February 1912. When the first scaffold blew down, a new one was built in 1924 to replace it, and this in turn was replaced by a third one in 1930, in time for the Western Canadian Championships in 1932. Ski jumping fell out of vogue in the late 1960s, and the jump was taken down.

The Camrose Ski Club, however, once again has a ski jump, one of only a few in western Canada. Occasionally in winter, you can watch this sport that so obsessed early settlers of the region in a setting that has changed little in ninety years.

TRESTLE RAILWAY BRIDGE/WALKING TRAILS

The Canadian National Railway bridge is visible from the parking lot of the Stoney Creek Centre at the ski hill. Consult the posted map of the city trail system, and follow the trail southward until you are standing underneath the bridge. Retrace your steps or continue in a loop that will bring you back to the parking lot.

AUGUSTANA UNIVERSITY COLLEGE (4901 46th Avenue)

Camrose Lutheran College was founded in 1910, and its first building, now known as "Old Main," had been constructed by 1912. Designed by Professor J. P. Tandberg, the first college principal, it is an impressive three-storey wood-frame structure that is still used for classes by students at Augustana University College.

49TH STREET RESIDENCES

It is well worth a stroll north down two blocks of 49th Street, just off the campus, to see some of the most attractive early-twentieth-century urban residences in the province. One well-known Camrose figure to have lived on this street, locally known as College Lane, was Chester Ronning.

DIGGING *DEEPER*: Chester Ronning

Born in China in 1894, Ronning served as a fighter pilot in WWI. He then taught in Edmonton until 1921, when he and his wife returned to China to teach in the Lutheran mission school founded by his parents. In 1927 he returned to Canada to become the Principal of Camrose Lutheran College for the next sixteen years. Elected MLA in 1932 for the United Farmers of Alberta, he was defeated in the election of 1935. A member of the Canadian Commonwealth Federation (CCF), Ronning was provincial leader of the CCF in Alberta from 1938 to 1942. He then served as head of intelligence in the RCAF until 1945. This experience led to a career change. Ronning joined the Canadian Foreign Service and returned to China as First Secretary and Chargé d'Affaires until 1951. Later postings included Ambassador to Norway, High Commissioner to India, and special representative to Hanoi and Saigon in 1966. Ronning's distinguished service to Canada has been recognized with six honorary degrees and Companion of the Order of Canada, among other awards. A remarkable man, Ronning retired to Camrose, where he died in 1984.

DIGGING *DEEPER*: Main Street Programme

Remember when all the action was on Main Street and window shopping was fun? The main street programme has been running in Alberta since 1987. It is a community-driven economic enterprise designed to promote downtown revitalization. Merchants can restore or enhance the historic character of their main street by bringing back the original appearance of their building or developing character signage—all with technical and financial assistance through matching grants through the Alberta Historical Resources Foundation. Camrose is one of fourteen communities, also including Lacombe, Didsbury and Wetaskiwin, which have participated in the programme.

CAMROSE CANADIAN CLUB (4857 50th Street)

Camrose's businessmen met here to play billiards or have a quiet moment with a newspaper in the reading room. The Government of Alberta bought the building for offices and a provincial courtroom. Moved to its present site in 1957 on the completion of new provincial building, it served for many years as the Camrose Public Library. Today it is home to the spacious and urbane Merchants Tea and Coffee.

Open Monday–Friday 7:00 AM–10:00 PM; Saturday 8:00–10:00 PM

CAMROSE RAILWAY MUSEUM, GARDENS AND TEA ROOM (44th Street and 47th Avenue, one block south of HWY 13)

This Canadian Northern Railway station house was built in 1911. By 1914 Camrose was served by the three great Canadian transcontinental systems: the Canadian Pacific Railway; Canadian Northern Railway; and the Grand Trunk Pacific Railway. Camrose was busy—up to twelve passenger trains passed through daily. Browse around the museum—our favourite exhibit is a G-scale garden railway, a train on 200 feet of brass tracks through an historic model Alberta landscape. You may also visit the library and archives of the Canadian Northern Society, which runs the restored stations at Meeting Creek (see page 72) and Big Valley (see page 177) as well as a gift shop. Two small buildings have also been restored: a 1919 tool shed, complete with tools, and a watchman's shed. You can

This impressive building was the home of the Camrose
Canadian Club for a decade, 1908–18.

catch a light lunch or a beverage in the tearoom before continuing on
your way.

Open Victoria Day weekend–Saturday of Labour Day weekend
Monday–Saturday 10:00 AM–5:00 PM

Tearoom open Thursday and Friday 1:00 PM–5:00 PM; Saturday
10:00 AM–5:00 PM

A themed "pioneer" lunch is served on Saturday lunchtime.
Wheelchair accessible.

Tel: (780) 672-3099

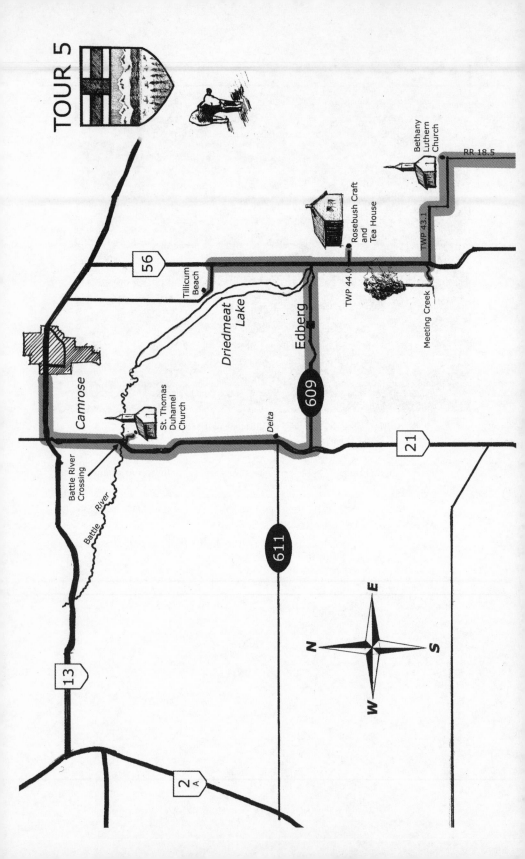

TOUR 5

Camrose

Battle River Crossing

Battle River

St. Thomas Duhamel Church

Driedmeat Lake

Tillicum Beach

56

Edberg

609

Delta

611

21

13

2 A

Rosebush Craft and Tea House

TWP 44.0

RR

Meeting Creek

TWP 43.1

Bethany Luthern Church

RR 18.5

N E W S

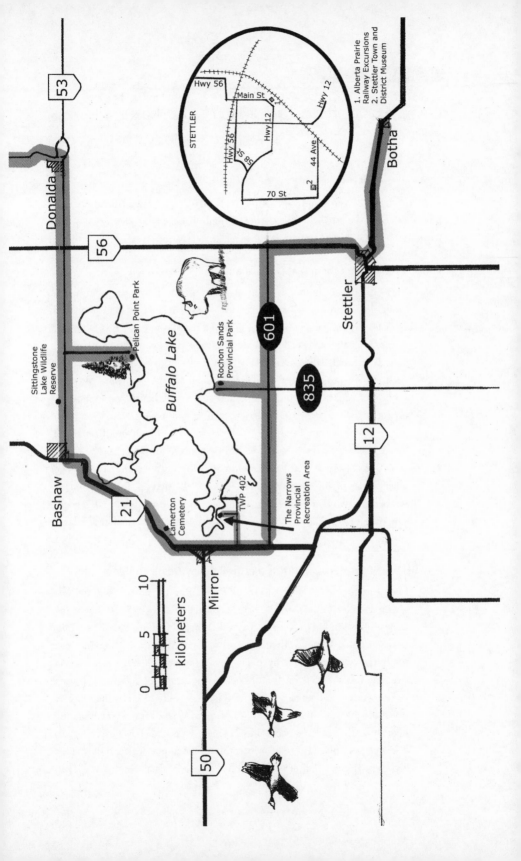

Camrose to Stettler, via Meeting Creek, Bashaw and Buffalo Lake

DIRECTIONS: From Camrose (see page 58) take HWY 13 west for 8 KM and turn south on HWY 21 for 7.8 KM. At St. Thomas Road on the south side of the Battle River Valley, turn east into the Provincial Recreation Area.

STOP: Battle River Crossing at Old Duhamel

This valley was home to Métis settlers from the 1870s, and when Dominion Land Surveyors arrived in 1883 they laid out the established river lots in this valley on both sides of the river. Names such as Dumont, Salois, and Laboucane echoed here. First called the Laboucane settlement, seventy families lived here by 1884, many of whom were freighters. The Battle River crossing was a major focus on the freight route between Edmonton and the end of steel in southeast Saskatchewan. Soon, however, the railway reached Calgary and the freight route moved west. An influx of immigrants came into the area, known as Duhamel from 1892 when a post office was established in François Adams's store. The eighteen-room Shamrock Hotel was built in 1901 close to the river's edge where boats plying the river to Driedmeat Lake tied up. Today nothing is left besides two Point of Interest signs located at the campsite on the south side of the river. The old Duhamel townsite was moved further south off HWY 21.

I *SPY*: Site of Former Grand Trunk Pacific Railway Trestle Bridge

Look east to where the Grand Trunk Pacific Railway line crossed the valley on an extraordinary trestle bridge constructed in 1909–10. It was the largest of its kind in the world. Six million board feet of BC fir—two million board feet alone for the piles—were used. Most of the timbers were thirty-two feet in length by twelve-inches square. A huge track-laying machine laid the rails on the bridge. At the height of activity, 120 men were working on the bridge, and local farmers were hired by the score to transport the heavy timbers from Camrose by wagon. Trains were running high above the valley by early fall 1911. Fire was a constant threat; barrels of water were placed at regular intervals on the upper deck and the bridge had to be inspected after each train had crossed to make sure a spark had

The sweep of the Grand Trunk Pacific
Railway trestle bridge over the Battle River at Duhamel.
PROVINCIAL ARCHIVES OF ALBERTA, A.11, 899

not ignited the timbers. By 1918, however, the GTP was in financial difficulties, and by 1923 had been amalgamated with the Canadian National
Railway. The GTP line was joined with the CNR line at Ferlow Crossing
south of the river and then ran north into Camrose, eliminating the need
to maintain the famous bridge, which was dismantled in 1924.

DIGGING *DEEPER*: The North West Mounted Police

The North West Mounted Police was established to police the North West
Territories in 1873. By 1888 several detachments were stationed in central Alberta to patrol the main trails. A detachment was opened in
Duhamel in 1894, but by 1895 it had relocated to Tail Creek further
south. From 1901–04 Constable "Blue" Smith was stationed at Duhamel.
Born William Walter Assheton-Smith, he is reputed to have earned his
nickname from the blue medicine bottle of whiskey he carried as he
patrolled on Rig, his faithful horse of seventeen years. Smith built a log
detachment building at Duhamel, complete with jail cell. Here he lived
with his wife Freda, daughter of John Edstrom, a homesteader at Edberg.
In 1910 Smith was curiously awarded the Imperial Service Order
Medal—the only member of the NWMP to receive this award instigated
in 1902 by King Edward VII, for meritorious service "in unhealthy places
abroad"!

DIRECTIONS: Follow St. Thomas Road uphill and around the curve as it heads east. Cross the railway line and take the first turn east. St. Thomas Duhamel church is on the south side of the road.

STOP: St. Thomas Duhamel Church Historic Site

French priest Father Beillevaire arrived in 1881 as Catholic missionary, and had a small church built by 1883. The church is post-on-sill log construction and was originally chinked with clay. The church, and later the settlement below in the valley, took the name Duhamel after Archbishop Joseph-Thomas Duhamel of Ottawa, who sent the bell. The steeple and sacristy were added some time later and the building was clad with siding. Original wall and ceiling paintings by a Mr. David of old Duhamel, along with nineteenth-century church furnishings, liturgical items, and vestments, make this one of Alberta's unsung heritage treasures. The church served the community from 1883–1962. Since then the Duhamel Historical Society has lovingly maintained it.

The church is always open to visitors. Please be sure to close the door when you leave.

A picnic table and privy make the church yard an ideal spot for a peaceful picnic. Take a walk to the cemetery behind the church. Here you will find Father Beillevaire buried, along with many of his early parishioners, who are listed on a commemorative wall.

St. Thomas Duhamel Church Historic Site.

DIRECTIONS: Retrace your route to HWY 21 and turn south.

ALONG THE WAY: Ancient Lake

At Duhamel, we again cross the Gwynne Channel (see page 54). At this point, the Battle River has taken over the wide valley as it flows to Driedmeat Lake and on to Saskatchewan. As you head south, notice how the topography flattens out. This area is composed of sand, silt, and clay that were deposited at the bottom of an ancient lake. In some places those deposits may be as much as eighty metres thick!

ALONG THE WAY: Delta

As you near the junction with HWY 611, look for the delta on the east side of the highway. A delta is the buildup of sand left behind when fast-moving water flows into a lake, then suddenly slows down and dumps the sediment it is carrying. This one was formed when an ancient river flowing from the south drained into the southern edge of a former lakebed.

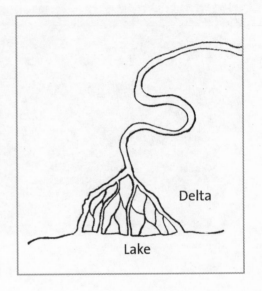

Delta

Lake

DIRECTIONS: After 15 KM, turn east at HWY 609. Follow HWY 609 17.6 KM to HWY 56 via Edberg.

ALONG THE WAY: Sloughs

The road runs between two large expanses of water. Neither has a name marked on the map, because they are sloughs that dry up during years of low precipitation.

I SPY: Saline Slough

These prairie sloughs are shallow catch basins for water draining from the surrounding area. As water continually evaporates, the salt content increases, sometimes reaching levels of one pound of salt for each gallon of water! Fish populations are not able to survive in such conditions, but waterfowl and shorebirds feed happily on the plentiful populations of aquatic plants and insects.

Although salt is necessary for the well-being of all birds, it can be lethal in high concentrations, so they need some way of filtering out the excess. Birds feeding at saline lakes have specialized salt glands located in their nasal cavities, that filter excess salt from the blood and excrete it via the nostrils.

FEATURED WILDLIFE: Killdeer

Shorebirds are well adapted for feeding along the margins of sloughs, picking out worms and other invertebrates from the soft, moist soil.

Killdeer eggs camouflaged against gravel.
FRED SCHUTZ

Watch for the killdeer as it flies just off the ground ahead of you, calling with its often heard "kill-dee-dee." It may be trying to distract you from finding its nest, which is simply a scraped hollow in the sand leaving the eggs completely exposed to the world. That would be a tremendous problem, except that the eggs are so well camouflaged that you are more likely to accidentally step on them than to distinguish their mottled colouring from the surrounding ground.

I *SPY*: South End of Driedmeat Lake

Shortly before the junction with HWY 56 the road follows the slope of the land downhill and you will get a scenic glimpse of the south end of Driedmeat Lake.

ALONG THE WAY: Driedmeat Lake

Once again we meet up with the glacial meltwater channel first seen at Coal Lake (see page 54). Looking at a map, you can see the characteristic shape of that channel in the long, narrow, river-like shape of this lake. A weir now controls the lake levels. Driedmeat was named for the pemmican recipe of First Nations: a mixture of dried buffalo meat and berries.

OPTION: You can access the lake at Tillicum Beach Park located on the east side of the Lake. (Turn north on HWY 56 for 9.6 KM and follow signs 2.4 KM west.) If you decide to stop for a swim in this lake or in any of central Alberta's lakes, be sure to towel off immediately afterwards. You are most likely to catch the "itch" during hot weather.

DIGGING *DEEPER*: Swimmer's Itch

The organism that causes swimmer's itch belongs to a family of worms called flukes, parasites that live on or in the bodies of animals. This species usually develops into an adult inside the body of a duck or other water bird. Eggs from the fluke exit the animal by hitching a ride inside its droppings. In the water, they transform into larvae that burrow into snails.

After leaving the snail, they must again find a warm-blooded animal, such as a duck, to develop into an adult fluke. When these tiny larvae come into contact with human skin, they mistakenly assume that they have found a duck. When they try to burrow into our skin, they die, causing redness and itching.

DIRECTIONS: Turn south on HWY 56.

STOP: **Rosebush Craft and Tea House** (3.4 KM south of HWY 609 on HWY 56. Turn east 1 KM on TWP 440)

You can look forward to a relaxing break from your drive as you turn into the Coles's drive and up to their pink foursquare house. Sip your tea or coffee, enjoy lunch, and look out on the surrounding peaceful farm fields.
Open May 1–Christmas Tuesday–Saturday 11:00 AM–5:00 PM
Tel: (780) 877-2243

DIRECTIONS: Continue south on HWY 56 for 8.1 KM. At the sign for Meeting Creek turn west into the hamlet.

STOP: **Meeting Creek**

Farmers from South Dakota settled the area around Meeting Creek in 1901–02. The news that the Canadian Northern Railway was to run through the valley in 1910 resulted in a townsite survey, and the post office, located five miles east, relocated into town. In 1912 another wave of immigrants arrived from Nebraska, lured by local businessman Harry Oium's rosy picture of the hamlet, whose pretty name originated much earlier and appeared on a map in 1884. Meeting Creek takes its name from the creek of the same name which flows east into the Battle River.

MEETING CREEK RAILWAY STATION MUSEUM

The CNR station depot at Meeting Creek was constructed in 1913 at the height of the railway boom. It is the last remaining example of a third-class depot building on its original site in Alberta, with its characteristic high hip roof broken by gable dormer windows. The station house has a waiting room, baggage room, office, and freight shed, as well as residential quarters for the stationmaster and his family. Although the station closed in 1966, passenger traffic into Meeting Creek continued until 1981. In 1986 the line was sold to a private railway company—Central Western Railway. Freight trains serving the grain elevators continued to pass through Meeting Creek until the line was completely closed in the late 1990s. The station has been restored by the Canadian Northern Society as a typical depot of the 1940s, along with a photo and artifact display on western Canadian railway station heritage. You can have a picnic in the adjacent park complete with bandstand and imagine a whistle blowing in the distance.

Open May–Thanksgiving. Key by local arrangement; check the sign at the station house for information.

MEETING CREEK GRAIN ELEVATOR MUSEUM

As the agent is no longer here to tell you how the mysterious workings behind the imposing exterior walls of the elevator function, we will!

The interior contains two open areas: an attached driveway and an open space, called the work floor, in the centre of the elevator. A large receiving scale takes up most of the driveway floor. The agent weighs the load with a balance beam to the side of the scale. The farmer dumps his wagon—or later his truck—through a grate on the scale floor. The grain flows through it to the pit below. This pit is an open triangular-shaped steel pan.

The "leg" rises from the pit to the top of the elevator. The leg—originally powered by a 15 HP one-cylinder gasoline engine mounted under the office, and more recently by electricity—is an endless belt with cups attached, running inside a wooden chute. As the leg turns it elevates the grain to the head distribution spout, or gerber. The gerber is moved from one bin spout to another to direct the grain to the desired bin, and is controlled from the work floor of the elevator with a wooden pedal and a large hand wheel attached to the front of the leg chute.

Most spouts in the cupola feed into the storage bins, of which there are at least eighteen. One spout leads directly outside the elevator on the track side for loading grain into grain cars. Another spout leads to the driveway where grain can be dumped into a waiting wagon or truck. To ship a quantity of grain the agent opens the bin and the grain pours into the hopper on the shipping scale to be weighed. Then the grain is dropped

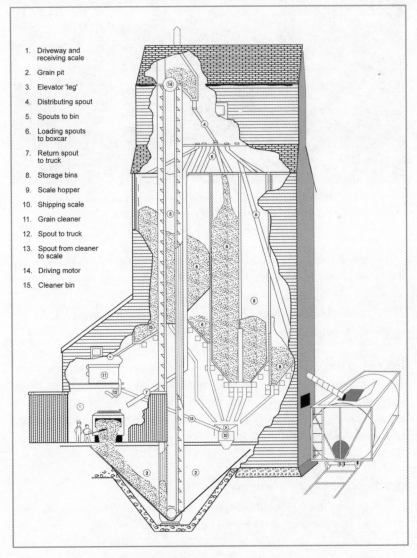

1. Driveway and receiving scale
2. Grain pit
3. Elevator 'leg'
4. Distributing spout
5. Spouts to bin
6. Loading spouts to boxcar
7. Return spout to truck
8. Storage bins
9. Scale hopper
10. Shipping scale
11. Grain cleaner
12. Spout to truck
13. Spout from cleaner to scale
14. Driving motor
15. Cleaner bin

How a grain elevator works.

CANADIAN INTERNATIONAL GRAINS INSTITUTE / WWW.CIGI.CA

The 1918 Alberta Pacific Grain Elevator is open to visitors. You can visit
the office and walk through to the work floor of the elevator.

into the back part of the pit where the leg re-elevates the grain to the top
of the elevator, through the gerber, and into the rail car loading spout and
into the grain car.

Open May–Thanksgiving. Key by local arrangement; check the sign
at the station house for information.

DIRECTIONS: Cross HWY 56 and take TWP 43.1 east up out of the valley.
After 5 KM take the second gravel road right and follow it south (this road has no
name or RR designation). You will get a good view of the Meeting Creek coulee
as you turn the bend to go east. At the Bethany Lutheran country church and
cemetery (6.6 KM) turn south onto RR 18.5 for 17.7 KM. You will soon see
Donalda on the far side of this impressive badlands valley.

DIGGING *DEEPER*: Driving uphill—in a wagon

As you come up the hill to Donalda you can imagine what a hard job it was
for farmers to bring their wagons full of grain up the sides of the coulee
to the grain elevators in the village. The horses needed to rest frequently,
with a stone placed behind the wheels. No doubt a downhill wheel brake
was useful—you can see one in the museum in Donalda.

DIRECTIONS: Cross the old railway bed and turn right onto Railway Avenue into the village.

STOP: Donalda

This sleepy village, one our favourites in Alberta, has seen busier days. The service station on Railway Avenue closed in 1985. The bank closed its doors in the summer of 1997, and the two grain elevators were demolished in 1998. The huge lamp overlooking the Meeting Creek Coulee is a beacon to visitors and an invitation to experience Alberta's almost lost small-town ambience along its leafy boulevard. Donalda has now become a destination for those seeking antiques and collectibles.

DONALDA AND DISTRICT MUSEUM (Southeast corner of Railway Avenue and Main Street)

Lamps, lamps, and more lamps! The museum has an extraordinary and important collection of over 850 lamps. From Aladdin parlour lamps to tiny nightlight lamps, local residents Donald and Beth Lawson collected them all. In 1979 the Lawsons donated their collection to the village and the museum was constructed to house them.

Other artifacts in the museum give you a chance to test your pioneer skills in the "What is it?" section. Also look out for the tea pouch made from the noses of two moose. Another unusual item is the Globe Cabinet patented in 1881, and brought from the USA by the Swan family in a covered wagon to the Donalda area in 1903. This tin kitchen cabinet is designed to be mouse-proof. It has a number of compartments for staple foods, including one for coffee beans—complete with grinder.

Open May–September Monday–Friday 9:00 AM–5:00 PM; Saturday, Sunday 11:00 AM–5:00 PM

Tel: (403) 883-2100.

Small admission fee for adults.

DONALDA GALLERY FOR THE ARTS (Northeast corner of Railway Avenue and Main Street)

The Canadian Imperial Bank of Commerce opened its doors as the Imperial Bank of Canada in 1932—ironically, during the Depression. Donalda had been without a bank for four years since the original Merchant Bank of Canada, built in 1912, burned to the ground in 1928. Banks were an important service in small towns before improved roads made it easy to travel to big centres. The imposing architecture of bank buildings lent a common air of stability across the prairies. In Donalda this building served the district for sixty-four years, finally closing in 1996. CIBC presented the building to the Donalda Community Arts Society along with a cheque for restoration that led to a ribbon-cutting in 2000. Today the cool high ceilings of the bank hall provide a wonderful art gallery space for the changing exhibits of the work of local artists, both professional and emerging.

Open May–June, September–October Saturday, Sunday 11:00 AM–5:00 PM

July, August Wednesday–Sunday 11:00 AM–5:00 PM

Tel: (403) 883-2255

www.donaldagallery.com

DONALDA CO-OP CREAMERY (Foster Street north of Railway Avenue)

The Donalda Co-operative Creamery Association closed its doors in 1987 after fifty years of receiving cream, eggs, and poultry from farm families in the area. But if you peek through the window it looks as though everyone has just left for the night. The office in the southeast corner of the building, along with the boiler and storage area, is separated from the manufacturing plant, with its pasteurizing vat and churns, and the egg grading area. This is what the plant would have looked like in the 1950s. By this time, the creamery was using both new churns as well as older technologies that included a Babcock Tester and centrifuge. The original cabinet for storing the butter papers remains in the building.

A butter paper. "Donalda Maid" was exhibited across Canada and won many prizes.
VILLAGE OF DONALDA

Tours available on request; ask at the museum.

I SPY: Antique Tractor (Corner of Foster Street and Alberta Avenue)

After 1920 many farmers switched from horsepower to tractor power. Tractors bought before 1945 were equipped with steel wheels studded with steel lugs. These tractors were slow, rough to ride, and dusty—but traction was excellent. When rubber tires became widely available after WWII, farmers preferred the smooth ride and left their steel wheels behind. Today steel wheel enthusiasts are to be found at tractor pulls only.

DIRECTIONS: Take HWY 53 west from Donalda.

STOP: Pelican Point Park—A Watchable Wildlife Site (18.1 KM from Donalda, follow signs 6 KM south)

Pelican Point Park is a well-equipped camping, beach, and day-use area with excellent hiking trails that are smooth and flat enough for wheelchairs. Pull into the marina, where you will find a Watchable Wildlife sign at the beginning of the trail system. The red shale trail follows the shoreline where shallow water has encouraged the growth of marsh vegetation. Cattails support red-winged blackbird nests. Willows are riddled with evenly spaced holes drilled by the yellow-bellied sapsucker. This is an ideal habitat for waterfowl such as the northern pintail and shorebirds such as the spotted sandpiper to nest, feed, and rest.

The trail then follows a peninsula that juts out into the lake, giving a panoramic view of the secluded bays in this corner of Buffalo Lake. Signs along the trail provide information about the wildlife and vegetation that inhabit the area. Fauna include the American kestrel, northern shoveller, Canada goose, Franklin's gull, ruddy duck, snowshoe hare, great blue heron, muskrat, white-tailed deer, and great horned owl. Partway around the trail, you will see an excavated area showing outcroppings of sandy soil, which settled out thousands of years ago as rivers from melting glaciers flowed over this spot. On the day that we explored the trails, the sun was low in the sky, lighting up the poplar trees on the opposite shore with a golden glow.

A secluded bay of Buffalo Lake.

FEATURED WILDLIFE: Moulting Waterfowl

Birds moult to renew old and worn feathers. Moulting reduces lice and allows the males to don a bright new coat of colour for the breeding season. For that reason the ducks have a partial moult in early April, immediately before breeding. In late June and July, a complete moult occurs. If you are trying to identify waterfowl during the summer, keep this in mind. The moult leaves the males with a dull, inconspicuous coat, called the "eclipse plumage." Renewing feathers takes a considerable amount of energy. Consequently, it must occur at a time when food is abundant and other activity is minimal.

Most birds moult their feathers gradually, so as not to lose the ability to fly. Ducks and geese, however, shed all of their flight feathers at once. These birds normally obtain their food walking or swimming, and they are still able to do these things without feathers. Nevertheless, there is a danger in not being able to fly away from predators. Consequently, they are very shy during this time of year, staying hidden in the reeds. The secluded bays in this end of Buffalo Lake offer plenty of food and cover for ducks during the time of the moult.

DIRECTIONS: As you continue west along HWY 53, the hummocky topography begins to fade.

STOP: Sittingstone Lake Wildlife Preserve (North side of HWY 53, 3.5 kilometres east of Bashaw)

This site was once a landfill site—not somewhere you might like to walk. Its reclamation has reintegrated the area back into the landscape and you can watch migratory birds from the observation point. Consult the trail map at the parking lot.

DIRECTIONS: Continue west on HWY 53 and turn north at the UFA tanks onto Bashaw's 50th Street.

STOP: Bashaw

Bashaw has been around since 1911, following the Grand Trunk Pacific Railway's announcement in 1910 of a new line south from Camrose, to run through Duhamel and south, passing close by the northwest tip of Buffalo Lake. Bashaw came into its own in the 1920s as the centre of an expanding agricultural district.

Dave More's mural on the curling rink wall.

HERITAGE PARK

The park is a convenient place for a quick road break, complete with picnic hut, playground, and washrooms. Don't miss the mural on the curling rink wall, painted by well-known artist Dave More. Watch for the transition of time as car designs change from the 1920s in the foreground to the 1940s at the north end of the street. Find the faces of early Bashaw residents, including Ed Kranston in the 1920s car, N.J. Holz and Jim Charlesworth leaning up against the manure spreader, police officer Doherty, and newspaper boy Lester Taylor. Now you are ready to turn onto Main (50th) Street and figure out how many buildings depicted in the mural still exist.

OLD BASHAW FIRE HALL MUSEUM (5020 50th Street)

This is one building in town that you cannot miss. It was built in 1914 to house the five-man volunteer fire brigade and the 1915 Waterous pumper, which remains in the hall. It is a plain frame building, embellished by a wood

The old Fire Hall, undergoing restoration.

cornice, ornate brackets, and a frieze. Fire was a huge concern in new settlements, and once the fire hall was completed Bashaw residents enjoyed a 5 per cent reduction in insurance premiums. The hall has a 37,000-gallon concrete water reservoir and an impressive tower that was used to dry the hoses. The Village of Bashaw had a system of sirens on telephones for a fire alarm until the 1950s.

Open summer months Monday–Friday 1:00 PM–5:00 PM; weekends by appointment.

Tel: (780) 372-3815 or (780) 372-3929

MAJESTIC THEATRE (5110 50th Street)

When the Majestic opened in 1915, magic lantern shows were all the rage. Legendary silent films such as *Jesse James* and *The Last of the Mohicans* with accompanying piano music entertained the citizens of Bashaw from the early 1920s. The Majestic has been through several incarnations. During the 1930s it served as Bashaw's first Catholic Church. In the early 1940s it returned to its roots as a house of entertainment rather than of prayer. Renovated for motion pictures, it opened as The Dixie and brought American popular culture to the district until 1984. The Friends of the Majestic Theatre Society are in the final stages of restoring the theatre to an art deco 1920s interior. A theatre museum will soon open in the foyer. Meanwhile, the Majestic is open by appointment.

Tel: (780) 372-2376

DIRECTIONS: From Bashaw head south on HWY 21 for 15.1 KM.

STOP: Lamerton Cemetery

Here lies one of Alberta's infamous characters: James Gadsby, who homesteaded in the district as early as 1885. Known as Longhair Jim, Gadsby soon had a reputation for his skill with a gun and his fondness for liquor. The story that he ran with the Jesse James gang south of the border, then returned to Canada and smuggled whiskey before settling down, goes undisputed.

DIGGING *DEEPER*: Lamerton

The cemetery is the only reminder of one of Alberta's earliest communities. Lamerton, which was northwest of the cemetery, had its origin in the Buffalo Lake Trading Post set up by Fletcher Bredin on the freight trail running north from Content. Bredin opened a post office named Lamerton in 1893. Mail came in twice a week over the trail from

The village of Lamerton circa 1910.

Lacombe. By 1895 the North West Mounted Police had a detachment at Lamerton, and by the early twentieth century Lamerton had all the makings of a town. Reached by a bridge over the creek, it boasted a hotel, stores, and creamery. All vanished once the railway brought Mirror into prominence, except for the two grain elevators that bore the name Lamerton from 1921–70.

OPTION: At the junction of HWY 21 with HWY 50 join Tour 6: Mirror to Rocky Mountain House (page 90).

DIRECTIONS: Continue south on HWY 21. Watch for the sign for The Narrows Provincial Recreation Area on the east side of HWY 21, 3.3 KM south of Mirror. Turn east on TWP 40-2, and follow signs to the Narrows.

STOP: The Narrows Provincial Recreation Area

This kilometre-long channel connects the main bays of Buffalo Lake to a small bay on the west end called Parlby Bay. Only about three feet deep and filled with aquatic plants, it is heavily used by waterfowl and other birds.

Fishing is very popular at Buffalo Lake, particularly for northern pike. Earthen, flat-topped mounds piled along the water, each with a picnic table and fish cleaning stand, were designed with the fisherman in mind.

During spawning, pike move west through the Narrows to Parlby Bay, and up Parlby Creek to the flooded hay meadows. The Narrows is closed for fishing from late March to late May each year to protect spawning pike.

The Narrows is a Watchable Wildlife site.

FEATURED WILDLIFE: Migrating Geese

The first geese to arrive are usually the Canada geese that stay here to raise their young. Others may go all the way to Alaska before stopping for the summer. Those just passing through, a group that commonly includes the snow goose, stop for rest and a bite to eat before continuing on. During the night, they will relax on the lake. By mid-morning, the geese will flock out to feed in the local sloughs and fields. Natural areas like these are important, not just for wildlife homes, but also as pit stops for such visitors.

Biologists are just beginning to understand what makes birds so good at finding their way over thousands of miles. The sun is very important; even on cloudy days, birds are able to pinpoint their location by perceiving the pattern of polarized light showing through the clouds.

At night, the moon and stars become important guides. And at any time of day or night, changes in the earth's magnetic field are thought to give clues to the birds about their location. They do not often get put off course, though it may happen, at least temporarily, due to fog, heavy rains or by being blown off course by strong winds.

Most birds usually fly at about 3,000 feet, though geese have been known to fly as high as 27,000 feet! At that altitude, they take advantage of jet streams—very fast-flowing winds that carry them along, making their long journey much easier.

DIRECTIONS: Retrace your route to HWY 21 and continue south. At HWY 601 turn east. After 18.1 KM, turn north on HWY 835 and travel 6.4 KM for Rochon Sands.

ALONG THE WAY: Knobs and Kettles

South of Buffalo Lake, great mounds of land bulge up on either side of the road. In between, shallow ponds fill in the low areas. Geographers call this hilly terrain knob-and-kettle topography. The knobs are the hills and the kettles—also referred to as prairie potholes—are the bowl-shaped ponds.

As the glaciers melted, they left behind a mixture of sand, silt, clay and boulders, called till, that had been scraped up over the years. In places where glaciers melted quickly, the layer of till was thinly spread over the ground. In other places, the glaciers slowed or stopped, dumping thick accumulations of till in one spot. Mixed in with the till were large chunks of ice that were insulated from rapid melting. When they eventually melted, the overlying till collapsed, leaving potholes in a hummocky landscape.

To recreate this landscape in a sandbox, mix ice cubes in with the sand. In places where the ice cubes melt, you will end up with depressions, leaving a lumpy topography like this one.

The rolling countryside of knob-and-kettle terrain.

STOP: Rochon Sands Provincial Park—A Watchable Wildlife Site

We parked near the lake, close to a prominent hill. It was identified as a Watchable Wildlife Viewpoint so we quickly climbed the stairs leading to the top. A thick crop of chokecherries and saskatoon bushes lined the way. At the top, we took in a tremendous view of Buffalo Lake. Using the boat launch spit as twelve o'clock, we could see Boss Hill at two o'clock, the Village of Rochon Sands at three o'clock, a wetland area at nine o'clock and Pelican Island at ten o'clock. Following the trail down the other side of the hill, we saw a couple of white-tailed deer and a ring-necked pheasant making their way about the park.

The view from the Watchable Wildlife viewpoint is well worth the climb.

I *SPY*: Ice-Thrust Hills

Prominent features in the village and park are the steep hills created by glaciers. These hills were translocated by the glaciers in a more-or-less intact state as thrust blocks, or deformed into thrust slabs and folds. The Watchable Wildlife viewing platform is perched on the top of an ice-thrust hill.

DIGGING *DEEPER*: Buffalo Lake

That famous explorer, David Thompson, gave Buffalo Lake its name. When he drew it on a map, he thought it resembled a buffalo with the head to the east and legs to the north. Buffalo Lake was a favoured Cree and Blackfoot camping area, very likely because the fescue grassland attracted large herds of buffalo.

The land around Buffalo Lake is a gently rolling glacial till plain, with much knob-and-kettle terrain. The vegetation is trembling aspen, wild rose, and saskatoon with rough fescue grassland on the drier south-facing slopes. Much of the area around the lake has been cleared for agriculture and is very productive for grain crops.

Buffalo Lake receives most of its surface inflow from Parlby Bay via Parlby Creek. Groundwater inflow to the lake is also significant; studies have shown that Buffalo Lake is moderately saline but has not increased in salinity over the years. That is somewhat surprising, since there has not been surface outflow from the lake for many years. The largest bay on the lake has a maximum depth of 6.5 metres.

This is one of the most important waterfowl breeding and staging areas in Alberta. It is estimated that seven thousand ducklings are raised at Buffalo Lake each year. In addition to waterfowl, colonies of great blue herons, terns, gulls, and grebes nest on or at the lake.

The ring-billed gull colony on Pelican Island is one of the three largest in Alberta, and the colony of Forster's terns is one of only a few in the province. The number of birds staging at the lake in autumn is impressive: 17,000 ducks, 3,500 swans, and 12,000 Canada and snow geese.

DIRECTIONS: Return south to HWY 601. Continue east 13.2 KM, turn south on HWY 56 and travel 9.2 KM for Stettler.

STOP: Stettler

On November 2, 1905 a new townsite on the Canadian Pacific Railway line from Kerrobert, Saskatchewan, to Lacombe, Alberta, went up for sale. Swiss immigrant Carl Stettler, the postmaster at Blumenau, two miles east, made the decision to pull up stakes and move there in December 1905. The post office moved in early 1906 and the hamlet was named after its first postmaster.

Things moved quickly in Stettler; businesses and residences rose out of the bald prairie. By June the village had its own newspaper, a police detachment, and a Dominion Lands Office. By the time the town was incorporated in November 1906, the *Stettler Independent* was able to report upwards of ninety district business and professional men. "It has graded streets, long stretches of sidewalk . . . has under construction a handsome fire hall and water storage tanks . . . handsome hotels, business houses, and residences of two- and three-storeys high grace the town. The population is creeping up close to a thousand . . . one of the churches is a structure that with its towering spire visible for many miles, would be a credit to a town of many thousand inhabitants." When you drive about it is clear that Stettler still boasts a number of its original fine homes. Some of the commercial buildings sport historical information plaques.

ALBERTA PRAIRIE RAILWAY EXCURSIONS (Station at 46th Avenue and 46th Street)

If you feel like parking your car for a while and returning to an earlier, more leisurely mode of transportation, we recommend a train trip. Climb aboard a vintage coach pulled by a steam-powered locomotive and go off for half a day. The train runs south to Big Valley. Onboard entertainment for children and information about the countryside is on offer as you travel. A rural buffet lunch or supper is included in the ticket price.

Tel: (403) 742-2811 or www.absteamtrain.com for more information, schedules, and reservations.

STETTLER TOWN AND COUNTRY MUSEUM (44th Avenue)

Did you know that Stettler once had a cigar factory? A tobacco leaf cutter, used in the manufacture of Van-Loo and Panama Queen cigars from 1912–16, is only one of thousands of items from Stettler's past to be found here. This is a museum for museum buffs! From the newspaper press, pin collections, a 1953 fire truck, and old toys, to old washing tubs and the story of the Stettler band, there is something for everyone. Twenty-three buildings, including a church, schools, machine sheds, and a railway station, are filled with artifacts.

The former courthouse is home to the ship's bell from the HMS Stettler, part of the town's wartime history. You can trace the improvements in dental equipment in the dental office of Dr. Albert Edward Aungier, and his son Dr. William Reid Aungier, who joined his father's practice in 1929. Between them, they offered dental services from 1911–77! Don't miss the display of artifacts from one of the province's earliest museum collectors, local Justice of the Peace, William B. Gray.

Open daily May–September 9:00 AM–4:30 PM

Small admission fee.

DIGGING *DEEPER*: Judge William Brigham Gray

Billy Gray was a Yorkshireman who came to the Canadian West and worked as a cowboy on the sweeping ranges southeast of Calgary in the

The former courthouse, part of the Stettler Town and District Museum.

1880s. He turned freighter and then rancher, and ran a stopping house and post office at Bullocksville, south of present day Alix, all before the turn of the century. In 1906 he finally settled to a new phase of life in the brand-new town of Stettler. At the age of fifty, he threw himself into making it a prosperous and law-abiding town. He served as Dominion Land Agent, and sold insurance and real estate. As Justice of the Peace, he heard local cases and imposed fines. He held a number of official positions, including auditor and notary public. He issued marriage licenses and later auto licenses. In his spare time Gray amassed an important collection of natural history specimens as well as artifacts and curios from around the world. Older Stettlerites have fond memories of going to Gray's large house, where the "Judge" never tired of talking about his collection, which was housed in the two front rooms. When he died in 1947, his obituary declared that the West had "lost one of the few remaining colourful characters of the early days."

OPTION: Excursion to Botha.

DIRECTIONS: Drive 13.1 KM east on HWY 12 from Stettler to Botha. Turn north into Botha and east along 50th Avenue.

I SPY: Heritage Mural—The Underwood Brothers and their Marvellous Flying Machine

Here on an end wall of the 1928 arena (50th Street, south of 49th Avenue) is a mural showing the Underwood brothers in flight. In 1907, George Elmer and John Underwood displayed their "flying wing" at the Stettler fair. It did not have a motor; rather, it was a kite. The elliptical fir wing was covered in canvas and wire spokes attached to the wing from a central hub on a platform, which propelled along the ground on motorcycle wheels. A series of experiments over the next two years ended with the kite smashing on a windy day.

While in Botha drop into the huge Botha Mercantile, which was built in 1909 and still boasts its name over the door. It has retained its original floors and an impressive expanse of pressed-tin ceiling.

DIRECTIONS: From Stettler, you may join Tour 11: Stettler to Trochu (page 175).

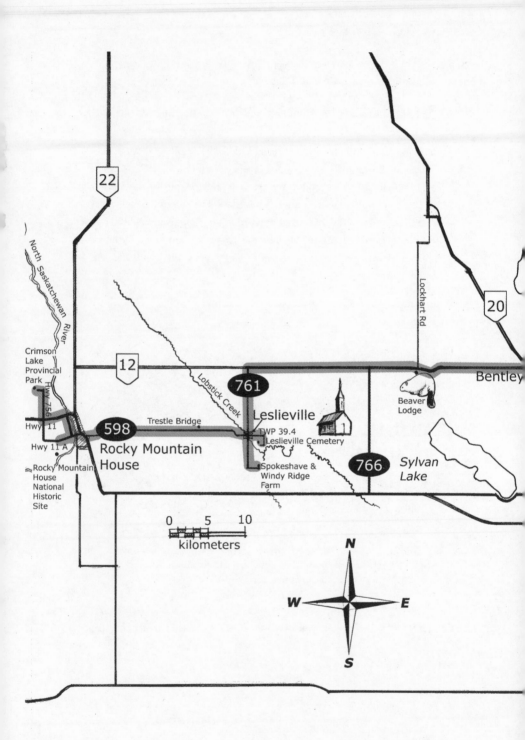

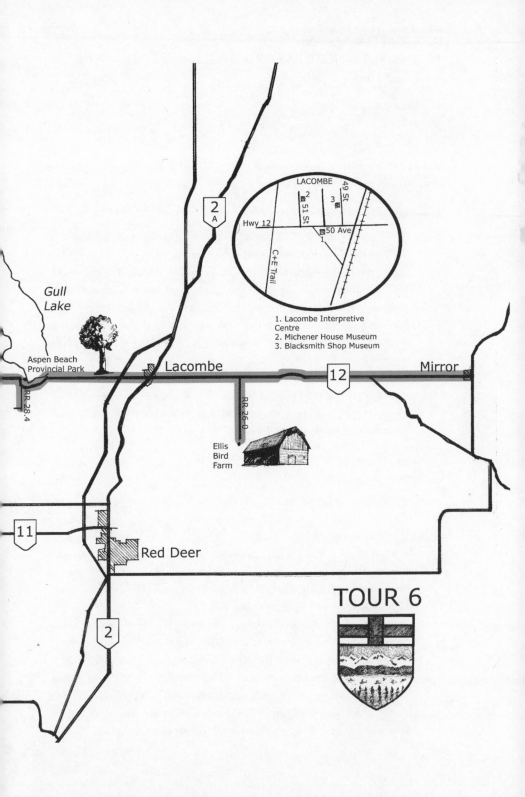

LACOMBE

49 St

2

51 St

3

Hwy 12

50 Ave

1

C+E Trail

1. Lacombe Interpretive Centre
2. Michener House Museum
3. Blacksmith Shop Museum

Gull Lake

Aspen Beach Provincial Park

RR. 28.4

Lacombe

12

Mirror

RR. 26-0

Ellis Bird Farm

2 A

11

Red Deer

2

TOUR 6

Mirror to Rocky Mountain House via Lacombe

DIRECTIONS: Mirror is located along HWY 50 just west of HWY 21, 17.2 KM south of Bashaw.

STOP: **Mirror**

The Grand Trunk Pacific Railway put this town on the map. Its namesake the London *Daily Mirror* reported on August 10, 1911, that the new town had two splendid boulevards: Whitefriars and Northcliffe. The GTPR soon built a roundhouse, repair depot, water reservoir, and living quarters for train crews. Hopes for Mirror were high; the townsite was surveyed and lots auctioned off—for a total of $251,648 in only eleven hours. Mirror never did become a city, and its days as a divisional point on the railway were over by 1924. The introduction of diesel locomotives in the 1950s meant that trains no longer even had to stop for water. Many of the spacious homes that once housed railway officials remain. The large number of vacant lots gives Mirror a rural feel, and the town's private gardens are a showcase in summer.

ST. MONICA'S ANGLICAN CHURCH (Corner of 49th Street and 50th Avenue)

St. Monica's, built in 1895, preceded the town of Mirror. In fact, the Anglican Church made a tidy profit on thirty-eight acres sold off during the great auction of 1911. Thirty-one volunteers from the area around the settlement of Lamerton (see page 80) just to the northeast built the church. Rancher Walter Parlby then applied for the land title from the Dominion Lands Office in Red Deer. By 1904 it was no longer a mission church and had its first resident minister.

In 1910, the *Stettler Independent* described the very pretty wedding between Miss Gladys Marrayat, of nearby Haunted Lakes, and Mr. R. E. V. Yerburgh, of Alix, which took place in St. Monica's on a cold Saturday morning in December. The guest list was a local who's who of British ranchers, including the bride's sister Irene and brother-in-law Walter Parlby. "The church was gay with the colour of pretty dresses; the prevalent tone being mauve, in accordance with present day fashion . . . the bride wore a semi-tailor-made costume of white cloth trimmed with a white silk braid, and a white hat trimmed with ostrich feathers." Imagine the scene as the couple left the church and climbed into a sleigh drawn by four white horses. Hear the snow crunch under the runners as the long cavalcade of sleighs follow en route for the wedding breakfast. You are welcome to visit the church; the key is available at the museum.

MIRROR AND DISTRICT MUSEUM (4910 53rd Street, opposite caboose)

Railway history and tales of a locality are well-told at this little museum. Find the wedding dress made from silk ordered from China by new immigrants to Mirror who wished to thank a local bride for English lessons. Among other town characters you will meet Dr. Douglas Chown, former physician in Mirror. Take time in the reading room to flip through the many photo albums of the town, people, and events in the districts.

Open Victoria Day weekend–Labour Day weekend Tuesday–Saturday 10:00 AM–6:00 PM; Sunday 10:00 AM–5:00 PM

Tel: (403) 788-3828

Admission by donation.

THE MIRROR HOTEL (Corner of 50th Avenue and 54th Street)

The Mirror Hotel is a typical boom-time Alberta hotel, originally known as the Imperial. Today it stands starkly alone on a corner above the railway line. If you are looking for a country bar experience, this is one you won't forget. Crowding the walls is an extraordi-

The Imperial Hotel in the mid-1950s.
GLENBOW ARCHIVES, PD-313-142

nary collection of animals who have been to the taxidermist—including moose, deer, bison, owls, hawks, a fox, and even a peacock!

DIRECTIONS: Head west on HWY 50 to join HWY 12 west for Lacombe. As you travel along HWY 12, look for the following common agricultural residents, easily spotted from your car.

FEATURED BIRD: Black-billed Magpie

The magpie is as common to rural residents as pigeons are to the city-dweller. Consequently, its beauty and uniqueness often goes unappreciated. Its strikingly long tail, black and white markings, and purplish sheen seem to belong more to an exotic species rather than a country commoner.

Black-billed magpie.
PETER LLEWELLYN / SPLIT SECONDS

Look for its domed stick nest in the trees along the road. The nest has one or more entrances from the sides, leading to a grass inner nest where the eggs are incubated. The magpie will eat everything from insects to roadkill, and scavenge on all food items that cross its path.

FEATURED WILDLIFE: Coyote

Look for coyotes as they race across a field to escape your view. They have a strong sense of self-preservation that includes working very hard not to be noticed. Coyotes hunt in pairs, feeding mostly on ground squirrels, mice, and hares. One coyote will openly approach the prey while the other stalks the intended lunch from behind.

If a coyote seems unusually friendly, do not approach it, since it may well be rabid. Rabies is a virus that attacks the brain and nervous system of its victim. It creates symptoms in animals that encourage them to spread the disease. The virus may induce calm, which allows predators to attack them, or humans to approach them. The virus also causes viciousness, giving the animal the urge to bite anything and everything. Rabies is a serious disease that must be treated promptly.

STOP: Ellis Bird Farm (34 KM west of Mirror, 8 KM south on Prentiss Road [RR 26.0])

The Ellis Bird Farm is an enchanting place to learn about local wildlife—especially feeding and nesting birds of many varieties. Charlie Ellis, "Mr. Bluebird," became enthralled with the western bluebird early in his life, and worried about the severe drop in their population. That spurred him to set up over 300 nesting boxes for the bluebirds and to establish a farm that provided habitat and food for all species of wildlife. Bluebird numbers alone increased from one pair to more than sixty pairs in the following two decades. To continue the hard work begun by Charlie and his sister Winnie, a special arrangement with Union Carbide resulted in the establishment of a non-profit organization that continues and adds to their work.

At the parking lot, pick up a self-guided trail brochure. A short walk will lead you past the world's largest collection of nest boxes—all functional (though not all in use at one time). Bluebird enthusiasts have sent them here from all across North America.

You will leave with some great ideas for your own backyard after seeing the demonstration water garden, rock piles, and log piles. These backyard possibilities provide shelter for a variety of creatures, including weasels, salamanders, and chipmunks. From the gazebo at the north pond, look for the cylindrical tunnels made of wire mesh and flax straw, donated by Ducks Unlimited, to encourage nesting ducks such as mallards and redheads.

Friendly staff and displays at the Visitor Centre will provide answers to questions about this unique site. You will particularly enjoy the closed circuit video of nesting and feeding birds. Ornamental fruit trees surround the tea house, and colourful gardens feature many plants intended to attract butterflies and hummingbirds.

Open Victoria Day weekend–Labour Day weekend Tuesday–Sunday and holiday Mondays 11:00 AM–5:00 PM

Tel: (403) 885-4477 (site) 346-2211 (office)

www.ellisbirdfarm.ca

Thanks to the many nest boxes set up in rural Alberta, the mountain bluebird is now commonly seen in open areas, winging through the air to snag insects.

DIRECTIONS: Return to HWY 12, continue west 10.3 KM, and cross HWY 2A onto Lacombe's Main Street.

STOP: Lacombe

The new townsite of Lacombe, on the Calgary and Edmonton railway, was ready for business in 1894. Edward Barnett had operated a stopping house some distance north on the Calgary–Edmonton Trail, on the east side of the lake that now bears his name. Seizing an opportunity, Barnett purchased the quarter section north of the land on which the C&E townsite had been laid out, and hired a surveyor to lay out an adjacent private townsite, north of what is now 50th Avenue. This created a unique angular aspect to Lacombe's street plan, highlighted by the distinctive triangular flatiron block built by the Merchant's Bank of Canada in 1904.

The Flatiron Building in Lacombe, around 1908.
GLENBOW ARCHIVES NA-3026-42

Lacombe boasted a population of 100 by 1900, and in 1902 was incorporated as a town. By 1905 the population had jumped to 900. Many of Lacombe's early residents built impressive homes in the architectural styles of the day, which have not lost their gracious ambience. Lacombe boasts possibly the best collection of Edwardian commercial buildings in Alberta outside of a major city.

LACOMBE INTERPRETIVE CENTRE (100–5005 50th Avenue)

In 1904 Merchants Bank of Canada placed its faith in the rapidly growing town and constructed this impressive building in the Beaux-Arts style. At the time there were only two other brick buildings in Lacombe, which suffered a disastrous fire in 1906. Today it houses first-rate exhibits—don't miss the video presentation in the Lux theatre in the basement.

Open daily 9:00 AM–5:00 PM
Tel: (403) 782-6666

MICHENER HOUSE MUSEUM (5036 51st Street)

This modest frame house, built as the manse for Lacombe's Methodist ministers in 1894, was the birthplace of Roland Michener, Governor

General of Canada 1967–74, and is the oldest surviving building in Lacombe. The museum has period-furnished rooms and displays on Michener's life and achievements. It also houses community archives and a camera and photograph collection belonging to early local photographer Ben Cameron.

Pick up a walking tour brochure from Michener House as a guide to the historic downtown core.

Open May–September Monday–Saturday 9:00 AM–5:00 PM; Sundays, holidays 12:00 PM–5:00 PM

Tel: (403) 782-3933

Admission by donation.

BLACKSMITH SHOP MUSEUM (5020 49th Street)

Blacksmiths were vital to the functioning of a community, not only for shoeing horses, but for making and repairing farm implements and machinery. A long line of traditional blacksmiths has worked long hot hours in this unassuming boomtown-front building since its construction in 1902. In that year Alfred Jacob Weddle opened the doors on this building and since then it has been in continuous use. The glow of the forge in the centre of the shop welcomes you into the dark smoky interior, where men originally stood around waiting and watching the blacksmith pound glowing metal. The building had two sliding doors to allow horses to enter, and one side of the shop was set aside for shoeing. To visit the blacksmith shop, owned by the Maski-Pitoon Historical Society, ask for a tour or demonstration at Michener House Museum.

Tel: (403) 782-3933

DIRECTIONS: Continue west on HWY 12 towards Gull Lake

I SPY: Pik-n-Pak Greenhouses (13.5 KM west of Lacombe)

This area of west-central Alberta is well known for its horticultural businesses, many of which are operated by families who originally brought their skills from Holland. Some specialize in decorative plants and flowers, others in vegetable production, especially tomatoes, peppers, and cucumbers.

STOP: Aspen Beach Provincial Park (16.8 KM west of Lacombe)

Drive into the Ebeling Day Use Area, turn left at the beach toward the boat launch, and park close to the red shale trail. Follow the trail past a horse corral, then across the road to a campground road. At site 164, you will see a glacial erratic and a sign a pointing toward the boardwalk. The boardwalk takes you over a dense marsh of cattails where viewing porches hold signs that describe wildlife inhabiting the area.

The hiking trail continues to Lakeview Campground and follows alongside the highway all the way to Bentley.

FEATURED **WILDLIFE:** Dragonfly

Be nice to the dragonfly; its diet consists mostly of mosquitoes! The dragonfly begins life as an aquatic creature, crawling in muddy lakeshore and pond bottoms. This is a feared insect carnivore, able to prey on tadpoles and even small fish. The extendible mouthpart, with hook-like teeth, shoots out to grab prey as they swim past. When sufficiently matured, the nymph drags itself onto the shore or up an emergent plant stem into the fresh morning air. As if only a masquerade, the skin splits open, from which the winged adult emerges. With a stiffening of the abdomen, air is sucked into the lungs and blood is pumped to the wings, which soon dry and take the transformed insect sailing through the skies to catch insects in mid-flight.

Red-winged blackbird.

FEATURED **WILDLIFE:** Red-winged Blackbird

Look for a flash of red. The red-winged blackbird is one of Alberta's most loved birds. It is a dependable resident of cattail populations seen on the shorelines of lakes, ponds, and roadside sloughs. The male of the species is commonly seen balanced atop a cattail singing his distinctive "ko-ka-ree." He does this to proclaim a nesting territory and to attract a female. The female bird is secretive, not wanting to attract attention to her nest. A mottled brown colouring effectively camouflages her against the cattail stems where the young are raised.

Red-winged blackbirds weave their nests between the cattails, hidden a few feet above the water using stems and leaves for construction. Red-necked grebes build nests from the same materials, but float them in open water.

Cattails are a source of food, building materials, and shelter for many wildlife. Their fibrous roots bind together the rich sediment that accumulates on the shoreline, eventually allowing the cattails to expand their territory. Other common wildlife to watch for in and around the marsh are muskrats, dragonflies, marsh wrens, and various waterfowl.

DIGGING *DEEPER*: Rocky Mountain House Trail

Part of the route from Lacombe to Rocky Mountain House follows the old Rocky Mountain House Trail out from the parkland. The trail was developed in the early nineteenth century. A section of it passes near the south end of Gull Lake, and continues west to ford the Blindman River, approximately two miles south of the present town of Bentley.

"It was near sunset when we rode by the lovely shores of the Gull Lake, whose frozen surface stretched beyond the horizon to the north . . . Night came down quickly upon the silent wilderness; and it was long after dark when we made our camps by the bank of the Pas-co-Pee, or Blindman's River."

So William Francis Butler described this section of the trail on his way to the Rocky Mountains in 1870, in his book *The Great Lone Land*, published in 1872. Butler was an Irish-born career officer in the British army, whose romantic descriptions of a wild northern land sold well among the British public into the twentieth century. The trail remained in use during the early twentieth-century settlement of this area.

OPTION: One section of the old trail is still visible. To see it, take the first road south, past the Aspen Beach turnoff (RR 28.4). Approximately 2.4 kilometres south, on the west side of the road after the railway line, you can see the esker (see page 186) that the trail followed. If you turn west at the next corner and stop, you can see the trail quite clearly. It is on high ground running southwest across the southeast corner of the quarter section, through the trees.

DIRECTIONS: Continue west on HWY 12.

STOP: Bentley

The crossroads in the centre of the village is on land filed in 1899 by an American Civil war veteran, Major McPherson, and his sons. McPherson opened a store, and within a couple of years the village was taking shape on this site. A good number of the early buildings have survived and the Museum has provided information plaques on many of the village's historic buildings, most of which are on the main street. The Bentley

The main street of Bentley is still recognizable in this photograph,
taken in August 1931, looking east towards Lacombe.

Mercantile, a cooperative store established in 1919, now houses a bar,
while the former service station is a chiropractic office.

BENTLEY MUSEUM (4929 51st Avenue)

Wander from room to room. Someone in the area was a fashion plate,
judging from the collection of hats! An auxiliary building has a great display of horse harnesses. The AGT operator won't talk back, but when you
meet her you can well imagine the days of the party line. Best of all at this
district museum are the interpretive guides—all old-timers of the district
and always ready to tell you a story or two.

   Open Victoria Day–Labour Day Wednesday–Sunday 1:00 PM–5:00
PM or by appointment

   Tel: (403) 748-3943 or 748-3891

   Admission by donation.

THE FARMER'S MARKET (Arena on Dick Damron Way—follow
signs from main street)

Each summer Saturday at 1:30 PM sharp the bell rings and the race is on—
to purchase the perfect pie, the perfect lettuce, the perfect gift among the

An old house is the home of the Bentley Museum.

wide range of craft items. From children's clothes to country collectibles, it's all here. Crowds from the nearby lake cabins and campgrounds mingle with locals buying, selling, and enjoying old-time music. The arrival of BC fruit and Taber corn is eagerly awaited each year. Get there early—things wrap up at 3:30 PM but often the best is bought long before that.

DIRECTIONS: Continue through Bentley and cross HWY 20, continuing west on HWY 12 for Rocky Mountain House.

I *SPY*: Bison Ranch (8.9 KM west of HWY 20)

Look out for a bison ranch just before the road begins to curve uphill for the Medicine Lodge Hills. Pilatus Farms, run by Armin and Rita Mueller, offer occasional tours. Catch them if you can or call for an appointment.
Tel: (403) 748-4218

DIGGING *DEEPER*: Bison Ranching

Buffalo is the common term for what is properly called bison. The bison on central Alberta's farms and ranches are descendents of the vast North American bison herds which once roamed from western Canada south to Mexico. These animals migrated to North America from Asia via the Bering Strait about 40,000 years ago, eventually becoming the most numerous of the large grazing animals, with a population estimated to have been between 30 and 75 million before the arrival of Europeans. By the mid-1880s, due to overhunting and the ravages of tuberculosis, the bison herds had disappeared from the prairies.

Bison ranching began as early the 1870s. Walking Coyote, a Flathead Indian who had built up a herd of six hundred animals by 1906, sold a few bison to Montana rancher Michel Pablo. These animals were dispersed across USA and Canada, some of them becoming the nucleus of the herds at Elk Island National Park and at Banff. Alberta bison ranch stock is derived from both the cream–coloured plains bison herd domesticated by Pablo and others and the black wood bison native to Alberta's Wood Buffalo National Park.

Central Alberta, especially west of Highway 2, has the highest concentration of bison ranches of any region in North America. Bison are large strong animals—a wood bison bull can weigh up to a ton—and are of uncertain temperament, so paddocks must be secured with either an extra-powerful electric fence or a strong wire fence at least six-feet tall. Most ranchers build special corrals in conjunction with a paddock strong enough to contain the animals and arranged to facilitate handling the unruly beasts when they need to be attended to by a vet, or for loading or moving them. Bison are capable of foraging year-round for their feed, but most are fed baled hay and silage in the winter months.

The yellow-red-coloured calves are born in spring after a gestation of nine months and weigh from twenty-five to forty pounds at birth. The bison calves may be fattened in a feedlot and slaughtered when they reach maturity or retained for breeding stock. Bison can live up to thirty years.

ALONG THE WAY: Medicine Lodge Hills

Long before William Francis Butler, explorer Anthony Henday passed this way and noted the Medicine Lodge Hills. They certainly captivate travellers from far in the distance. These are not hills of soft deposits such as sand and gravel as you might expect. If you dug straight down, you would find that the "soft" materials are only about three metres thick. Below that is bedrock composed mostly of sandstone, siltstone, mudstone and shale.

DIGGING *DEEPER*: How Do Leaves Change Their Colour?

During autumn, the colours in the forest, combined with the soft glow of the September sun, make a spectacular drive through the Medicine Lodge Hills. As leaves die, they go out in a blaze of glorious colour. But why do leaves change colour in the fall, and why do they drop from deciduous trees while evergreens keep their needle leaves?

Deciduous trees such as the aspen poplar have soft leaves that lose water very quickly. During summer, the roots are constantly sucking up water and nutrients to feed the tree. In winter, no water is available since the ground is frozen. The tree must close up all places where water escapes or it would dry out and die.

A cork layer forms where the leaf stem connects to the branch, cutting off the water supply to the leaf. The layer of cells holding the leaf to the tree weakens and the leaf flutters to the ground. Over time, it will decay into soil that feeds the tree.

Just as pigment in our skin turns brown when we suntan, a pigment in leaves, called chlorophyll, turns green in the sun. As the leaf dies, the green chlorophyll fades, allowing other pigments of yellow, red, and orange to show through.

Evergreens have a different strategy for surviving winter. Their leaves are narrow, tough, flexible, and waxy. They lose water very slowly and continue to absorb energy from the sun during the warm days of winter. Evergreen needles do drop off as they get old, but only a few at a time, and new ones soon replace them.

I SPY: Beaver Lodge

Look out for a beaver lodge on the south side of HWY 12 immediately past Lockhart Road.

This close-up of a beaver lodge is similar to the one described here.
ALBERTA COMMUNITY DEVELOPMENT / PARKS AND PROTECTED AREAS

Beavers are nature's dam builders and very efficient engineers at that! They dam creeks to create water environments that serve their needs. Lodges such as the one that can be seen from the highway are constructed in a depth of water sufficient for the beavers to enter through an underwater entrance to the dry chambers high up in the lodge. That limits the predators that are able to follow them into their home. They also stash young branches into the bottom of the pond to be retrieved during the winter for sustenance.

The water levels must also allow for the formation of water-filled channels that allow access to new stands of poplar. To survive, the beaver must stay close to water at all times, since its mobility on land is severely limited.

I SPY: Gilby Gas Plant

Your eye cannot miss the Gilby Gas Plant—and neither can your nose! Here the oil and gas from the surrounding oil field is gathered by pipeline and truck. The oil and natural gas is separated from sulphur and other impurities. The oil is put into tanks on site and the gas is directed into Alberta's gas pipeline system.

I SPY: Bedrock

As you pass the intersection of HWY 766, look to the north. The lonesome hill that can be seen just a few miles north is a massive chunk of bedrock that was ripped from the ground by the driving force of glaciers that gouged and scraped their way across the landscape.

I SPY: Oil Well Donkeys

Why are they called donkeys? Simply because of the shape of the pump. The head that goes up and down is attached by long lengths of sucker rod to a lift cylinder in the oil well below the level of the oil pool. A low-speed one-cylinder gas motor or an electric motor powers it. Each cycle of the pump brings another quantity of oil to the surface. The oil is either pumped into a tank on site or directly into a pipeline.

DIRECTIONS: Continue west on HWY 12 for 17.7 KM from HWY 766 for your first glimpse of the Rocky Mountains. Take HWY 761 south for 9.1 KM to Leslieville.

ALONG THE WAY: White-tailed and Mule Deer

If the kids constantly ask: "Are we there yet?", get them to scan the road-

A hungry mule deer pays little heed to the camera.
FRED SCHUTZ

side for wildlife. Perhaps the first person to spot a deer could choose where you will stop for your next meal or snack.

The chance of seeing one or more deer browsing along the road is good since the local terrain is prime habitat for ungulates. During the middle of the day, deer are most commonly bedded down in a protected grove of trees. But early and late in the day they search for the tender leaves of shrubs that are found in great abundance along wooded road-sides.

As you pass a white-tailed deer, it will flash its white tail as it bounds into cover. Biologists believe tail flashing is intended to let the predator know it has been seen. Knowing it has been spotted, the predator realizes that chasing the deer would be fruitless, particularly if the deer has enough of a head start. This is supported by the fact that deer do not flag when a predator is already very close.

STOP: Leslieville

Leslieville is named for Leslie Reilly, whose family settled in the district in 1903. A post office was established in 1907, and from then on the hamlet was known as Leslieville.

THE GENERAL STORE

This store on Main Street is among the last of its kind. Drop in for coffee and a snack. The historic photos of Leslieville on the walls will give you a good sense of what this community was once like.

DIRECTIONS: Follow the signs east from HWY 761 on TWP 39.4A, take the first turn south, and then the first west at the sign. The cemetery is 3 KM from Leslieville.

LESLIEVILLE CEMETERY

Here rest Edward and Theresa Pepper amidst the rustle of the pines. Edward Pepper, of Liverpool, England, met his Irish wife, Theresa, in

On the stone lies a name, and behind a name there is always a story.

Argentina. There they both worked on a ranch—he as an overseer and she as governess. They tried ranching on their own but by 1910 they were forced to sell out and sailed for Liverpool with their three children. Undaunted, Edward then embarked for western Canada, while Theresa went to Ireland for the birth of her fourth child. She then set off across the Atlantic bound for Leslieville in 1911 with baby Maureen and her son Jimmie. The two older girls, Anita and Eileen, remained in Ireland to go to school.

It was two years before the Pepper family was reunited in Leslieville. Imagine the excitement when the two girls arrived from Ireland to rejoin their family, and just in time before the outbreak of war in 1914! The girls finished their schooling in Leslieville, before training as RNs in New York. The Peppers all had the travel bug—Maureen later worked all over the world with the Canadian Department of External Affairs, and Jimmie went south to Bozeman, Montana, where he taught at the State University. Only Edward and Theresa remained in Leslieville, and were buried among those with whom they had raised families, shared picnics and box socials, gone to dances, and watched baseball games.

DIRECTIONS: Head south on HWY 761 for 4 KM from the railway tracks. Turn east at the Spokeshave sign.

THE SPOKESHAVE & WINDY RIDGE FARM

Carl Sewell's woodwork is a real treat for the connoisseur of handcrafted wooden objects. Sewell works with black walnut, Manitoba maple, cherry-wood, willow from his property, and spalted birch. Spalting is an aging process which gives the wood weathering and colour patterns. Sewell now does custom work only. Turned vases, bowls, candlestick holders, cheese boards, three-legged stools, and darning mushrooms can all be ordered at the workshop in his yard, where he also restores and repairs antique furniture.

If you are a fan of the donkey (also know as *equus assinus*), talk to Sybil Sewell, who runs Windy Ridge Farm at the same location. Sybil raises large standard donkeys as well as the mammoth jackstock, which, she will tell you, was developed by George Washington in the eighteenth century from large imported European asses.

Open May 15–October 15 Tuesday–Saturday 10:00 AM–5:00 PM
Rest of the year by chance or call ahead for appointment.
Tel: (403) 729-3047

A donkey at Windy Ridge Farm.

DIRECTIONS: Retrace your route to Leslieville. Cross the railway line and turn west on HWY 598 for Rocky Mountain House.

I SPY: Rail Siding

Notice the rail siding to the south of the highway where the town's grain elevators once stood, just before you cross the bridge over Lobstick Creek.

ALONG THE WAY: Lobstick Creek

What does lobstick mean? A lobstick was the name given to a very tall pine tree that had all but the uppermost branches stripped from its trunk. Native people used such trees as landmarks and commemorative sites. There may have once been a lobstick in the vicinity from which the creek took its name.

Drumlin comes from an Irish word—*druim*—meaning rounded hill. The geological term was first coined in Ireland, where there are thousands of drumlins.

ALONG THE WAY: Drumlins

As you look to the north, you'll see an oddly shaped hill with a steep slope on one end and a gradually tapered slope in the other direction. It looks misplaced, as if it had been randomly plunked onto the flat expanse of farmland. One could imagine it was fashioned by a local farmer who bulldozed a heap of unwanted clay and rock into the middle of his field. In fact, the last glaciation produced this interesting landform.

In some parts of Canada and elsewhere in the world, thousands of them—called swarms of drumlins when grouped—can be seen, all oriented in the direction that the great ice sheets moved. When the glaciers began to melt and unloaded large quantities of silt, sand, clay, and gravel into cavities under the ice, the combination of rushing water and pressure from the ice sculpted these streamlined hills. The "stoss" or steep face of the hill is the side from which the ice came. The long, tapered slope is the lee side, which points in the direction of glacier movement.

I SPY: Trestle Bridge (6.2 KM west of Leslieville)

Look out for a glimpse of the magnificent wooden trestle railway bridge, built by the Canadian Northern Railway, which spans Lasthill Creek.

ALONG THE WAY: The Trail to Hell

Rocky Mountain House trail ran some distance north of the road you are on. The last section from Leslieville was notorious. As the *Rocky Mountain House Echo* declared in August 1911: "When a man is living at Leslieville a distance of just twelve miles, straight east of the ferry at Rocky Mountain House, and that man drives here via way of Eckville, Evarts, Markerville, Raven and Stauffer, a distance of eighty miles, it is a sure sign that there must be a very bad piece of road between there and here. A man walked, waded and swam over the trail from Leslieville a week ago, we had a talk with him just after he landed, his opinion of things in general wasn't the best, the water was cold, the mud was deep and the flies were bad, he said that back on the trail he noticed a sign board which read: Three and a half miles to hell in any direction, except straight up, and its mud all the way." Your journey over the next fifteen minutes should be less eventful!

SATURDAY MORNING AUCTION AT COLE'S AUCTION MART (Located on 46th Street, the service road running north from HWY 598 immediately before the junction with HWY 11)

Test your bidding skills or have fun guessing what things will go for. It's a lot of fun! Bidding on miscellaneous items begins at 10 AM on Saturdays year-round. You might find anything from a washer and dryer to garden rakes to a covered wagon to collectible furniture. Hay, straw, and cattle are also sold. Cole's also does close-out farm auctions. Everyone is welcome—but be warned that household items and collectibles usually sell first-thing.

DIRECTIONS: Cross HWY 11 into Rocky Mountain House.

STOP: Rocky Mountain House

Rocky Mountain House is central Alberta's gateway to the Rocky Mountains. It sits at the foothills on the western edge of the Great Plains. At the townsite, the land is relatively flat and undisturbed by mountain-building forces, but immediately west of town the sandstone and shale bedrock begins to show folding and tilting, appearing as a series of long ridges. The region is heavily forested, with grasslands in the broader valleys, and waterlogged muskeg where clay soils, which were dumped during glacier-melt, clogged the drainage of water. Rocky Mountain House is a gateway for the David Thompson highway, provincial wilderness areas, and the Rocky Mountain National Parks. To explore Main Street, turn south at the four-way stop by the hospital.

ROCKY MOUNTAIN HOUSE MUSEUM (Off HWY 11 at the Tourist Information Centre—look for the fire lookout tower)

Get your exercise for the day by pumping a range of old and contemporary tunes on the 1917 Amherst player piano. The harder you pump your feet the louder it goes! This wonderful instrument was found in a house in Calgary occupied by seventy cats. Now restored, it is none the worse for wear. Piano players with their tunes on paper rolls were all the rage before WWI. Amherst Pianos Ltd. of Nova Scotia had a huge "scratch and dent sale" after the great explosion in Halifax harbour in December 1917. The company offered terms as low as one dollar a week and freight charges, as well as rail fare, to the sale. By 1925, however, other forms of entertainment had become popular and the player piano became an oddity of the past.

The museum is located in a large new building along with the Tourist Information Centre. It is packed with artifacts that offer a trip down nostalgia lane into the 1930s and 1940s in particular. On the grounds are the 1910 Glacier School and a fully equipped Ranger Forestry Cabin, used in the Meadows Forestry area until 1954.

Open Victoria Day weekend–Labour Day weekend Monday–Saturday 9:00 AM–5:00 PM; Sunday 10:00 AM–5:00 PM

Rest of year Monday–Friday 9:00 AM–5:00 PM

Tel: (403) 845-2332

Small admission charge.

GLACIAL ERRATIC

Follow the walking trail north and then west from the museum to check out a 500-tonne boulder. It is composed of quartzite, a hard rock that is not of local origin, but rather is the rock that makes up much of the Rocky Mountains. So how did it get to this spot? It is believed that rockslides of 18,000 years ago dropped boulders onto the Athabasca valley glacier that was moving to the east. It collided with the Laurentide glacier that covered most of Canada, forcing the Athabasca ice to move southward, parallel to the mountains. When the ice finally melted, boulders were dropped in a twenty-two-kilometre-wide band, parallel to the mountain range. This is called the Foothills Erratics Train, stretching all the way from the Jasper area to Montana.

One mighty big rock!

DIRECTIONS: Head west on HWY 11A over the North Saskatchewan River. On the west side of the bridge turn immediately right to follow a gravel road north along the river for 4.3 KM to HWY 11.

OPTION: Continue west on HWY 11A (4.1 KM) to the sign for Rocky Mountain House National Historic Site. Turn left over the railway track and left again into the site, which is 7 KM from the town of Rocky Mountain House.

STOP: Rocky Mountain House National Historic Site of Canada

Catch the echoes of the fur trade along the banks of the North Saskatchewan River. Little is left of the four different successive forts of the North West and Hudson's Bay companies which once rang with the sound of axes and voices through the trees, but there is much to find at this site. There are two separate trails through the site with interpretive panels and listening stations, that bring back those days of fiercely competitive trade with no fewer than nine Aboriginal groups. The centre, operated by Parks Canada, has comprehensive displays and artifacts on the fur trade, western exploration, and life of Aboriginal peoples in the area. Choose what interests you from a range of videos to watch in the theatre—great for a wet day.

Catch a special event such as the Brigade Days, when you can learn about loading a muzzle rifle with black powder. Kids love the play fort and puppet shows about the life of David Thompson, surveyor and mapmaker. You can easily spend several hours at the site. The best place to picnic is at the Brierly Rapids.

Open Victoria Day weekend–Labour Day weekend 10:00 AM–5:00 PM

The Visitor Centre is closed the rest of the year, but you are welcome to walk the trails during office hours which are 9:00 AM–4:00 PM.

Tel: (403) 845-2412

www.parkscanada.gc.ca/rockymountainhouse

Admission charge

ALONG THE WAY: The Mighty North Saskatchewan

The old Hudson's Bay trail from Lacombe came in from the north along the east cliff, and continued west from the river crossing that was just south of the rail bridge. When settlers came to the area at the beginning of the twentieth century they found the crossing to be extremely difficult and dangerous. A ferry was installed on the river in 1908. From the outset it had problems—not least in getting built! A load of lumber for its construction was swept away while trying to cross the river. When it was finally constructed, the ferry came to grief on its maiden voyage and ended up on a sandbank—presumably the one you can see a short distance to the north of the road and pedestrian bridge. "Ferry Goes Down"—ran a headline in the *Rocky Mountain House Echo* in May 1912. "Last Saturday morning the ferry filled and sank, no one was on board at the time, the old tub has been in no shape to handle large amount of traffic which has to be plied across the river here this summer, ferryman Austin having had to bail her out one or more times each day. On Saturday contractor Mike Madden, had twelve teams pull it out of the water and up on the shore, then the Nor construction company put on three men who understand that kind of work, to make it water tight and it is expected that she will be launched again this afternoon. The sinking of the ferry means considerable delay and loss to railway contractors who have many teams freighting west."

Less than two months later the dangerous state of the ferry nearly led to a major tragedy and caused the death of two horses and the loss of a wagon. A three-horse team was on the ferry which, when midstream, "made a sudden dip, the upstream side going completely under water, this caused a great wave to roll over the ferry which frightened the horses, they started to back up and in spite of the efforts of the driver . . . backed off the ferry taking the wagon with them." In attempting to turn the ferry bow upstream, *Rocky Mountain House Echo* reported, the cable broke from the west tower and the men on the ferry barely escaped with their lives. Despite such difficulties a ferry was the only way to cross the river by car until the early 1940s when the traffic bridge was built.

DIRECTIONS: Turn west on HWY 11 at the T intersection. Turn north on HWY 756 for Crimson Lake Provincial Park.

ALONG THE WAY: Muskeg and More

On the road to Crimson Lake Provincial Park you will immediately see the low-lying muskeg typical of this area. Growing in the muskeg is the sickly-

Though interesting to look at, muskeg makes for difficult hiking!

looking black spruce mixed with the only conifer that loses its needles each winter, the tamarack. Down the road, higher ground produces an interesting mix of aspen, white spruce, lodgepole pine, and balsam poplar. The mixed forest, with such a great variety of foliage, is truly pleasing.

STOP: Crimson Lake Provincial Park

Follow the signs to the day use area. Walk to the trailhead located immediately across the main road. The trail shortly branches off in three directions. The left trail takes you to the lake and the right trail to the campground. We suggest taking the middle trail to the boardwalk.

Not far along the middle trail, a spur forks off to the left, leading to a viewpoint explaining oil extraction methods in the park. The Crimson Lake area is rich in oil and gas and is criss-crossed with cutlines, oil pipelines, and wellsites.

The trail drops in elevation until you reach the wooden boardwalk. Crimson Lake, named for the spectacular sunsets reflected in its still waters, is an opening in a large expanse of muskeg that covers this area. The expanse of flatland around you is a sedge fen, with the water table just under the surface. It is too wet for trees to become established. Only scattered willows and dwarf birches grow on small raised areas.

Be careful. The top layer of sedges and interwoven mosses form a mat

Labrador Tea makes a tasty brew.
ALBERTA COMMUNITY DEVELOPMENT / PARKS AND PROTECTED AREAS

which floats on the surface, looking like solid footing. Not until you step on the mat and break through into the water do you realize your mistake!

In wet areas like this, where black spruce and sphagnum moss grow, you can depend on finding a plant that has dark, green, leathery leaves, with orange fuzz on the underside. It's called Labrador tea and, yes, it does make a tasty brew.

If outdoor types were to be polled on their favourite moss, it would be sphagnum—also called peat moss—of which there are actually about twenty species in Alberta. Each mound of moss is made of individual plants. Gently grasp the compact head of one and pull it from its nest. The feathery branches of this unusual plant can hold twenty times their weight in water!

You will also find a small shrub with birch leaves, called the dwarf birch. In contrast to its relative, the paper birch, this little guy likes to have wet feet.

Trail map signs are spaced regularly along the way. Use them to decide whether you want to explore further or loop back to the parking area.

DIRECTIONS: To return to Rocky Mountain House take HWY 11. From there you can connect with Tour 7: Rocky Mountain House to Sundre (page 115).

OPTION: From here you can travel west for the Rocky Mountains via Nordegg, one hour west of Rocky Mountain House. Don't miss the Nordegg Heritage Centre and the Brazeau Collieries Industrial Museum—now a National Historic Site of Canada.

Open daily mid-May–late September 9:00 AM–5:00 PM

Telephone (403) 721-2625 for further information and times of minesite tours.

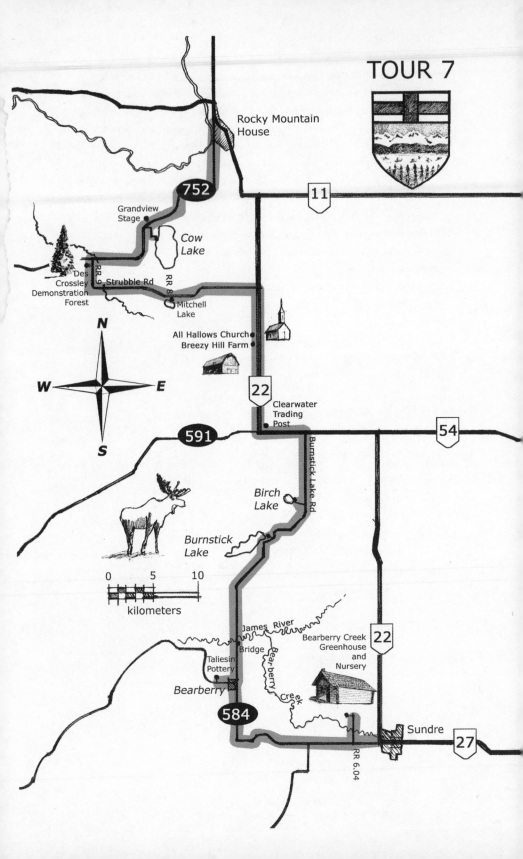

TOUR 7

Rocky Mountain House

11

752

Grandview Stage

Cow Lake

RR 9
Strubble Rd

Des Crossley Demonstration Forest

RR 8

Mitchell Lake

All Hallows Church
Breezy Hill Farm

N
W **E**
S

22

Clearwater Trading Post

54

591

Birch Lake

Burnstick Lake Rd

Burnstick Lake

0   5   10
kilometers

James River

22

Bridge

Bearberry Creek Greenhouse and Nursery

Taliesin Pottery

Bearberry Creek

Bearberry

584

Sundre

RR 6.04

27

Rocky Mountain House to Sundre, via Burnstick Lake

DIRECTIONS: From Rocky Mountain House (see page 108), turn south onto HWY 752 from HWY 11A, shortly before the bridge over the North Saskatchewan River. Follow the highway through the outskirts of Rocky Mountain House.

FEATURED WILDLIFE: Crows and ravens

As you pass through the transitional area from aspen parkland to foothills, a new species of blackbird becomes more common—the raven. Crows are found throughout Alberta, but ravens favour more remote habitats such as mountains and colder regions. Can you tell them apart? As their colour, overall shape, and behaviour is identical, telling them apart is sometimes tricky. Remember that the raven is one-third larger, and has shaggy feathers around the throat and a heavier bill. The most obvious iden-tifier is the voice. Crows are most commonly heard "cawing" whereas the raven makes a deep, unmistakable "croak." It also creates a sharp, metallic "tock" that echoes through the woods. Keep in mind that both birds are great mimics and can fool you with unexpected sounds.

ALONG THE WAY: Lodgepole pine

As you move into the foothills, lodgepole pine trees are one of the main indicators of the new terrain. This tall, slender evergreen has a straight trunk with little taper. It is found mostly in the mountains and foothills, where it prefers well-drained, sandy, and coarse-textured soil. The name comes from Aboriginal use of the long, straight trunk for making lodge or tipi frames. Lodgepole pine is used for tele-phone poles, railway ties, log cabins and

The common raven.
FRED SCHUTZ

fence posts. It is one of the most important forest resources in the province for pulpwood. The lodgepole is one of the first trees to grow after a forest fire. The resin which seals its cone softens during the heat of a fire. The seeds are then released to the soil, which is freshly exposed and fertilized with ashes. In the absence of fire, there are generally some "open-coned" trees that drop seeds to ensure survival of the pine forest. Aboriginal peoples had many medicinal uses for the pine, such as chewing on the buds to relieve a sore throat.

You will be dwarfed as you walk through the towering forest of lodgepole pines.

DIRECTIONS: After 15.5 KM you will arrive at Grandview Stage at corner of TWP 38.4.

STOP: Grandview Stage

This is a popular but tranquil rustic stopping place for visitors to this area. Here you will find a general store, gas bar, and restaurant. There is also a gallery featuring art and gift items, and western-style three-star cabin accommodation. Get your supplies for the west country at the timbered trading post that boasts a mounted cougar. You can find everything from worms to cold drinks, groceries, and camping supplies, as well as fishing and hunting licences. Everything is made from scratch—buffalo burgers, soups, and pies are the specialty of the licensed restaurant. Relax on the outdoor patio that has magnificent views of the Rocky Mountains and Cow Lake.

Grandview Trail to Cow Lake Recreation Area is a pleasant one kilometre walk to the lake. The trail begins as a gravel drive immediately across the road from Grandview parking lot. When you reach a fork, follow the "trail" sign straight ahead through the grass. The right fork leads to a private residence. The trail is described in the section: Cow Lake Recreation Area below.

Open daily 6:30 AM–9:00 PM
Tel: (403) 845-6404

DIRECTIONS: Continue on HWY 752. Cow Lake comes into view as the road swings south from Grandview. The turn for Cow Lake Recreation Area is 0.8 KM south of Grandview Stage.

STOP: Cow Lake Recreation Area

Cow Lake is a small, shallow lake, which drains the surrounding muskeg and then flows north into the North Saskatchewan River. Explore the shoreline from the same vantage point as the ducks and grebes by renting a canoe, fishing boat, or paddleboat.

Check out the following habitats by walking along the named trails. Maps are available at the park entrance.

Boats moored at Cow Lake.

SPRUCE GROVE TRAIL

From the boat launch and beach area, head east to follow the Spruce Grove Trail. It leads you into the cool, dark surroundings of a mature spruce forest. Here the undergrowth is sparse, except where rays of sunshine are able to break through the dense canopy to warm the ground. The soil is very moist in this habitat, since the water table is quite close to the surface. The soil here is a woody, fibrous, and mucky peat, which developed over years of swampy conditions.

FEATURED *PLANT*: Black Spruce

Take a look at how the black spruce is able to root itself from its stem and branches. This is an absolute requirement for a plant that grows in wet soils. Otherwise, growing hummocks of moss would soon engulf the young spruce trees. The living part of the spruce roots must also remain above the water table to absorb adequate oxygen, so the root system is quite shallow and the black spruce is easily uprooted. Unlike its better-looking cousin, the white spruce, this tree is too small, twisted, and knotty to be used for lumber, and its appearance is not considered desirable for landscaping. The branches are short and droopy. Its needles are short and the top of the tree has a clustered appearance consisting of a tight growth of branches and cones.

DEER RUN TRAIL

To see how much difference higher ground can make to the vegetation, follow the road from the boat launch area until you see the Deer Run Trail crossing the road. Head west on the trail. It takes you to higher ground where the drier conditions allow growth of aspen trees and dense undergrowth of shrubs and flowering plants. If you are feeling energetic, you can follow this trail all the way to Grandview Stage (approximately 1 KM).

FEATURED *PLANT*: Red-osier Dogwood

If moose and deer were able to speak, they would rave about the red-osier dogwood—the tastiest shrub in Alberta, judging by the extensive browsing of this plant. Red-osier dogwood is one of the most common shrubs in the aspen forest, easily identified by its reddish stems, which contrast with the white snow during winter. Its pasty white berries, though eaten by wildlife, are not a preferred fruit for humans. Aboriginal people ate them only when mixed with sweeter berries. Other uses for the dogwood shrub include weaving the flexible, colourful stems into baskets, and boiling the roots to make a medicinal tea.

DIRECTIONS: Continue on HWY 752, south and then west, for 7.8 KM. Directly after Prairie Creek Bridge look for the sign: Crossley Demonstration Forest. Turn south onto RR 9. The site is 0.5 KM south of the intersection on the west side of the road. Be aware that logging trucks commonly use these roads.

STOP: Des Crossley Demonstration Forest

Fifty years ago, Des Crossley, a researcher with the Canadian Forest Service, used this forest to investigate thinning, harvesting, and regeneration of lodgepole pine. The results of Crossley's work, which you can see here, have been applied to lodgepole pine management across Alberta. Sunpine Forest Products Ltd. spearheaded the development of interpretive trails on this quarter-section. The centre is operated by Inside Education (formerly FEESA), a non-profit educational society promoting understanding of environmental issues.

Open daily May–October

Parking lot and outhouse facilities.

Telephone (780) 421-1497 for information on educational tour bookings.

Check the orientation signage and begin your hike on the self-guiding trail at the edge of the parking lot. Interpretive panels along the trail explain the results of forest management experiments and point out a captivating variety of lush vegetation and wildlife that inhabit the area. Watch the trail markers carefully to know when to loop back. A well-maintained 2.5-kilometre trail weaves through old-growth forest with a soft floor of brown needles and green mosses. Look for the endless variety of colours and shapes of fungi rooted in the spongy soil or growing on fallen trees.

FEATURED *PLANT*: Fungi

When you pick a mushroom, it gives the impression that you have successfully picked the plant and left only roots behind. If you then dig at the soil under the mushroom, only a powdery dust is left behind, which only reinforces your perception. In fact, that white powder is the main body of the fungus. It is made up of a mass of delicate threads called mycelium. They grow far into the soil where they absorb nutrients and produce their "fruit": the mushroom. The mushroom produces billions of microscopic seeds called spores, releasing them into the air. Look for different escape hatches for the spores. You may be most familiar with gills, but you will also find mushrooms with pores on the underside of the cap and those that must be stepped on to release the spores. Puffball fungi release a brown smoke of spores into the wind when the skin is broken. Poke one with your finger to help spread this interesting species.

A mushroom is fun to look at but don't taste it unless you're an expert. We do have poisonous varieties in Alberta.

FEATURED *PLANT*: Old Man's Beard

The scraggly hair hanging eerily from dead or dying pine and spruce branches is a lichen appropriately named Old Man's Beard. Lichens are very successful partnerships between fungi and algae. The fungus makes up the strands of the lichen plant. It absorbs moisture, provides living space for algae, and anchors the plant to the tree. The algae are microscopic-sized particles that live in those strands and give them a green colour. Algae produce food from the sun's energy to supply both partners with nourishment. Old Man's Beard travels to other trees when the feet of squirrels or birds pick up reproductive clumps. This lichen has served both people and animals with a wide range of uses: lichen-covered branches for kindling, winter food for deer, nest-building material for birds, boiled for a meal by the First Nations, and used to make troll dolls by Scandinavians.

DIRECTIONS: RR 9 becomes Strubble Rd. as it turns east. 11.6 KM from Des Crossley Forest look for the sign for Mitchell Lake. Take RR 8 south at the mailboxes. The road is marked "No Exit" and takes you over a Texas gate. Follow for 1 KM to the lake.

ALONG THE WAY: Crown Lease Pastures

Many farmers take out crown leases to pasture their livestock. The crown owns the land and the private leaseholder pays an annual rent to the government based on the number of animal units that the land can support in relation to the quality and the quantity of grass. One cow and calf is considered one animal unit. When the lease changes hands the new leaseholder buys improvements such as fencing and dugouts from the previous leaseholder. The leaseholder also pays taxes due on the land every year. There are also community pastures where a group of farmers have a board of directors to manage the lease. Each member is allowed to pasture livestock according to how many animal units are available when the total is divided amongst the group. As a steward of the land, the rancher takes care of the crown lease that provides his livelihood, and the public does not have free access to the land without permission.

STOP: Mitchell Lake

This lake must be many people's "secret fishing hole," since it is a remarkably beautiful pond tucked inside of and surrounded by dense forest. Provincial conservation officers stock the lake with brook trout and have fenced the lake to keep cattle from accessing the shoreline, thus helping to maintain the natural water quality. As you walk down to the boat

The serene waters of Mitchell Lake.

launch, an informal trail leads along the lakeshore to a floating dock and bench. From this vantage point, you have a splendid view of the entire lake for bird watching. Mitchell Lake has campsites with fire pits and picnic tables, pit toilets, and a boat launch.

FEATURED WILDLIFE: Goldeneye Duck

When goldeneyes first arrive in Alberta in early spring, they search for tree cavities close to a lake or pond. Nest boxes, such as the one prominently seen nailed to a tree along the shoreline, encourage nesting, though it is surprising that the adult is able to fit through the small entrance hole. A few days after hatching, the nestlings jump—or are pushed by their mother—from the nest box, bouncing to the ground below. Then they obediently follow the hen to the water where they feed and grow until they are able to fly. During this time, the tall weeds around the lake are important for sheltering the young birds, since they are very susceptible to predators such as hawks and weasels.

FEATURED PLANT: Water Smartweed

The waxy leaves of water smartweed, which contain tiny pockets of air, float on the water surface and adorn the lake with spikes of pink to scarlet flowers. Smartweed grows from creeping rootstalks and appears in large masses of flowers with colour that is most prominent in July and August.

DIRECTIONS: Retrace your route to Strubble Rd. and continue east 10.3 KM. Turn south on HWY 22. This is cattle country—few crops are grown here on this scrubby land.

I *SPY*: All Hallows Church and Chedderville Cemetery

Look for the tiny church 4.8 KM south of the junction.

ALONG THE WAY: Breezy Hill Farm

This farm is home to hundreds of Romanoff-Suffolk sheep. Owner Rena Waite uses sheepskin for her cozy slippers and wool cushions, which she sells throughout Alberta as well as directly from the farm.

Open by chance or appointment.

Tel: (403) 845-2707

DIGGING *DEEPER*: "What kind of cow is that?"

Most of the cows that you will see driving in central Alberta are beef breeds. Pure beef breeds include: Hereford—red with white faces; Angus—all black or all red; Simmental—shades of red to tan with a white face, white irregular markings on body; Charolais—white to cream-coloured, sometimes with white face; Limousin—solid colour, a browner shade of red. Hereford and Angus are smaller animals than the others. Many beef cattle are crossbreeds, resulting in a mix of traits. A cross between a Hereford and an Angus, for example, may get a black animal

A courteous cow waits for us to pass before crossing the road.

with a white face, a red body with a red-spotted white face, or a black body with a black-spotted white face. Most of the dairy cows in Alberta are Holstein—but they are rarely seen, as they are generally kept indoors in the huge dairy barns that are now seen all over central Alberta.

DIRECTIONS: Look for the Clearwater Trading Post at the junction with HWY 54. Turn east onto HWY 54 to cross the Clearwater River. After 4.9 KM turn south on Burnstick Lake Road. 12.7 KM south of HWY 54, look for the Watchable Wildlife sign. Turn west, follow the oil industry road, and park off the road at the oil well site. Caution: Drive with care as there may be trucks or other service equipment on this road.

STOP: Birch Lake Great Blue Heron Colony—A Watchable Wildlife Site

This is one of Alberta's most interesting Watchable Wildlife Sites and well worth the short drive in. Take the first wide trail to the right of the well site. It drops steeply to the lakeshore. For another good view of the lake, go back to the well site, and take the trail up the hill until you reach a fork. Step a short way to the right to overlook the lake.

A great blue heron contemplates searching for its next meal.
FRED SCHUTZ

Across the lake is an island of spindly-looking aspens with huge nests of sticks atop them. During nesting season, from April to May, you will see the tall, gangly birds that build them, making quite a racket. Nesting in colonies provides safety in numbers for great blue herons, and being on an island makes it that much more difficult for predators to reach them. Being so high up in the trees is another advantage. Some of these birds may have been nesting here for more than twenty years! They have a strong attachment to the colony and to their own nesting site. They add on to the nest each year until it becomes a large and very sturdy structure up to a metre across.

We watched as a heron lifted gracefully off its nest and floated down toward the water. As it approached the shallow end of the lake, it stretched out its impressive wings, landing in the water with barely a ripple. The large wings are crucial to the heron, as being able to land softly ensures that its legs are not damaged and also prevents scaring away food. The heron is not too particular about what it eats—if it moves and fits into the heron's mouth, it is considered edible! They have been known to eat young muskrats and ducks, gophers, and even kittens. Mostly, they eat fish, frogs, mice, and salamanders. The heron hunts by standing very still, waiting patiently, until a frog or fish happens too close. Without warning, the heron uses its long, sharp beak to spear the prey, and then gulps it down.

The trees on this nesting island have seen better days—life under a colony of nesting herons is not an ideal habitat for a tree. The amount of excrement that falls on the trees and down to the ground each season does provide nutrients, but becomes too much of a good thing. Herons are not very tolerant of people and nest only in remote locations. Only about seventy-five colonies exist in all of Alberta.

DIRECTIONS: Return to Burnstick Lake Road. Continue south 1.2 KM, and turn west to Burnstick Lake Municipal Campground.

STOP: Burnstick Lake

Burnstick Lake sits at the edge of a wilderness of expansive marshes, bays decorated with pond lilies, and undisturbed forest along the shoreline with

Burnstick Lake.
FRED SCHUTZ

a backdrop of foothills and mountains on the horizon. Historically, beaver dams controlled the water level. Today a weir maintains more constant levels. West Stony Creek is the most prominent stream that feeds into the lake from the surrounding watershed. East Stony Creek then drains the lake into James River, which in turn feeds into the Red Deer River. Burnstick lake is quite shallow, with large areas under one metre in depth. Consequently, it supports a great deal of emergent vegetation, including bulrushes, cattails, and pond lilies. This type of habitat attracts diverse wildlife, including moose, mink, muskrat, herons, and large populations of frogs. Adventurous types may wish to explore some of the backcountry by crossing the road at the weir near the campground entrance.

Facilities include a picnic area, campsites, and a playground.

FEATURED BIRD: Belted Kingfisher

This is a bird not likely to be mistaken for any other. Bluish with a white collar and breast, it seems to have an oversized head because of its blue, ragged crest or "Mohawk hairdo." Its distinctively long bill is used to spear and grasp fish, frogs, and large insects. The kingfisher is often seen scanning the water from a perch on the branch of lakeside trees. To catch its prey it will dive headfirst into the cool water, often completely submerging itself to snatch a meal. Kingfishers have a loud rattling call, often made in flight, which sounds much like a teacup clattering on a saucer. The male and female work together in making their nest, tunnelling out a burrow using their bills to dig, and feet to scrape as far as six feet into the side of a steep lakeside bank. At the end of the burrow, eggs are laid on the bare sand.

FEATURED WILDLIFE: Moose

Picture this: a bull moose standing shoulder-deep in water munching on masses of pond lilies that surround its thousand-pound frame. Sometimes the head goes completely

The massive moose is quite common in the extensive marshes and muskeg that surround Burnstick Lake.
FRED SCHUTZ

underwater as the moose struggles to free a deep-rooted plant from the muddy pond bottom. Then, like a monster rising from the depths, it bursts back to the surface, mouthing a long-stemmed and obviously tasty root-stalk. Moose have twelve sets of broad molars with sharp ridges that grind against each other when chewing. They are very useful for pulverizing woody stems, especially when the moose eats the tough branches from shrubs and trees, its usual diet during winter. A moose spends most of its time feeding, since it must eat almost fifty pounds of vegetation a day to maintain its substantial frame. So that the animal can keep watch for danger, its eyes are placed at the sides of its head and can rotate independently so that the moose can simultaneously look forward and backward.

DIRECTIONS: Continue south on Burnstick Lake Road.

I SPY: Reforestation

About 5 KM south of Burnstick Lake there is an area of reforestation on both sides of the road.

STOP: James River (12.6 KM south of Burnstick Lake)

Pull off the road to explore the James River, one of the streams that drain water from mountain glaciers. Perhaps the most common fish in these waters is the bull trout, also called the Dolly Varden. Designated as Alberta's provincial fish, it is found in all Alberta rivers originating in the mountains. Throughout the year, look for this trout in slow-moving waters. During early fall, the mature fish will spawn in the small creeks that feed into James River. At that time of year, keep in mind that you may be sharing space with bears and ospreys (fish hawks) that enjoy picking off the spawning trout. Like all trout, bull trout are cold-water fish, slow to mature. Consequently, all bull trout caught in this area must be released to ensure that sport fishermen do not put undue pressure on populations.

In Alberta, there are a number of regulations that help to protect fish populations. Size limits prevent fish from being harvested before they have had a chance to spawn, so every fish is potentially able to contribute to its population. Other regulations include season dates, daily catch limits, catch-and-release for vulnerable species, and restrictions on the type of bait used. About 30 per cent more caught-and-released fish die when baited hooks instead of bare hooks are used.

DIRECTIONS: Continue south. The gravel road turns to pavement as you travel uphill to spectacular views of the mountains.

ALONG THE WAY: Foothills

Looking toward the west, the view is magnificent. To what do we owe this awesome panorama? This is the western boundary of the Great Plains of North America, blending quickly into the foothills of the Rocky Mountains. The Rocky Mountain range and its foothills were created by the collision of gigantic plates of the earth's crust: the North American continental plate and another plate which now forms the basement of British Columbia. At the boundary of these plates, the rock layers had no choice but to be pushed, tilted, and thrust upward. At the edges of the thrust zone are these foothills, which contain the same sandstone as you have seen in the river valleys of central Alberta, except now the sandstone layers are tilted.

DIRECTIONS: Take the west fork in the road downhill to Bearberry.

STOP: Bearberry

The picturesque, laid-back hamlet of Bearberry lies at the foot of Bishop Hill. Luther and Jennie Bishop, along with their son Reginald, arrived here in 1907. Jennie Bishop was postmaster between 1911 and 1918. Father and son each broke a quarter section at the foot of the hill, which has officially borne the family name since 1991.

DIGGING *DEEPER*: How do geographic names get chosen?

There are established rules for naming geographic features in Alberta. Applications are sent to the Geographical Names Program Coordinator at Alberta Community Development. Program staff conduct research before it is submitted to the body that makes naming decisions. First consideration is always given to those names that are well established in local usage, such as was the case with Bishop Hill.

THE BEARBERRY SALOON

Once a store, this building is still the hub of the community and the place to get a bite to eat. Relax on the veranda on a long, lazy summer evening for a western experience. There are rustic cabins are for rent if you wish to tarry awhile.

Open Sunday–Thursday 7:30 AM–11:30 PM; Friday, Saturday 7:30 AM–2:30 AM

BEARBERRY HERITAGE & ARTS CENTRE

This barn from the James River Ranger Station was built in 1942. The Bearberry Community Association moved it here and lovingly restored it. On the ground floor you can learn about the history of the Bearberry area. Above the horse stalls, in the old hayloft, is an art gallery which displays paintings, pottery, and outdoor metal sculpture. Also on sale are stained glass and hand-crafted wood furniture. Well worth a visit, and on the long weekend in September you can catch a Country Market here.

Open May–September Saturday, Sunday, and long weekend Mondays 11:00 AM–4:30 PM

The Bearberry Heritage & Arts centre is located to the northeast of the community hall.

TALIESIN POTTERY STUDIO (West on TWP 33.04 from Bearberry Saloon, north on first gravel road—RR 7.03—first driveway on east side of the road)

Barbara Bell welcomes visitors to her airy pottery studio/gallery. She has functional ware on display as well as distinctive raku-fired pieces, and sculpture. Barbara paints upstairs in mixed media and watercolour, inspired by the landscape and trees that surround her.

Open by chance or appointment.

Tel: (403) 638-2704

Barbara Bell working outside on a warm fall day.

DIRECTIONS: Take the right fork east out of Bearberry and follow HWY 584 south and east toward Sundre.

ALONG THE WAY: Bearberry Creek

Not far from here the major rivers of central Alberta are born. They begin at the melting glaciers, high in the mountains, pass through the foothills, and emerge here where they collect additional runoff from smaller rivers and creeks that feed into them. Bearberry Creek is one of those feeders, flowing into the Red Deer River at Sundre. The width of this valley seems much too wide to accommodate the narrow flow of Bearberry Creek. At one time this valley was filled with glacial ice. As the climate warmed, a glacial lake filled the valley, leaving an immense space for the present-day water flow.

FEATURED *PLANT*: Bearberry

This valley was named after a common ground cover, its fruit a favoured food of black bears. Bearberry is a low-growing evergreen shrub with leathery leaves which turn from a shiny green to reddish in the fall. It is found most commonly on sandy soils, often associated with jack pine and lodgepole pine. The flowers are pinkish-white, forming bright red berries later in the summer. In earlier days the berries were mixed with whitefish eggs for a flavourful dish and the dried leaves were smoked in pipes. The native name for Bearberry is *Kinnikinnik*.

Bearberry Creek Greenhouse and Nursery (3.2 KM north on RR 6.04 and then west on TWP 33.02)

Heinjo Lahring likes to do things the hard way—building his own house and breeding and growing exquisite water lilies in an area with a harsh climate and short growing season! For twenty years he has pioneered an aquatic plant farm, specializing in native species and water lilies. Reclamation of Alberta's wetlands depends on native plants, and Lahring's dedication and knowledge has borne fruit in his new field guide *The Water and Wetland Plants of the Prairie Provinces*. The growing area has sunken frame ponds—ask for a tour to see how it is done. The sales area offers numerous water plants for you to experiment with in your own backyard. Lahring has a range of products such as liners, and is generous with advice. In May and June the greenhouse offers traditionally popular bedding plants and hanging baskets.

Open daily May 1–June 30 9:00 AM–6:00 PM

July, August by appointment.

Water lilies begin to bloom at the end of June so call ahead if you wish to see them.

Tel: (403) 638-4231

ALONG THE WAY: McDougall Flats

Just west of Sundre, you cross a wide, flat plain named McDougall Flats, after rancher David McDougall, brother of John McDougall, missionary at Pigeon Lake. David McDougall and his son, David Jr., ran cattle here from the 1890s, until the loss of half their herd in the hard winter of 1906–07 forced them to sell out. Whereas an ancient lake formed Bearberry valley, this expanse is within the floodplain of the Red Deer River. It was created over thousands of years as the river flattened a wide valley by repeatedly changing course and flooding its banks. Look for old channels where the river once travelled.

STOP: Sundre

Sundre is a major centre for outdoor activities, including trail riding, whitewater rafting, canoeing, and fishing. People from all over the world come to explore the high mountain meadows west of the town. Sundre's roots are in logging and ranching. Today many residents continue to make their living in guiding and outfitting, following in the hoofprints of Charlie Logan's pack horses that once transported the food and instruments required by geophysical and land survey parties in this area.

The perfection of a crimson hardy hybrid water lily.
HEINJO LARHING

SNAKE HILL (north on Centre Street from four-way stop)

Snake Hill is a conspicuous landmark on the north side of Sundre. To reach it, head north on Centre Street to 6A Avenue. Parking is clearly indicated. Snake Hill was glacially formed. A stream flowing within the ice deposited sand and gravel in a massive mound that is now a fine place to walk, ski, toboggan, and luge. Walk the perimeter of the hill to get a fine viewpoint of the southwest.

Can you spot these landmarks?

Rocky Mountains • Sunpine Forest Products mill • Rodeo grounds • Foothills forests • Red Deer River

FEATURED *PLANT*: Juniper

No, this shrub was not planted on Snake Hill. The common juniper is a native species that is found growing all across the northern hemisphere. Bluish berries are found on the female plants, but look again! They are actually fleshy cones that have the appearance of berries. Though the Cree used the cones for medicinal purposes, they are not generally considered edible.

FEATURED WILDLIFE: Woodpeckers

In a mature forest such as this, downy woodpeckers find plenty of food. They search the cracks and crevices of tree bark for insects and their lar-

Hairy woodpecker.
FRED SCHUTZ

vae. They excavate nest holes in both dead and live trees with entrance holes that are barely more than one inch in diameter. The downy woodpecker and its slightly larger cousin, the hairy woodpecker, are the most common woodpeckers of central Alberta.

Featured Plant Growth: Galls

As you hike down this forest trail, you will find swellings on various plant stems, buds, and leaves, each of which may be the home of an insect. On willow shrubs, look for a rounded "pinecone" on the tip of a branch. In fact, it is a swollen bud. A tiny insect laid its eggs inside the bud and released a plant hormone, causing the plant cells to multiply and become abnormally enlarged. The developing insect is suitably housed, with the inside of its home serving as a food supply. On goldenrod stems a small fly causes the gall. In the worm stage, it feeds inside the gall, eventually chewing a tunnel almost, but not quite, through to the outside. After it transforms into a small fly, it is able to push its way through the thin skin to freedom. On older, dried-out galls, you will see the escape holes. If you cut open a fresh, green gall, you will find the larva inside.

SUNDRE RODEO

The cowboys are still at it—trying to prove who is the toughest and the most skilled at roping a calf. The first Sundre Rodeo held in 1919 was second only to the Calgary Stampede. It was the first place in Alberta to hold chuckwagon races. Howard Steen was a well-known Sundre competitor— look for a photograph in the museum of his outfit leaving Sundre on the long haul to the Calgary Stampede in 1926. Sundre rodeo turned professional in 1979 and is held the third weekend in June.

SUNDRE AND DISTRICT MUSEUM (Reception Centre on 2nd Street, south of 1st Avenue SW)

One of the museum buildings is a log house built by Norwegian settler Haagen Eggen and dedicated by Lieutenant-Governor Grant MacEwan in 1970 to the men and women who first homesteaded in the area. Indeed many of their descendents helped to furnish the house thirty years ago. The museum tells you who donated what and gives the history of the particular item, from chairs to linens. Eggen might not now recog-

Sundre Stampede 1924

nize the interior of his home, but it holds community memories. Also on site is an outdoor display of agricultural machinery, and a schoolhouse complete with functional wood stove. Inside the barn you will find a range of displays—but it was individual objects, such as a sidesaddle used by Mrs. McRae who came to Eagle Valley in 1903, and a berry picker made from a can with spikes welded on, that took our attention. Look for a wicker baby carriage, cushion-lined with a pink parasol, brought to the Bergen area from Wisconsin by the Olson family. It is hard to believe it survived in such good condition, having been used by four children in rural Alberta!

Open Victoria Day–Labour Day Wednesday–Saturday and holiday Mondays 10:00 AM–4:30 PM

From here you can join Tour 8: Sundre to Bearberry Loop (page 135) or Tour 9: Sundre to Olds (page 145). See also Tour 14: Innifail to Sundre (page 211).

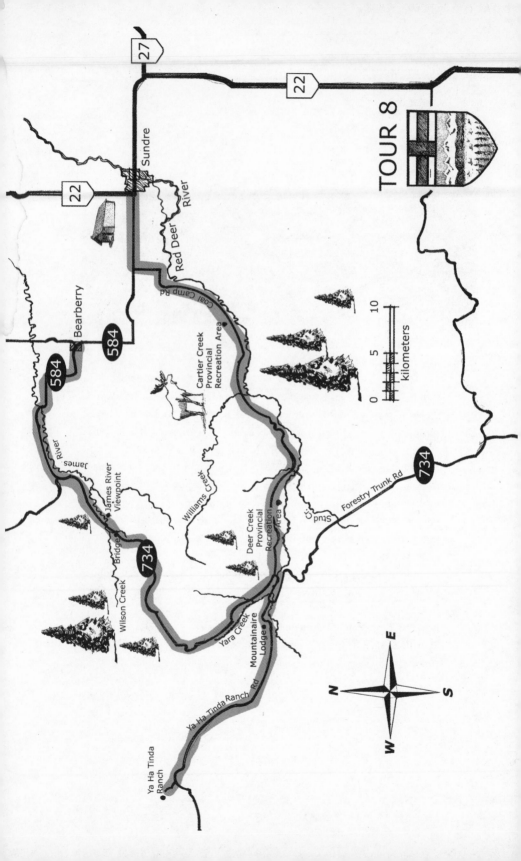

Sundre to Bearberry Loop, via the Coal Camp Road and the Forestry Trunk Road

This tour is ideally a day's outing, at minimum a three-hour drive. Approximately half of the 107-kilometre distance is over slow gravel roads. Logging trucks and oil industry vehicles may be encountered along the way, and special care is required on dry dusty days. Watch for livestock and wildlife on the road. There are no services—check your fuel gage before setting off. It is, however, a wonderful introduction to the backcountry of Alberta's foothills with magnificent scenery.

DIRECTIONS: From Sundre take HWY 584 west from junction with HWY 22.

I SPY: Sawdust Pile

A huge pile of sawdust marks the Sunpine Forest Products mill, which gives employment to 1,000 people in the Sundre area, both at its two mills and in the forest.

DIRECTIONS: After 7.2 KM turn south onto the Coal Camp Road and follow west. Distances for this tour are given from the Coal Camp Road turnoff. We suggest you zero your odometer here.

ALONG THE WAY: Coal Camp Road

The Coal Camp road leads to the hamlet of Coal Camp, where coal was first mined in 1898 and used in local homes. This area was also prime timber country, and from 1907–15 the Great West Logging Company had its main logging camp at Coal Camp, which retained its name despite the change in industry. While coal was no longer produced commercially, the blacksmith at the logging camp, where huge bunkhouses each housed up to 120 men, used it in his forge. Early farmers and ranchers in the area worked in the woods. Each spring most of the logs were driven down river to the Great West sawmills at Red Deer. The finished lumber was soon in stock at Alberta's lumber yards, which could hardly keep up with the demands of newly arrived settlers in the years before WWI. As you follow the road through magnificent ranching country, especially stunning in the fall, you will catch glimpses of the Red Deer River.

Bright fall sun glints off the Avery steam traction engine.

I SPY: Steam Engine

Watch for an Avery steam traction engine, located on a bend on the north side
of the road where the river comes into view. This once-again-brightly-paint-
ed monster with its enormous boiler was hauled from the Red Deer River in
the 1990s. It had sunk beneath the water during the flood of 1915 when logs,
lumber, and the steam engine were lost to the Great West Lumber Company.
The Avery was used to power a small sawmill at Coal Camp.

I SPY: Log Cabin

Look out for an original log cabin on the south side of the road as you
enter the hamlet of Coal Camp.

ALONG THE WAY: Rock Outcrops

Where the road begins to run parallel with river (12.7 KM on the route) it cuts through rock outcrops composed of hard sandstone and shale. Although this bedrock underlies all of central Alberta, it is usually exposed only in deep river valleys. In the foothills, the bedrock has been forced up from the ground by the immense energy of the mountain-building forces that created the Rockies. Look for limestone and red or white sandstone boulders carried here and left behind by glaciers. The sand and gravel that forms the bed of the Red Deer River was also left by melting glaciers and has since been augmented by the floods of water that flow from the mountains.

Getting through the rock cut was a little more hazardous around 1913. You are travelling the same road today.
GLENBOW ARCHIVES NA-1941-17

STOP: Cartier Creek Provincial Recreation Area (13.5 KM on the route)

This is a good spot to pull in and explore the gravel banks of the Red Deer River where the wolf willow grows. Look east to get a good view of the rock outcrops above the road.

Sit and watch the icy blue water rush over the rapids with their backdrop of dense spruce forest. The Red Deer River begins in the mountains near Lake Louise and flows through the foothills and across the plains, eventually joining the South Saskatchewan River. Scottish settlers named the river after the magnificent elk seen in the vicinity, assuming it to be the same species as the European red deer.

Much of the sand and gravel along the banks of this rushing river were deposited when glaciers helped to widen the valley. Today, the constantly moving and sometimes flooding waters continually add to those deposits. Over time, they move massive amounts of rock from the mountains and carry it into the plains. As long as the Rockies do not uplift further, this sort of erosion will eventually wear down the mountains until they are level with the prairies. In these cold, fast-moving waters, life is scarce. Look for insects that are adapted to survive in such waters. Turn over a stone to see the mayfly nymphs clinging to the underside and the strange "house" of the caddis fly larvae.

FEATURED WILDLIFE: CADDIS FLY

In its larval form, this is no ordinary caterpillar. Firstly, it is entirely aquatic. Secondly, it builds a "house" around itself by first spinning a silken cocoon, then embedding sand grains or plant bits for protection. It may surprise you to see such an inanimate-looking object suddenly move. Watch carefully to see the caddis fly head and front legs emerge, looking for floating bits of food to eat. Eventually, the larva will escape the cold water when it metamorphoses into a moth-like insect.

FEATURED WILDLIFE: SPOTTED SANDPIPER

The spotted sandpiper has a characteristic and comical habit of teetering back and forth after a run or flight. It feels very much at home along the banks of the river, where it searches for insects in the sand using its long, pointed bill. Its nest is a simple depression in the ground, lined with grasses and established under the cover of grasses or shrubby growth. This is one of the few bird species in which the male is left to tend the nest while the female searches for food and defends the territory.

ALONG THE WAY: Red Deer River Ranches

Just east of Williams Creek bridge (21.9 KM on the route) look out for the entrance to Bar 75, one of the Red Deer River ranches.

At the turn of the century Harry Graham staked his claim here and opened a store to trade with Aboriginal people in the area. John Morgan and Arthur Heaton bought the land and buildings and set out to develop a ranch. The first winter of 1906–07 was a disaster—only 90 cattle out of a herd of 350 survived the frigid temperatures and deep snow that gripped the province. The ranch was bought by Dick Brown in the 1920s and later by Colonel Snyder, who built a hunting lodge on Williams Creek that became known far and wide. In 1953 the lodge burned—and all of Snyder's trophies with it. Only the fire and chimney remained, and have been incorporated into the new lodge on the site.

DIRECTIONS: Continuing west, the pavement turns to gravel at 24.6 KM on the route.

ALONG THE WAY: Cache Hill and Bull Hill

As you head west, you will pass two large hills. They are the result of rivers that flowed inside or on top of glaciers, piling up massive amounts of sand and gravel within the confines of the ice walls. In more recent times, the gravel deposits have proved very useful for road building. After many years of use, those gravel pits have now been landscaped and re-seeded with native species. Look to the west for log harvesting sites on the slopes of the foothills. At one time square cutblocks were the norm when harvesting for timber. Today, logging simulates more closely the effects of a forest fire, and plant debris is left behind to provide nutrients for regeneration of the forest.

DIRECTIONS: At 33.8 KM on the route you cross Bull Creek.

I SPY: Deer Creek Flats—Prescribed Burn Sign (37.1 KM on the route)

Look to the north where a deforested ridge is evident. The Alberta Forest Service conducted forest burn experiments on those slopes, which have since been grazed by cattle. Note how the aspen poplar has grown on the burned areas.

STOP: Deer Creek Provincial Recreation Area (37.8 KM on the route)

Fishermen have great success here. Where fish are abundant, you can count on spotting an osprey looking for a meal; stroll along the informal trails along the riverbank and keep your eyes peeled. Facilities include a boat launch, picnic shelter, and washrooms.

FEATURED WILDLIFE: Osprey

Watch for the osprey patrolling along the river, look-ing for movements of fish in the water. When it spots a fish, the osprey dives downward, then positions itself so that its outstretched claws point directly at the prey. If neces-sary, it will submerge itself completely beneath the water to grasp its meal. Two forward-pointing claws and two that point backward are very effec-tive in grasping and holding slippery fish.

Also called the fish hawk, the osprey has no lack of trees and cliffs on which to nest in this region.
PETER LLEWELLYN / SPLIT SECONDS

ALONG THE WAY: River Confluence

At 43.5 KM on the route you will come to a rockslide slide area as the road begins to plunge downhill. We suggest you park safely at the pull-in just past the #10 sign on the road and walk back up the hill to catch the magnificent view to the southwest, where McGee Creek joins the Red Deer River.

DIRECTIONS: At 46.5 KM on the route you will arrive at the junction of Coal Camp Road and the Forestry Trunk Road (HWY 734). Turn right and continue north on the Coal Camp Road. The sign indicates that you are now heading to Nordegg, although this tour will guide you to Bearberry.

OPTION: If you wish to explore Ya Ha Tinda Ranch, turn left at the same junction. The Mountainaire Lodge is located approximately 3 KM past the turn, and is a popular staging place for river rafting and trail rides in the area. After 25 KM you will arrive at Ya Ha Tinda Ranch. It is located on a plateau surrounded by mountains, where the winter climate is mild. Since 1930 it has been used by Parks Canada to breed and train the horses used by wardens to patrol the backcountry of the Rocky Mountain Parks.
Tel: (403) 637-2229
From nearby Bighorn Campground you can walk to the spectacular Big Horn Falls.

ALONG THE WAY: Willow Clumps

The tight clumps of willows and dense grasses seen on either side of the road have the appearance of groomed shrubbery. This habitat promotes luxuriant growth of willows and sedges—grass-like plants that like wet feet—although it is too wet for larger trees. Fireweed growing along the ditches indicates past disturbance, such as road-building, since it is one of the first plants to invade new sites of freshly disturbed soil. Both willows and fireweed are staples in the diet of ungulates such as the Canadian elk.

FEATURED WILDLIFE: Elk

Of the Canadian deer species, the elk is second only to the moose in size. It is easily distinguished from other deer by the pale-coloured patch on its rump. The male grows a massive rack of antlers each season, which may reach halfway back over the length of the body, adding nearly forty pounds to the weight of the animal. Massive neck muscles are needed to put those giant antlers into action when sparring with other bulls.

Antlers are the fastest growing bones known, lengthening up to one inch per day. At the beginning of summer, they start as spongy cartilage. A close look at the velvet covering the antlers reveals grooves and ridges, the veins that carry blood to the growing antlers. By August, they are completely mineralized into a hard bone of calcium and phosphorus, the velvet begins to dry up, and bulls can be seen scraping it off on trees and road signs. Elk are a vocal species, expressing themselves with a distinctive bugle, especially during the fall, when the males advertising for females sound much like a first-time trumpet player.

ALONG THE WAY: Forest Fires (50.4 KM on the route)

On September 30, 2001, flames raced from tree to tree through this area at Yara Creek and shot into the sky, which was soon filled with black smoke. The fire, which began in the Dogrib Creek area, was out in twenty-four hours, but it had burned 11,000 hectares. Although no people were hurt, forty-five cattle, seven wild horses, and innumerable wildlife were killed, and three million dollars worth of logging equipment was destroyed. How did the fire start? Someone left a campfire unattended.

Sunpine salvaged almost a year's worth of lumber for their Sundre mill from the area when the fire was out. It had to be done immediately, as lumber that has been heated or is standing dead for any length of time will crack. In this Forest Management Agreement Area, Sunpine is monitoring natural rehabilitation of the burn area as well as doing reforestation.

This devastation is the result of the Dogrib Creek fire of 2001.
SUNPINE FOREST PRODUCTS LTD

DIGGING DEEPER: Forest Regeneration

Wildfires have burned much of the forest in this area during the past hundred years. You may think of forest fires as disasters which ideally would never happen. In fact, fires are a natural part of the life of a forest. After a forest has matured, the trees begin to decay and large amounts of deadfall litter the forest floor. This attracts woodpeckers and animals that feed and live on dead trees, but after a time, the wildlife population diminishes. When fungal rot, dry and withered branches, brown needles and too many insect pests take over, nature has a way of clearing it all away with fire to start afresh. The ashes left in the wake of fire contain nutrients on which new growth can feed. Soon the blackened soil comes to life with scores of plants and animals eager to move back in.

Aspen trees, their underground roots barely harmed by the fire, sprout in dense patches, giving the original trees immortality through their clones. The intense heat of a fire cracks the cones of pine trees. As the resin melts, the seeds are released to begin a new generation. Fireweed, whose bright purple blooms provide a striking contrast to the blackened trees, grows easily in the ashes. Elk, mule deer, and moose browse hungrily on the new, tender growth.

I *SPY*: Charred Trees (56.2 KM on the route)

Charred tree trunks for the next few kilometres indicate the fires that have whipped through here in the past. This area once looked just like the burned area you drove through earlier.

I *SPY*: River Meander

You will get a good view as you drop downhill into the James River Valley (61.4 KM on the route) and will catch a glimpse of a meander in the river

as you follow its course. After another kilometre you cross Bridgland Creek, named for Dominion and Alberta Land Surveyor Morrison Parsons Bridgland, who mapped large tracts of the Rocky Mountains.

I *SPY*: Shell Canada

At 68.9 KM on the route is a sign for Shell Canada Road—a reminder that you are sharing the road with oil industry traffic.

Look west for a view towards James Pass and the front ranges of the Rockies as you meet the valley floor on a curve in the road.

FEATURED *PLANT*: Aspen Clones

About one kilometre past the Shell Canada Road, look for regenerating meadows of aspen poplars and occasional glimpses of the river. Though each female aspen tree sends out millions of seeds each year, most new trees sucker from underground roots. One parent tree may produce several hectares of genetic duplicates, called clones. Clones will go through changes in unison: changing leaf colour, dropping leaves, and developing buds all at the same time. It is easiest to tell the male and female trees apart in spring or early summer. Take a close look at the catkins, the flowers that grow in long fuzzy clusters. Does it have long wispy shoots growing out through the fuzz, with yellow pollen on the ends? That is a male catkin. Does it have shorter, pear-shaped shoots growing through the fuzz? Do the ends look smooth? That is a female catkin, which will eventually produce seeds.

STOP: Wooden Bridge (78 KM on the route)

A steel bridge crosses James River here. Pull off before the bridge. Down by the river's edge you can see the remnants of an older wooden bridge. If you walk west about 100 metres, alongside the river, you can catch a spectacular river view to the north. Erosion has worn a small canyon for the river to rush through.

FEATURED WILDLIFE: Black Bears

If you find animal droppings shaped like cow patties, black in colour and containing berry pits, you know you have crossed trails with a black bear. This species is one of the most successful in the province and is found just about anywhere there is a forest. Surprisingly, this powerful animal with a mouth full of predatory teeth rarely goes after live prey, preferring berries, insects, and carrion, though streams full of spawning trout present a meal too tempting to pass up. Note: All wild animals are very unpredictable. NEVER approach a bear!

ALONG THE WAY: James River Viewpoint (85.2 KM on the route)

Look out for a grassy crescent-shaped loop on the right side of the road. Here you can pull in safely. There is a wonderful view from the bank high above the James River—keep children closely supervised here. Stroll through the trees on the abandoned logging trails for a leg stretcher.

DIRECTIONS: At 88.3 KM on the route, take HWY 584 east. It is 19 KM to Bearberry (see page 127). The last part of this section is on a paved highway. At Bearberry you can join Tour 7: Rocky Mountain House to Sundre (page 115), and then from Sundre, Tour 9 to Olds (page 145).

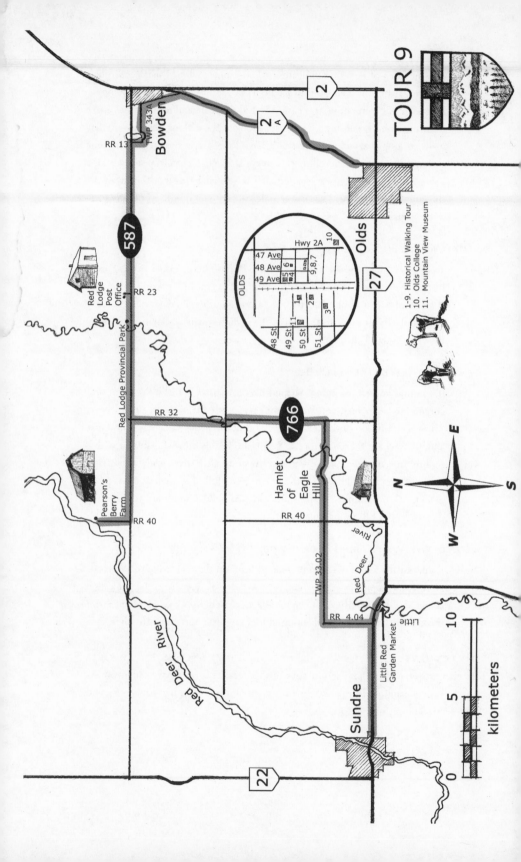

TOUR 9

2

2
A

Bowden

TWP 343A

RR 13

587

Red Lodge Post Office

RR 23

Red Lodge Provincial Park

RR 32

766

Pearson's Berry Farm

RR 40

Hamlet of Eagle Hill

RR 40

TWP 33.02

Red Deer River

RR 4.04

Little Red Garden Market

Little Red Deer River

Sundre

22

Olds

27

1-9. Historical Walking Tour
10. Olds College
11. Mountain View Museum

OLDS

Hwy 2A   10

47 Ave
48 Ave   6
49 Ave   5   9,8,7
                4

48 St
49 St   11   1
50 St   2
51 St   3

N
E
W
S

Red Deer River

0   5   10
kilometers

Sundre to Olds via Eagle Hill and Bowden

STOP: Sundre (See page 130)

DIRECTIONS: Drive east from Sundre. As you leave Sundre, HWY 584 becomes HWY 27.

ALONG THE WAY: Sundre Hill

As you leave Sundre, you will climb Sundre Hill just east of town. Take the opportunity to look west for a spectacular view of the mountains when the weather is clear. To take a photograph, park safely in the parking lot adjacent to the golf course on the north side of the road.

DIRECTIONS: After travelling 8.3 KM on HWY 27, turn north onto RR 4.04 at the sign for Forest Heights Golf Course. Continue north for Eagle Hill.

OPTION: To visit the Little Red Garden Market, continue on HWY 27 for another kilometre. You drive down into the valley past the Little Red Deer River Store. As you climb out of the east side of the valley, you will find the market on the south side of the road.

LITTLE RED GARDEN MARKET

Jim Dickson grows a wonderful garden—two acres of vegetables including beans, chard, kohlabri, rutabagas, carrots, parsnips, and peas. All are pesticide free. As well, there are raspberries, and in 12,000 feet of poly tunnels a variety of succulent summer tomatoes ripening on the vine. If he is not too busy, Jim is happy to give you a tour of his growing facilities.

Open May–mid-October, Monday 10:00 AM–6:00 PM; Tuesday–Sunday 10:00 AM–8:00 PM

Tel. (403) 556-8809

www.littleredmarket.com

I SPY: Floodplain

As you head north, you will drive through the floodplain of the Little Red Deer River.

ALONG THE WAY: Kame Terrace

Kames are land formations that developed along the rim of glaciers. Looking to the east, the long flat-topped ridge indicates that during glacial activity, a lake was trapped between the ice and the valley side. The lake gradually filled in with sediment, leaving a flat surface. When the glacier melted, the water drained away leaving a flat-topped ridge bordering the valley.

DIRECTIONS: After 2.5 KM, take the first gravel road (TWP 33.02) to the east.

I SPY: Eagle Hill

Eagle Hill is a landmark in the valley that also shares the name with its creek and the hamlet to the east. The name is thought to be of native origin, coming from an eagle sighting in a tree on the hill. An old Indian trail, no longer visible, crossed the township road about 1.2 KM east from the turnoff.

I SPY: Microwave Tower

Microwaves are super-high-frequency radio waves that transmit signals for radio, television, phone, and computer across the continent. Microwave systems are line-of-sight media, so towers must be situated on high points of land. In the relatively flat terrain of central Alberta, locating these lines of sight is certainly simpler than in areas of more hilly or mountainous terrain.

DIRECTIONS: East of Eagle Hill you come to a junction with RR 40. Continue east.

I SPY: River Valley

This is beautiful rolling countryside above the Little Red Deer River Valley.

ALONG THE WAY: Mountain Bluebirds

Look for bluebird nesting boxes along the road. Mountain bluebirds flash a soft blue colour as they dart across the landscape catching insects on the wing. They are particularly gentle in nature and so are unable to resist the aggressive actions of starlings and house sparrows, which often overtake the bluebird nests. Their sensitivity to insecticides (not surprising in an insectivorous bird) has also endangered their populations. Nest boxes attached to fenceposts through central Alberta, called bluebird trails, have been a tremendous boost to the population.

DIRECTIONS: At the hamlet of Eagle Hill, now only a handful of farmyards, the road twists downhill and crosses a bridge over the Little Red Deer River. Keep right, and at the junction of paved HWY 766, turn north. At the T junction, turn west across the bridge over the Little Red Deer River. Immediately west of the bridge, turn north for 6.7 KM on RR 32, a winding gravel road which runs beside the river. Turn west on HWY 587 for 6.4 KM. Watch for a sign for Pearson's Berry Farm. Turn north on RR 40 and follow the gravel road for 2 KM down the hill to the farm.

STOP: Pearson's Berry Farm

This is one of many U-pick berry farms in central Alberta. Situated in a valley just off the highway, it is one of our favourite destination points. The smell of warm Saskatoon pie is irresistible—have a piece with ice cream or take one home. Jams, syrups, jellies, soft hot ciders, and berry-flavoured lemonades are also for sale. Visit the craft shop with quality items from across western Canada, located in a wing of the cozy log home on the grounds.

Open daily in the summer season.

Tel: (403) 224-3011

Here you can pick your own saskatoons during the season that begins about July 25, or you can buy frozen berries by the pound.
FRED SCHUTZ

DIRECTIONS: Retrace your route east on HWY 587 and continue east toward Bowden.

ALONG THE WAY: Dugouts for Cattle

A dugout is either an existing slough that has been mechanically deepened so that it will hold water year-round, or a large hole dug in a suitable spot where it will fill with water. In those few areas of central Alberta where it is difficult to drill a well, dugouts are used as a source of water for house and farm use. However, most dugouts are developed mainly as a convenient place to water cattle. Usually one end has a gently sloped approach that allows the cattle to walk up and drink. Dugouts, usually well tended and fenced, are sometimes stocked with trout in spring. The trout are fed each day and soon grow to a good size. They are usually caught before freeze-up, as few will survive the winter beneath the ice. In winter, once the ice is thick enough, dugouts make great skating rinks.

STOP: Red Lodge Provincial Park

In any populated area, agriculture, towns, highways, and other man-made obstacles fragment wildlife habitat. This means that unless wildlife is somehow able to move from one area to another, their food supply will diminish. For example, deer will overbrowse the vegetation and weasels will decimate their prey populations. Inbreeding also becomes a problem, and disease may easily spread throughout the confined population. Rivers provide one of the few corridors along which wildlife are able to move from one habitat area to another. Moose, deer, beaver, and black bears are a few of the animals that are able to move freely, with little disturbance from man, through the riverine forests and grasslands along the Little Red Deer River.

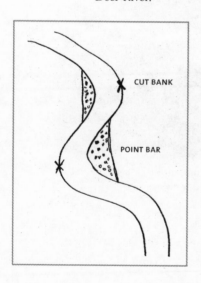

CUT BANK

POINT BAR

Follow the gravelled trail from the day use parking area. It follows the river in both directions and offers a great opportunity to see riverine plants and wildlife. The geology of river formation can be clearly seen where the river bends.

Facilities: camping, picnic areas, showers and toilets, public phone, swimming, playground.

CUT BANKS

A short walk along the riverside hiking trail, in either direction, will take you to a bend in the river. On the inside of the bend, notice how the sandy soil accumulates. This is called a point bar. On the outside of the bend, a cut bank occurs. Why does this happen? The physics of water flow causes water on the outside of the bend to flow more quickly, thus slowly cutting soil away from the riverbank. On the inside, the water flows more slowly and so soil is gradually deposited. Eventually, vegetation will cover the point bars as the path of the river moves in the direction of the eroding cut.

FEATURED *PLANT*: Reed Canary Grass

This dried grass once served as an effective insulation. When softened by rubbing it was stuffed into clothing and footgear. The stems, which grow to about six feet, were easily woven into mats or simply spread loosely on the ground for bedding.

Reed canary grass is seen growing prominently along the shoreline.

I *SPY*: Red Lodge Post Office

On the north side of the road, 1.2 kilometres from Red Lodge Provincial Park, you will see a white farmhouse in the middle of the quarter-section. This was the Red Lodge Post Office from 1899, where Colin Thompson also kept a store. The line of trees west of the farmhouse marks a segment of the old trail that once ran from Bowden to Rocky Mountain House. You can travel north on RR 23 a short distance to see it clearly.

DIGGING *DEEPER*: Bowden to Rocky Mountain House Freight Trail

Just before WWI the Canadian Northern Railway and the Central Alberta Railway were competing to construct their lines west from Red Deer to the North Saskatchewan River. Bowden was touted as the most logical place from which to freight goods for the construction gangs west from the Calgary–Edmonton railway. The trail west from Red Deer was cited as being poor due to the swampy country it passed through. *The Bowden News* noted, "It is not generally known that the road in question is partly over the old Hudson Bay road used during the last century by that company for the purpose of freighting to and from the old Hudson Bay post." The trail from Bowden, already being used by Fred and Jack Brewster to freight supplies to the collieries at Brazeau, joined the old HBC trail from Morley to Rocky Mountain House in Township 35 Range 3, to the northwest of Red Lodge Provincial Park.

DIRECTIONS: Turn south on RR 1.3 to follow the route of the old trail into Bowden. Turn east at TWP 343A. The road curves south of Bowden Lake to bring you across the railway line into Bowden at 17th Avenue, exactly where the railway station house once stood.

Bowden Pioneer Museum (2201 19th Avenue)

Located in the old curling rink, the Bowden museum has a unique exhibit: a refurbished Chapter Room of the Eastern Star Lodge, the ladies' wing of the Freemasons. Complete with hand-hooked rug, chairs, and symbolic pedestals, it includes objects from the organization from all over Alberta. Robert Hoare was the town photographer until 1914. His images form an important record of the days of early rural settlement around Bowden, and many are on display along with a collection of early cameras.

Open May 24–July 1 Wednesday, Saturday 10:00 AM–4:00 PM
July 1–September 30 Tuesday–Saturday 10:00 AM–4:00 PM

DIRECTIONS: Take 20th Street south as it turns into HWY 2A south for Olds. It follows the railway line closely.

I SPY: Freight Train!

This is a good spot to see a freight train close up. The tanker cars carry compressed natural gas or propane; square hopper cars carry sulphur or fertilizer; round hopper cars carry grain; boxcars and other containers carry a wide range of goods, but the familiar caboose is a thing of the past.

STOP: Olds

The town of Olds had its beginning as Sixth Siding on the Calgary–Edmonton railway line in 1890. Soon Olds, named for railroad man

George Olds, was the market town for an area that became known for mixed farming and dairying. Huge stacks of hay were to be seen waiting for boxcars to ship it to other points in the province, giving Olds the nickname "hay city."

Olds hit national headlines in 1907 when railroad officials decided to

A crowd gathered on the line for the "Battle of Olds."
GLENBOW ARCHIVES, NA-624-4

close off a second railway crossing that the town had installed—with their blessing—to the tune of $500. The CPR, who operated the railway, dismissed the townsmen's protests. When it became clear the town meant business, a train bearing gravel was sent from Calgary with fifty workmen, several CPR detectives and twelve North West Mounted Police. Undeterred, the townspeople—many of them armed—blocked the line. A riot of sorts ensued, during which the NWMP arrested a good number of the town's prominent merchants and the town constables arrested several CPR detectives and workmen! The town ultimately lost what the *Toronto Globe* called the "Battle of Olds," but not without taking the matter to the Supreme Court. CPR lawyer R. B. Bennett was too wily for the town's legal advisor and the crossing remains closed to this day.

MOUNTAIN VIEW COUNTRY FAIR

The best time to visit Olds is during this old-style fair with livestock judging, heavy horse show, crafts and horticultural exhibits, antique tractor pulls, a fiddlers' jamboree, and of course fireworks and a midway. Sponsored by the Olds Agricultural Society, it is held at the fairground downtown each summer from Thursday through Sunday on the weekend following the August long weekend.

Their website address is: www.oldsagsociety.com.

MOUNTAIN VIEW MUSEUM (5038 50th Street)

Located in the former Alberta Government Telephone building, the museum tells the story of those singing wires complete with switch-board. The community is represented through a series of exhibits, one being the local store—quite a range of items were for sale in this railway town. Imagine yourself sliding onto the barber's chair or coming home to supper in the dining room after a day at the business office. Changing exhibits reflect community interests and events. The museum building also houses an archive, where the local newspaper, the *Olds Gazette*, can be read on microfilm.

Open September–June Tuesday–Thursday 12:00 PM–5:00 PM
July, August Monday–Friday 9:00 AM–5:00 PM
Tel: (403) 556-8464

WALKING TOUR OF OLDS

Despite the devastation of Main Street in a huge fire in 1922, the town has a number of historic buildings of interest. We have picked out several close to the downtown area. For a longer walking tour check the museum's web site at www.telusplanet.net/public/ohschin or pick up a map at the museum.

Building 1: The Public Lunch (4916 50th Avenue)

This is probably the oldest Chinese restaurant in Alberta. Wong Yet arrived in Olds from China in 1898, opened the Star Laundry, and by 1903 was able to send for his son Wong Pond. Together they operated a popular restaurant, along with the laundry until fire shattered their dreams. In 1918 they reopened as the Public Lunch, which, despite changes made by the family over the years, retains the atmosphere of a small-town meeting spot for business people and visitors alike.

Building 2: Davey Block (5008 50th Avenue)

This block dates from 1926—one of the new boomtown-fronted brick buildings to be constructed as a result of fire. It was home to Davey's grocery store and a number of offices upstairs. Today the Touchstone Gallery anchors this important commercial block.

Wong Pond outside the Public Lunch with its impressive boomtown facade around 1911.
GLENBOW ARCHIVES, NA-1926-1

Building 3: Canadian Imperial Bank of Commerce (5009 51st Street)

Today a drug mart and photo shop occupy this impressive brick building, constructed in 1909. The bank opened its door in September that year, with Mr. W. C. Duncan as manager. After the bank closed on December 31, 1934, the building housed the post office and library. The best place to look at the exterior of the building is from the opposite side of the street. Notice its fine boxed decorated cornice with plain frieze. The window surrounds are in cut sandstone and the recessed doorway has a decorative sandstone surround, with an arched fanlight over the door.

Building 4: The Brown House (4809 49th Avenue)

Mrs. Brown, a storekeeper and a milliner—a maker of ladies hats—maintained her house as a rooming house for respectable young ladies. They were subject, the story goes, to "Brownie's" curfew at 10:00 PM. Visiting gentlemen left the parlour immediately on the ring of an alarm clock set for the hour! From 1913–25 the house was rented out as a dormitory for students at Olds College.

Building 5: The Hunter House (4801 49th Avenue)

Mr. Brown built this magnificent house in 1901. In 1907 he sold it to

The Brown House, built in 1902, is designated as a Registered Historic Resource.

W. W. Hunter, a local rancher, who lived in it to 1947. The house was then sold to the United Grain Growers, whose lucky elevator agent lived there until 1955. Originally located opposite a livery stable, the house fortunately escaped the sparks when the livery stables burned in the early years of the twentieth century. Today it is occupied by a business that has preserved original architectural details such as a Palladian window on the gable end facing the street, eave brackets, gingerbread, and decorative fish scale shingling.

Building 6: Eaton's catalogue house (4722 49th Street)

Imagine it is around 1920—you choose your house from the Eaton's catalogue, sending in the order to Winnipeg. The stationmaster lets you know your crates have arrived. Once the concrete foundation has been poured you follow instructions and watch the house rise from the ground. It is not known what name Eaton's gave this design—but it offers a pleasing appearance on the street with its hip-roofed enclosed front veranda.

Buildings 7–9: The Craig Houses (4706-50th Street; 4718 50th Street; and 4726 50th Street)

These impressive houses belonged to the Craig brothers, who came from Quebec and established themselves as the most prominent merchants in Olds. They were brothers four—generally known by their initials—R. L.; S. J.; W. M.; and C. G.! The Craigs had a grocery store as well as a large dry goods store known as the People's Store, which was established in 1900. Although it operates under a new name, it remains the oldest business in town, located at 5102 50th Avenue. W. M. Craig bought 4706 from his brother C. G. shortly after it was built in 1904, and lived here until 1944. The most striking feature of this very large house is its octagonal tower with bay windows on all three stories. From 1920 on S. L. Craig lived at 4718, which was built by David Shannon in 1906; and R. L. Craig lived at 4726.

OLDS AGRICULTURAL COLLEGE (At the east edge of Olds on
HWY 2A)

Since 1913, Olds College has provided practical education and training
in the fields of agriculture, horticulture, land and environmental management, agribusiness, and rural entrepreneurship. The campus is widely
recognized as one of the most beautiful and interesting in western
Canada. In a short walking distance you can explore a modern farm,
flowering gardens maintained by the horticulture program, and a wide
variety of both modern and traditional College buildings.

Olds College Farm, spread
over 1,200 acres, is Alberta's largest
for teaching and demonstration. You
can watch farm operations for
dairy, sheep, swine, beef, equine,
and more! A farm manager and
technicians operate the farm, working with instructors to provide
hands-on experience for students,
while simultaneously running an
efficient operation that boasts over
3,000 animals. Farm staff also work
with other agencies to research and
test new farming methods.

On the other side of the campus are the Flowering Gardens—a
living laboratory of gardens and
plantings used for show and educa-

Interpretive panel—Olds College.
Take a walking tour of the college
buildings and gardens by following
the trail of interpretive signs. Pick up
a trail brochure at Duncan Marshall Place
located adjacent to parking lots 1 and 2.

tion. You may want to try some of the species or garden designs in your
own yard. Along the way, you will discover techniques used in the greenhouse, herbs that repel insects, the best irises for our climate and what
grows best in the shade. Feel free to ask questions of college staff. They are
always willing to explain their areas of expertise. Call ahead to arrange a
staff-led tour for groups.

Tel: 1-800-661-6537 (toll-free) or (403) 556-8281

From here you can join Tour 10: Olds to Trochu (page 157).

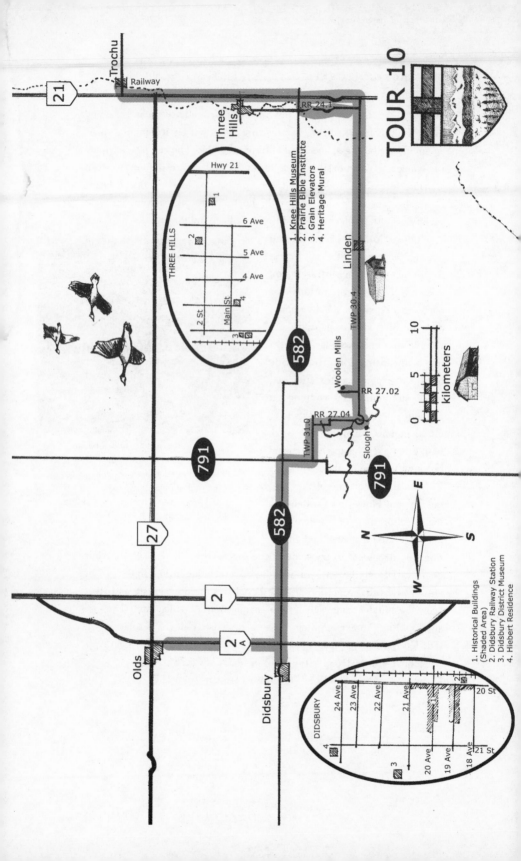

TOUR 10

Trochu

Railway

21

Three Hills

RR 24.1

Hwy 21

THREE HILLS

6 Ave

5 Ave

4 Ave

Main St

2 St

1. Knee Hills Museum
2. Prairie Bible Institute
3. Grain Elevators
4. Heritage Mural

Linden

TWP 30.4

582

Woolen Mills

RR 27.02

RR 27.04

TWP 31.0

Slough

791

791

27

791

0   5   10

kilometers

N

E

W

S

2

582

2 A

Olds

Didsbury

1. Historical Buildings (Shaded Area)
2. Didsbury Railway Station
3. Didsbury District Museum
4. Hiebert Residence

DIDSBURY

24 Ave

23 Ave

22 Ave

21 Ave

20 Ave

19 Ave

18 Ave

20 St

21 St

Olds to Trochu, via Didsbury and Linden

DIRECTIONS: Take HWY 2A south from Olds.

ALONG THE WAY: Grassland Songbirds

You may think forests are the natural habitat of birds, but many species prefer open areas as their home. Roadside ditches are a perfect habitat for nesting and feeding. Watch for birds singing on the fence posts lining the fields. Grassland songbirds do not exhibit flashy colours, since they must blend in with the dry dirt and grasses of the meadow. They nest on the ground or in shrubs, fashioning nests made with the most available material: grasses and shed animal hair.
A diet of seeds and insects is always abundant. There is little protection from the cold during the blustery prairie winters, so grassland songbirds must head south for the winter, returning by early May.

The Savannah sparrow is one of Alberta's more common grassland species.
PETER LLEWELLYN / SPLIT SECONDS

DIRECTIONS: At junction of HWY 2A and HWY 582, turn west for the town of Didsbury.

STOP: Didsbury

Didsbury, named for a town in England, was a stop on the Calgary–Edmonton Railway in 1890. By 1894 it had became a centre for Mennonite settlers, led west by Jacob Shantz. Prior to 1914, Mennonite settlers in Alberta were of predominantly Swiss-German background who

This tiny building, constructed in 1914 after the fire, currently houses Mugs Coffee House.

migrated from the Waterloo area of Ontario, except for a group of Russo-German Mennonites from southern Manitoba. Both groups, who belonged to two different "conferences" (Mennonite Brethren in Christ and General Conference respectively), settled in the Didsbury area. In early Didsbury, which had become a town by 1906, street names included Waterloo and Berlin.

Didsbury developed quickly and by 1903 had it own newspaper: *The Didsbury Pioneer*. Fire burned part of the downtown area that year and the grain elevator the next year. The town rebounded, and by 1910 even had lit streets. 1914, however, was to prove disastrous for the town because fires destroyed three business blocks, two hotels, a livery stable, and the creamery. The town, like so many others in Alberta, passed a bylaw ensuring that new buildings in the business area must be constructed of brick, stone, or concrete. Many of those later commercial buildings are still in use.

WALKING TOUR

Take a stroll along the Main Street (20th Street) and 19th and 21st Avenue, where the past is present again. Many of the buildings have plaques telling their histories.

DIDSBURY RAILWAY STATION

The people of Didsbury were glad to see the completion of this building in 1902, which offered shelter for travellers and telegraph facilities for the operation of trains. It was one of the original stations on the Edmonton–Calgary Railway, and is the only station house left standing in Alberta with a mansard roof with wide bell cast eaves.

Didsbury railway station

DIDSBURY & DISTRICT MUSEUM (2118 21st Avenue)

The museum is located in Didsbury's impressive school, which opened in 1908, born of an optimism that the town would grow. The local school board hired an architect in 1907 to design the orange brick and sandstone building at an estimated cost of $28,000. It is worth visiting the museum just to get a sense of what it must have been like to go to classes here— one room is kept as a schoolroom. Among a variety of other displays, including military and naval uniforms, are medical items such as local physician Dr. Boyd's examining table from 1905. The oxygen case on display is a reminder that the school was used as an emergency hospital during the Spanish influenza epidemic of 1918. The school finally closed its doors to students in 1984, but remains a Didsbury landmark.

Open Summer Wednesday–Saturday 2:00 PM–5:00 PM
Winter Wednesday–Friday 2:00 PM–5:00 PM

HIEBERT RESIDENCE (2102 24th Avenue)

Cornelius Hiebert was a Mennonite who came to Didsbury from Manitoba in 1901. He opened a successful general store and soon had a lumber and implement business on the go. The ambitious Hiebert made his debut in politics by becoming village overseer from 1901–04. He had his sights set on a loftier title and in 1905 he was elected as a Conservative

MLA to the province's first legislature. In 1907 Hiebert chose a secluded residential street to build his fancy mansion and show off his affluent and influential position.

It is a large brick and stone two-storey house with gable windows on each face of the truncated pyramidal roof complete with widow's walk. Note the stone windowsills, lintels, and quoining at the corners. Hiebert went to a lot of trouble to have a variety of window designs, including unusual keyhole fireplace windows, as well as eyebrow windows. Steps lead to a gracious curved veranda supported by wooden pillars with ionic capitals, welcoming visitors to the house, whose formal layout is embellished with elaborate woodwork.

Life was not destined to work out well for Hiebert. He had the distinction of being the first MLA to promote prohibition in the province in 1908 and championed the idea of non-partisan politics. He lost his seat to a Liberal in 1909. He went homesteading in the Peace River country, later returning to Didsbury, where he died in 1919. The house remained a private residence until 1942 when it was used by the Didsbury Health Unit. It is once again privately owned and is a designated Provincial Historic Resource. It is well worth driving past before you leave town.

DIRECTIONS: Take HWY 582 east, crossing HWY 2A and HWY 2. Turn south on HWY 791. At the T junction turn east on Bergthal Road (TWP 31.0), then take the third gravel road (RR 27.04) south, past the Midway School. Continue south until you come to a large slough.

STOP: Spotting Ducks

As you pass the bridge, look for a good spot to pull off the road to do some bird watching. Waterfowl make use of sloughs for resting, feeding and nesting. When they return north in the spring, their plumage is the brightest, because the males must be in prime shape to attract the females during breeding season. Midsummer is a difficult time to identify species, as ducks moult their feathers during that time (see page 78). However, you can use other clues. Here are some characteristics you may find helpful.

Puddle ducks, such as the mallard, pintail, and shoveller, spring directly into the air when taking flight. They feed mostly at shorelines or in shallow waters, tipping into the water to grasp at food. Puddle ducks can walk and run quite well on land.

Diving ducks, such as the canvasback, redhead, and goldeneye, patter along the water before they can lift off. They tend to feed in deeper waters and will often dive to great depths to catch fish or escape danger. If you approach too closely, they disappear into the water, emerging quite a distance away, and will perhaps only show their heads before diving again. A good birdwatching guide will give you more details.

I *SPY*: Duckweed

Sloughs and ponds are often covered with a dense layer of duckweed. This is not your garden-variety plant. It floats on the pond surface, along with thousands of others, like a tiny leaf with a short root or two hanging down into the water. Duckweed reproduces most commonly by growing bulblets that separate and grow into new plants. Only rarely do they bloom, producing the tiniest of flowers. The flowers are single-sexed, each producing a single microscopic stamen or pistil.

DIRECTIONS: Continue around the slough, heading east toward Linden on TWP 30.4.

STOP: Carstairs Custom Woolen Mills (2 KM north of TWP 30.4 on RR 27.02)

Open the door at the Custom Woolen Mills display store and you are in knitters' heaven. That wonderful smell of wool is pervasive. You can buy any kind of wool you desire in a spectrum of colours—two-ply, three-ply, bulky four-strand, lopi soft-spun for knitting Icelandic sweaters, mohair, quivviut (musk-ox wool), and buffalo wool. Not a knitter? Never mind—work socks, a range of designer sweaters, toques, stuffed wool toys, blankets and a range of comforters are for sale. Customers of the mills who bring their wool here to be processed on site make many of these items.

These mills are a working museum and use machinery dating from 1869–1910. Owners Fen and Bill Purvis-Smith bought machinery in 1975 from two small defunct woolen mills—one in Sifton, Manitoba, and the other in Magrath, Alberta. The machinery was gradually reassembled and renovated—a process that continued until 1990, ending with the restoration of a 1910 William Spiers circular knitting machine.

Take a tour around the mill and follow the processes. Customers bring in garbage bags stuffed with sheared wool. It is washed, rinsed, and put in a centrifuge to rid it of vegetable matter and grease, and then dried. Once the wool is dyed it is brought to the carding machine where the fibres are aligned by brushing. Next comes spinning—here you can see the only operating spinning mule for yarn processing in Canada. Built in 1910, it spins 192 bobbins at a time, and gives a higher quality yarn than wool spun on a frame.

Open Monday–Friday 9:00 AM–5:00 PM
Note: The machinery shuts down at 3:00 PM.
Tel: (403) 337-2221

DIRECTIONS: Return to TWP 30.4 and continue east for Linden.

I *SPY*: Grain Bins

Plenty of grain is grown around here; farmers store their grain in bins at harvest. They slowly empty the bins through the year as grain is needed or markets open up.

Look for over forty-five grain bins in a row on the south side of the road!

DIGGING *DEEPER*: Zero-Till Farming

Some farmers, especially in the drier areas of eastern central Alberta, use an air-seeder to plant their crops directly into the stubble and crop residue from the previous year. The air-seeder literally blows the seed and fertilizer into the undisturbed ground. The system minimizes moisture loss through evaporation, the stubble protects the seedlings from the wind, and fewer greenhouse gases are released than when land is cultivated. Zero-till farmers control weeds with herbicides instead of cultivation.

STOP: Stream Vegetation

This scenic drive takes you across several coulees. Look out for a bridge through a wide riparian area, and take the opportunity to park and have a look at the vegetation along a stream. They include sedges, mint, dock, clover, fireweed, and wolf willow. You may be lucky enough to spot deer and other wildlife that are inclined to follow these watercourses.

Riparian areas—those lush, green strips of land alongside streams, rivers and wetlands—are of prime importance to the natural world and to our own well-being. Riparian areas stay greener longer and produce more forage than uplands, partly due to soils and mostly due to an elevated water table. The succulent green vegetation provides abundant water, shelter, and forage for both livestock and wildlife such as deer, bluebirds, and jackrabbits. Riparian areas also buffer the destructive impacts of floods and droughts. When rivers flood their banks, water soaks into the flood plain, which stores water like a sponge. During drier times of the year, the water is slowly released. Healthy streams are densely vegetated, slowing down the flow of water, so that erosion is also slowed.

SEDGES

Wherever the ground is moist, you will find one of the more than 150 species of sedge, grass-like plants that often have a triangular stems and tiny flowers arranged in spikelets. Since sedges often grow in dense tufts, wildlife find them very useful as places to hide, nest, and feed.

WILD MINT

Do you enjoy mint tea? Wild mint serves the same purpose. It has been used for hundreds of years to make a tea for bad breath, headaches, upset stomachs, fevers, and colds. The flowers on this plant are unique. At the base of each pair of leaves, you will find pink, purple, or white flowers that circle the square stem.

WESTERN DOCK

You may not notice this tall, narrow plant until the fall, when the fruits ripen to a reddish-brown that contrasts conspicuously with the surroundings. The flowers and seeds grow in long, dense clusters.

Wild mint.
ALBERTA COMMUNITY DEVELOPMENT / PARKS AND PROTECTED AREAS

STOP: Linden

As you approach Linden you will notice how the farmsteads are tucked into the sides of the coulee for shelter. The people who settled here are Church of Brethren in Christ Mennonites.

COUNTRY COUSINS RESTAURANT (Located off Central Avenue, behind the Alberta Treasury Branch)

This ethnic restaurant is famous for miles around for its peanut butter pie. It offers Mennonite homestyle cooking and the menu includes verenecki, otherwise known as perogies.

Open Monday–Saturday 7:00 AM–8:00 PM
Tel: (403) 546-4444

JO-AL STYLES (Central Avenue)

Mennonite women in this district continue the tradition of making their own clothes. A huge range of print fabrics is available at this store, where good sewing advice is also offered.

Open Monday–Saturday 9:00 AM–5:00 PM
Tel: (403) 546-3882

DIGGING *DEEPER*: Who are Albertans?

Ethnicity has been important in establishing the character of different areas in Alberta—not least in architectural details and patterns of speech. Political and religious conflict, both within and among different ethnic groups, has resulted in a proliferation of church denominations and cultural organizations over the last hundred years. Ethnic diversity has shaped communities and is central to understanding where we live and who we are today.

Albertans, like all Canadians, are a diverse bunch. The interaction of central Alberta's Aboriginal peoples—including the Cree, Blackfoot, and Nakoda—with French, British, and American traders, and subsequent emergence of the Métis, preceded an influx of peoples from all over the world. From the turn of the twentieth century, Anglo and French Canadians came to Alberta along with British, Irish, and American immigrants. Germans, Scandinavians, Greeks, and Italians followed them, along with settlers from central and Eastern Europe, including Ukrainians, Romanians, and Hungarians in the boom years before WWI.

People came in search of land, employment, and adventure. For some, such as Hutterites and Mennonites, the goal was freedom of religious expression, and for others, such as those of African descent, a search for racial respect. Some immigrants—most particularly the Chinese, who were subjected to a head tax on entering Canada—came alone, some as part of an extended family, others as part of a colonization scheme or religious group. Both World Wars brought further waves of immigrants to rural Alberta, notably the Dutch after 1945. Recent immigrants to central Alberta include men and women from Central and South America, Asia, including Macao, Vietnam, and Korea, and Africa. Although many of these later immigrants have settled in urban areas, others have made their homes in small towns.

DIRECTIONS: Continue east on TWP 30.4 through Linden.

I *SPY*: Barkman's Store

As you drive east look out for Barkman's general store—now closed—which once served the community from its rural crossroads location. Improved roads, more widespread ownership of cars, and rural depopulation, gradually made these rural hubs, which often also had baseball diamonds, halls, or churches, redundant after WWII.

Barkman's general store.

DIRECTIONS: Take the Coulee Loop, a rewarding short drive (8.2 KM) through a stunning prairie coulee. Turn north onto RR 24.1. This gravel road is narrow, and may be muddy in wet weather; drive with caution.

ALONG THE WAY: The Prairie

The prairie is often called "big sky country." Notice the vast expanse of landscape, where the highways stretch as far as the eye can see. People from the prairies often feel claustrophobic anywhere else, where hills or mountains box in the landscape. Why is the prairie different, and what happened to the trees? There were never many trees in this part of the country. The Rocky Mountains control the prairie climate by blocking the warm, humid winds coming from the coast, forcing the air masses upward where they cool and drop their moisture before reaching the prairies. The combination of dryness and exposure to the wind discourages the growth of trees. Grasses, on the other hand, both native and crops, are well adapted to these conditions.

DIRECTIONS: At the next intersection you meet the correction line. Jog west some yards before continuing north on RR 24.1

DIGGING *DEEPER*: The Grid System of the Dominion Land Survey (see illustration next page)

Across the prairies, Dominion Land Surveyors divided the land by numbered ranges that run from east to west from the principal meridians. The Fourth Meridian forms the Alberta-Saskatchewan boundary and the Fifth Meridian runs through Gull Lake west of Lacombe. Townships lines numbered south to north intersect with the ranges, and the resultant squares are called townships. Each township contains thirty-six one-mile by one-mile sections divided for the purposes of land ownership into quarters of 160 acres. Each quarter is described as the NW, NE, SW, or SE of a given section number, in a particular township in a given range, west of a principal meridian. Hence the location for a farm is given as, for example, SE8-TWP41-R2-W5 i.e. the southwest quarter of Section 8, Township 41, Range 2, west of the Fifth Meridian. Road allowances were surveyed between the sections.

As you travel from east to west, you will encounter a north-south range road at one-mile (1.6 KM) intervals, and as you travel north to south, you will encounter an east-west township road at two-mile (3.2 KM) intervals. As one goes north, the distance between the meridian lines becomes progressively less due to the curve of the earth's surface. At twenty-four-mile intervals the grid is adjusted to fit between the meridians. These east—west roads are called correction lines. You can spot them when the north—south junctions are offset by a couple of hundred yards.

ALONG THE WAY: Coulee

Coulees are dry valleys carrying runoff only after heavy rains or snowmelt. The life-giving water creates a wildlife oasis of trees, shrubs, and other lush greenery. Today, most of the prairie is cultivated. As a result, coulees and river valleys are a refuge for wild prairie plants and animals.

I SPY: Railway Bridge over the Coulee

Look north for the bridge located in the locality of Twining.

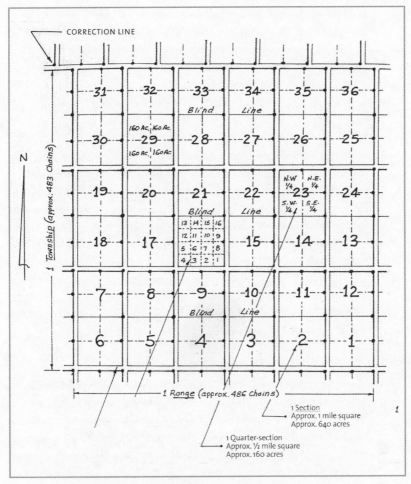

The Grid System of the Dominion Land Survey in Alberta.

COURTESY OF DOUGLAS BARNETT

DIRECTIONS: Continue north out of the valley. Caution: Stop at this dangerous railway crossing. This is the main CNR line and trains are frequent. Turn east onto HWY 582, and cross the rail line again to meet HWY 21. Turn north. At the sign for Three Hills turn east.

STOP: Three Hills

Three Hills is most well known as home to the Prairie Bible Institute. It all began in 1922 when Bible school teacher Leslie Maxwell came north from Kansas to teach at the invitation of several families. The first classroom was a small abandoned house, but soon the interest of more families led to the building of a new school in 1924 and the Prairie Bible Institute was born. Both the first wood frame two-storeyed school built in 1924, and the Miller chapel built in 1929, are located on the north side of 2nd Street as you come into downtown. By 1940 graduate missionaries of PBI were to be found all over the world. By then, more buildings, a farm, a printing press, and dormitories were signs of the large campus, which today has 1,300 students from kindergarten to graduate school.

KNEE HILL MUSEUM (located on access road south of 2nd Street)

This is the kind of museum where you can find the unexpected: uniforms, photos, and maps from the military and RCMP; broadcasting equipment from CFCN in Calgary; old surgical instruments and a wheelchair that conjures up post-WWI convalescence from the trenches. The CNR station is located on the grounds along with a number of rail cars.

Open May 1–September 30 Monday–Saturday 9:00 AM–5:00 PM; Sunday 1:00 PM–4:00 PM

Tel: (403) 443-2090

DIRECTIONS: Drive down 2nd Street and turn south onto 1st Avenue N to see what is left of the grain elevator row.

DIGGING *DEEPER*: The Demise of the Grain Elevator

These prairie sentinels, as they are often called, have been landmarks on Alberta's skyline since 1900, when railway expansion soon had grain companies building in feverish competition. Companies such as Alberta Pacific Grain, National Elevator, Security Elevator, and N. Bawlf Grain, to name but a few, were once familiar to rural Albertans. Elevators were built along the rail lines every seven miles or so, to accommodate horse-and-wagon delivery of grain. By 1934 the number of country elevators in Alberta peaked at over 1,700. By the late 1990s, new concrete silo regional terminal elevators were replacing the traditional local elevator—the anchor of many smaller rural communities. As elevators went down in a pile of dust, the loss of jobs and the lost taxes affected everyone. Services such as banks and restaurants gradually closed as farmers took their business to larger centres.

Alberta Wheat Pool's Number 3 grain elevator tumbles down
in a cloud of dust in summer 1997.

JUDY LARMOUR, COURTESY OF ALBERTA COMMUNITY DEVELOPMENT /
CULTURAL FACILITIES AND HISTORICAL RESOURCES DIVISION

Nostalgia for busy days at elevator row.

DIRECTIONS: Turn east onto Main Street.

I SPY: Heritage Mural

DIRECTIONS: At 6th Avenue turn north, and at 2nd Street turn east to return to HWY 21. Head north for Trochu.

FEATURED WILDLIFE: Swainson's Hawk

As you travel on the open prairie, you will find an increasing number of Swainson's hawks. The windswept grassland is their chosen domain,

Swainson's hawk.
FRED SCHUTZ

where they hunt for ground squirrels and other small delicacies. They also enjoy a good crop of insects. In some locations Swainson's hawks are known to congregate by the thousands in late summer to feed on grasshoppers. In flight, this hawk holds its wings tilted slightly upward. Look for dark upper feathers with creamy white underparts. You may also see a colour variation where the entire bird is quite dark, with the underparts being somewhat lighter. Swainson's hawks will nest very close to the ground on top of a thick bush if there are no trees available. Otherwise they like to take over abandoned magpie or crow nests.

STOP: Trochu

Armand Trochu's dream of genteel ranch life in this beautiful valley led to an oasis of French and Catholic settlement at the turn of the century, and a town that bears his name. Joined by Joseph Devilder and L. C. Eckenfelder in 1905, his dream was realized on the establishment of the St. Ann Ranch and Trading Company. It became the nucleus of a flourishing community of French families from Brittany. Nuns from a French order—the Sisters of Charity of our Lady of Evron—provided schooling and set up a hospital overlooking the ranch in the coulee. By the time the railway arrived in 1911 there was a thriving town at Trochu; the general store was reputed to be the biggest between Edmonton and Calgary. On the outbreak of the Great War in 1914 many of the ex-Cavalrymen of the town returned to France. Armand Trochu followed his family home in 1917. Most who left never returned to Alberta. One who did was Eugene Frère, whose descendents are the present owners of the original ranch house.

ST. ANN RANCH MUSEUM AND INTERPRETIVE CENTRE
(St. George's Avenue, off HWY 585 south of Railway Avenue)

The ranch is tucked away beneath the townsite that bears the name of its founder. The Frère family has retained the French connection—in 1995, fifty French descendants of Trochu's early settlers came to a reunion at the ranch. You can learn the fascinating story of the ranch in the interpretive centre through a photo exhibit and artifacts. On display are letters, memorabilia, and even dresses, which the daughters of Armand Trochu preserved in the family home in France. As children they played in the coulee at Trochu before returning to France in 1914.

Bed and Breakfast at the St. Ann Ranch is an idyllic experience.

Refurbished buildings at the site include a chapel, school, and hospital, and the first post office. The barn is an original building constructed in 1906 in the unusual monitor style. It was designed to house ranch cattle, rather than for multipurpose use. Our favourite building is the 1904 log-and-frame cabin where Capt. Leon Eckenfelder lived, furnished as if the family has just left for the day. Wander about at your own pace, and leave a donation to assist the Frère family in continuing their ambitious project.

The imposing ranch house, built by Joseph Devilder in 1904, was designed on a rather grander scale than most. Queen Anne-style features include the bay windows and curved veranda, along with the classical features of symmetry and gable roof pediments. Designated as a Provincial Historic Resource, the ranch house offers a perfect weekend retreat. The main house has seven wonderful rooms open for bed and breakfast, along with a two-bedroom pioneer house.

Open daily 9:00 AM–9:00 PM

Tel: (403) 442-3924

TROCHU AND DISTRICT MUSEUM (Arena Avenue)

Trace the development of Trochu at this small museum that has not only the printing press but original copies of the *Trochu Tribune*. Extensive photo displays and artifacts tell the story of why there were two townsites laid out prior to the coming of the railway, as well as of the buildings and personalities of the French settlement. Other exhibits focus on the history of mining and of agriculture in the area.

Open May–August, Tuesday–Saturday 9:00 AM–12:00 PM; 1:00 PM–5:00 PM

TROCHU ARBORETUM AND GARDENS (North Avenue)

Tucked away at the northern edge of Trochu is the Arboretum and Gardens. You can identify over a hundred species as you wander through the gardens on the red shale paths, or you can simply sit by the water garden, enjoy the lilies, and watch the birds. Trees include species of spruce,

Trochu Arboretum and Gardens is a gem of tranquillity and shade on a hot day.

the bur oak—the only oak species that will grow when planted on the prairies—and the Selkirk flowering crab. Annuals and perennials abound; look for spectacular delphiniums, peonies, and oriental poppies in season. The shade garden has a variety of lilies. If you are a rose lover do not miss the rose collection, an experiment in the variety of roses that will grow in the Trochu area.

The story of the Arboretum and Gardens dates from 1911 when local doctor J. B. Milne bought the quarter section from the Calgary and Edmonton Railway Company for speculative purposes. The town lots were never developed. After WWI, local businessman William Gerrick bought them, built a house and garage, and planted many of the trees on the site. In 1947 the house passed to Trochu's Dr. Hays, who lived here until 1973. His residence has been turned into an interpretive centre, complete with washrooms and small gift shop.

Open daily Victoria Day weekend–Thanksgiving weekend to 5:00 PM
Bring your lunch to eat at one of the picnic tables.
Note: pets are not allowed.
Tel: (403) 442-2111

WILDFLOWERS OF THE PRAIRIE

The unbroken prairie range was a mass of colour and settlers went out picking flowers to brighten their homes. In 1907 Marguerite Trochu was very taken with prairie spring at Trochu, which she described to a family member in France. "The prairie is full of crocuses in all shades of violet or white and some yellow flowers that resemble brooms and smell sweetly." Crocuses and other species are much reduced in numbers due to cultivation, and more recently, spraying of ditches.

From here you can join Tour 12: Trochu to Lacombe (page 186). See also Tour 11: Stettler to Trochu (page 175).

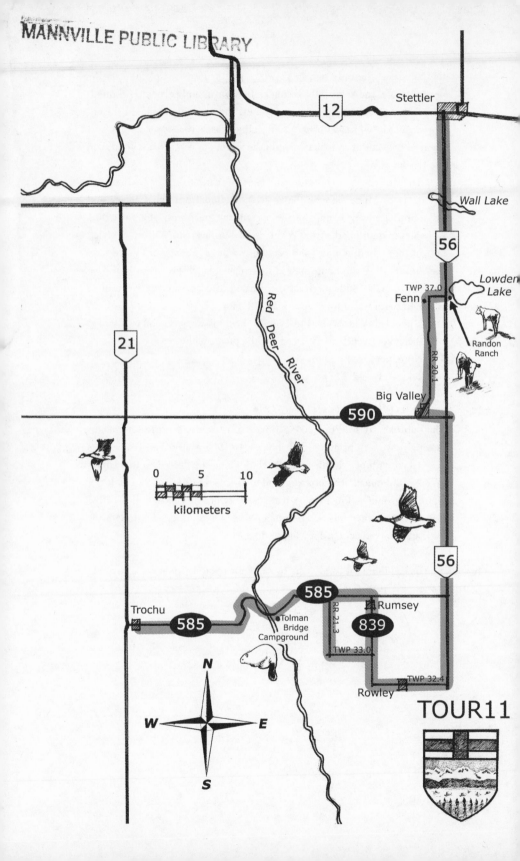

12

Stettler

Wall Lake

56

Lowden
Lake

TWP 37.0
Fenn

Randon
Ranch

RR 20.1

21

Red Deer River

Big Valley

590

56

0   5   10
kilometers

585

Trochu

585

Tolman
Bridge
Campground

RR 21.3

Rumsey

839

TWP 33.0

TWP 32.4
Rowley

N

W   E

S

TOUR 11

Stettler to Trochu, via Big Valley

STOP: **Stettler** (see page 85)

DIRECTIONS: Take HWY 56 south from Stettler.

DIGGING *DEEPER*: Prairie Fires

Prairie fires were a hazard in the early years of settlement, and were often caused by sparks or ashes from locomotives along the rail lines. It was initially the responsibility of the Northwest Mounted Police to patrol and organize the fighting and control of fires with local ranchers. Able-bodied men could all be pressed into fire fighting. Those who set prairie fires or "allowed them get away" were prosecuted under the Provincial Fire Ordinance; the usual fine was twenty-five dollars. Although settlers built fireguards by ploughing around their houses and their hay stacks, fires were virtually impossible to stop once they took hold, and much property and livestock was lost. As a 1906 editorial in the *Stettler Independent* pointed out, a prairie fire backed by a high wind would jump almost any fireguard and the lives of women and children were frequently endangered by the absence of the men on the ranches. One such tragedy occurred in the area of Stettler in 1909, when a woman and her two children were burned to death while attempting to flee a fire.

ALONG THE WAY: Lowden Lake and Early Ranching

The road passes through the middle of Wall Lake and then comes to Lowden Lake on the east side of the road. The Randon family settled in 1906 on the west shore of Lowden Lake, where they formed the nucleus of a French settlement in the district. About 500 head of cattle were run on the ranch. Travellers on the trail south from Stettler found a ready welcome at the Randon house, which the family ran as a stopping house for many years.

DIRECTIONS: At TWP 37.0 (opposite the Randon Ranch) turn west. Then turn south on Fenn Rd. (RR 2.01) at the first intersection.

I SPY: Fenn

To the west of the rail line you can spot the now-closed general store that marks the former hamlet of Fenn, which grew up around a station built on the Canadian Northern Railway in 1911.

Sharp-tailed grouse.
PETER LLEWELLYN / SPLIT SECONDS

FEATURED WILDLIFE: Sharp-tailed Grouse

Whereas you are more likely to see and hear the ruffed grouse in forested areas, here in the open expanses of grassland, shrubs, and clumps of trees, the sharp-tailed grouse or "prairie chicken" is more at home. It is best known for the entertaining display put on during mating season. The male, along with perhaps fifty others, struts proudly, inflates the purple air sacs at its neck, and stomps the ground with its feet, hoping to entice a fertile female. Unfortunately, sharp-tail populations are in decline due to lack of habitat. The Alberta Conservation Association is working with landowners to retain natural grasslands and shelterbelts on their land, to allow places for the grouse to nest, feed, and seek shelter.

DIRECTIONS: Continue south onto Big Valley's Railway Avenue.

STOP: Big Valley

Big Valley was first a mining town and then a railway town. Coal seams abound in this area, and by 1912 commercial exploitation was underway. The largest of several mines was the Big Valley Collieries, located one and a half miles north of town. After a modest start, it produced 400 tons of coal a day by 1920. By the mid-1920s, reduced quality of the coal and water seepage problems led to a slowdown, and in 1927 the mine closed. The big wooden tipple and all the buildings have disappeared. The Warder Collieries just a quarter mile north of town underwent several changes of name and management, ending its days as strip mine in 1952.

The railway boom began in 1913, when the Canadian Northern Railway built its line south from Vegreville via Stettler and Big Valley to Munson. It was in competition with the Grand Trunk Pacific line that ran further west through Camrose, Mirror, and Trochu. Big Valley was a terminal base with a roundhouse that had a crew of forty men. Hundreds of railway employees bought property, thinking that the valley would permanently be home for their families, but it was not to be. In 1919 the two railway companies amalgamated as the Canadian National Railway, and much of the traffic through Big Valley was diverted to the former Grand Trunk line. Then in 1924 a branch line was built between Hanna and Mirror. The roundhouse at Mirror became more important, and despite protests from the railway men of Big Valley, employees were transferred. Property values in Big Valley plummeted, and a population of 1,025 in 1921 fell to 447 by 1931.

BIG VALLEY STATION MUSEUM (Railway Avenue)

The station house, built in 1912, is a Canadian National Railway's second-class station, refurbished to depict the 1940s. There is lots to see in this museum, owned by the Canadian Northern Society, where it feels as though the train might still arrive—which indeed it does: Alberta Prairie Railway excursions arrive from Stettler regularly during the summer months. The annual Live Steam Days on the mid-July weekend are not to be missed. Interpretive guides will lead you through the exhibits in the steel CNR baggage cars on the track.

Open daily mid-May–August 31 10:00–6:00 PM and during arrivals of Alberta Prairie Railway Excursion trains.

Tel: (403) 876-2593

THE ROUND HOUSE INTERPRETIVE CENTRE (Railway Avenue)

Join the self-guiding trail at the tracks just north of the grain elevator.

ALBERTA WHEAT POOL GRAIN ELEVATOR (Railway Avenue)

This elevator has been saved from demolition through concerted local efforts, and has been restored by the Canadian Northern Society.

Open daily mid-May–August 31 10:00–6:00 PM and during arrivals of Alberta Prairie Railway Excursion trains.

Tel: (403) 876-2593

ST. EDMONDS ANGLICAN CHURCH

High on the hill west of town is the blue church built in 1919. It was funded through the efforts of one devout Caroline Leffler of England, whose knitted garments raised $500. She sent the money to the bishop of Calgary to donate to a church of his choice. He chose Big Valley, where Anglican parishioners held services in private homes. Walk up to have a look—it's worth it for the view of the town alone. If you would like to go inside, ask one the guides at the station house.

DIRECTIONS: Continue south of Railway Avenue. Turn east on HWY 590. Head south on HWY 56.

ALONG THE WAY: Grasses Are Built for Survival

Take a second look when you see "common" grasses. They are one of the most remarkable plants on earth, able to thrive on the dry, windy prairie, a place too inhospitable for most plants. How do they survive? How is it that you can trample them, cut them, burn them, dry them to a scorched yellow colour, and yet they keep on growing? Plants that stick their necks out too far dry very quickly in the parched prairie winds. Grasses stay close to the ground and carry few, narrow leaves, thus retaining moisture. Although the above-ground structure is limited, the root system is massive. Roots may grow to a depth of ten feet and spread horizontally at least that far. During a long dry spell, billions of root hairs reach into any pockets of moisture left in the ground. If the stems are grazed to the ground or burned, grasses are able to rejuvenate from the growing tips located at the base of the plants. The hollow stems, which are separated into sections with tough nodes, are very flexible. This allows them to be trampled and tossed by the wind without breaking.

Foxtail Barley.

FEATURED *PLANT:* Foxtail Barley

There are about 100 grass species in Alberta, many of them indistinguishable from one another. The most visible and easily identifiable is foxtail barley. Its tufted stem grows commonly along roadsides, and does somewhat resemble an animal's tail. Do not let your dog chew at the plant, since the barbed seeds, when embedded into soft tissue, can puncture organs, causing bleeding and infection.

FEATURED WILDLIFE: Richardson's Ground Squirrel

Richardson's ground squirrels, often seen perched alertly at the entrance to their underground tunnels or trying to cross the highway, are commonly known as gophers. In actual fact, the only true gopher in Alberta is the pocket gopher, which rarely shows its face during daylight.

Though ground squirrels live in colonies, with about eight individuals per acre, each adult digs its own burrow and defends it from the others. If you could use X-ray vision to see into the ground, you would be amazed at the intricate network of long tunnels and excavated chambers for storage, nesting, and hibernation. Ground squirrels will eat baby birds and frogs if given the opportunity, though most of their diet consists of plants, seeds, roots, and insects.

Richardson's ground squirrel.
FRED SCHUTZ

DIRECTIONS: At the sign for Rowley turn west onto TWP 32.4. Turn south into Rowley.

STOP: Rowley

The Canadian film *Bye Bye Blues* brought fame to this almost forgotten hamlet, now billed as "Rowleywood!" Create your own movie of the past as you wander "the set." Pause at the livery barn built by Henry Swallow in 1917. Swallow kept teams of horses to provide a taxi service from the railway, with a buggy or a cutter depending on the season, and also delivered coal, groceries, and milk in the village. The village office that served the community from 1915 closed in 1941, and it is a long time since the big foursquare hospital built in 1919, clad with blue clapboard, has had patients. In fact, the whole hamlet is really a museum—a collection of buildings run by the Rowley Community Hall Association and open to the public during museum hours (below). Visit the hardware store for an ice cream or shoot a game of pool in the pool hall top of the street opposite the United Church.

On pizza night, the last Saturday of every month, you will find Sam's saloon still open after 4:00 PM—packed for the jam session with a local musician.

Open daily May–August 10:00 AM–4:00 PM

Year-round Sunday 10:00 AM–1:00 PM

Admission by donation.

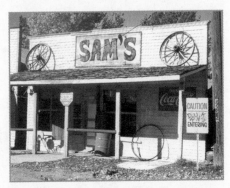

You will not meet Sam, the owner of the western saloon, but you can find his portrait behind the bar. Sam Leung took over the Yale Cafe in these premises in 1941. His business soon expanded to include a grocery and butcher shop until his retirement in 1968.

Sit in the sun at the railway station and gaze over to the abandoned
farm west of the three grain elevators.

DIRECTIONS: Return to TWP 32.4. Continue west to the paved road (Hwy
839) north to Rumsey. At HWY 585 turn west for Trochu.

OPTION: Panoramic View of the Red Deer River Valley Loop.

DIRECTIONS: Travelling north on HWY 839, turn west after 3.3 KM onto
TWP 33.0, and drive uphill.

I SPY: Dry Island Buffalo Jump

From the crest of the hill there is a commanding view of the Red Deer
River Valley to the west. You can see the cliffs at Dry Island Buffalo Jump
(see page 188) on the far side of the Red Deer River on a clear day. Native
people gathered in this area to the east of the river to camp. Tipi rings,
clearly defined by stones in the grass, and several medicine wheels have
been found in the Rumsey area.

DIGGING DEEPER: What is a medicine wheel?

There are many theories but no clear-cut answers to this question. One
of the medicine wheels in the Rumsey area is made up of a cairn of
stones, originally eighteen feet in diameter and four-and-a-half-feet
high, surrounded by a stone circle. An irregular human-shaped effigy lies

on the southeast side. Archaeologists have excavated the site, once in the 1930s and once in 1961. They found beads, projectile points, pottery, pipe, and bone fragments. This type of medicine wheel accounts for approximately one-third of the medicine wheels on the Plains. Other medicine wheels show a variety of patterns, including a stone ring with stone spokes radiating from it, or a central cairn from which radiate stone spokes, enclosed by a stone circle.

DIRECTIONS: Head north on RR 21.3. At HWY 585, turn west for Trochu.

ALONG THE *WAY*: Tolman Crossing at the Red Deer River

You will soon come to the spectacular Red Deer River Valley. Imagine negotiating these hills with a horse and wagon! Today you can whiz over the river in your car on the Tolman Bridge, built in 1964. Before then, you would have had to take a ferry across.

For those settling the area east of Trochu around 1906–07, the Red Deer River was a big obstacle. In 1907 the government decided to run a ferry here and the crossing became known as "East of Olds." In 1912 when the railway went through Trochu the crossing's name was changed to Trochu, and finally, in 1916 it became known as the Tolman crossing because it was on land owned by the Tolman brothers. Locally, it was also known as "Stonepile" because of a stone monument on a nearby hill.

The Trochu Tribune carried a report of an accident at the crossing in May 1911. Either the ferry was not running, or Messrs. A. and W. Hibbert of Knee Hill Valley decided not to use it. As they were crossing, the "wagon box became lifted from their running gear; the gear itself separated, and the gentlemen, after extricating themselves from the resulting wreckage, finally reached the shore with the team, losing guns ammunition, bedding, snake-bite medicine etc." A month later the Chandler family were crossing to go to the Coronation Day sports at Rumsey, when their horse became excited. The buggy overturned but they luckily escaped with little more than a good soaking in six feet of water.

By 1924 the railway had been built between Drumheller and Stettler and a crossing was deemed less necessary as fewer settlers arrived in the area. This, however, left sixty miles of river with no crossing and endless petitions resulted in another phase of ferry operation from 1946–64.

DIGGING *DEEPER*: Alberta's Ferries

Ferries were first privately owned in Alberta, but settlers and freighters soon complained about high tolls and poor service. In 1877 the government of the North West Territories passed the first Ferries Ordinance Act to regulate the operation of ferry crossings. It set out running times and toll charges for a licensed ferry. Many ferrymen lived in a house near the riverbank. Most ferries used in the early years of the twentieth century were cable-operated flat scows with a planked deck. These cable or "swing" ferries with a cable tower on each side of the river had to be of sufficient capacity to safely carry one double wagon loaded to 3,000 pounds drawn by two horses. The management of teams on board was tricky, as horses could take fright at unexpected events.

Bridges were built at strategic positions on important trails from the 1880s. However, as they required a good deal of maintenance and were subject to destruction during spring breakup, they did not always provide a satisfactory crossing, and many of Alberta's ferries remained in use until the 1960s.

STOP: Tolman Bridge Campground (East side of river)

The landscape in the Red Deer River valley is worlds apart from the prairie terrain you have crossed to arrive at this location. The Tolman Bridge Campground allows you to linger in this peaceful place and explore some of the vegetation, geology, and long history of the river.

Facilities: pit toilets, playground, campsites, day use shelter.

FEATURED PLANT: Plains Cottonwood

Park staff are attempting to slow down the industrious logging activities of beavers. The magnificent tree with wire mesh protecting its trunk is a type of poplar found only along rivers and streams. Chances are, you will not find any young cottonwoods around this mature tree, because it rarely reproduces from the roots, as do the trembling aspen. The cottonwood needs the unique environment of an occasionally flooding river to reproduce.

During June, snowmelt from the mountains, combined with spring rains, sends flooding water down the Red Deer River. Fresh mud is deposited along the river channel and is sometimes washed over the riverbanks. At the same time, plains cottonwoods will send millions of seeds, tufted with cottony fluff, floating through the air. If they land in a layer of fresh mud and are not disturbed, new cottonwoods will sprout. It sounds simple enough, but the timing must be right, seeds need enough but not too much moisture, and flooding may wash the seeds away. Along the Red Deer River, the right conditions for sprouting cottonwood seeds happens about every five years.

Popcorn rock

I SPY: Popcorn Rock

As you leave the park, notice the mudstone on the opposite side of the highway. It contains large amounts of clay minerals called smectites. When it rains, these minerals swell up to ten times their dry volume with water, becoming slimy and slippery. Smectites are made up of microscopic plates that slide against one another when wet. When dry, the surface of the mudstone shrinks into large crumbs, earning it the name popcorn rock. Smectite originates from airborne volcanic ash that drifted into this area from eruptions west of Alberta. When volcanic ash is preserved as a thin layer of rock, it breaks down into bentonite—a clay that is high in slippery smectites. Be careful when walking over any of the badland rocks. They get VERY slippery when wet!

DIRECTIONS: Continue on HWY 585 for Trochu.

I SPY: St. Ann Ranch

Open farmland, broken only by a few shelterbelts, lines the road on which you are travelling. As you approach Trochu you will see the St. Ann Ranch west of the road, tucked beneath a coulee hill (See page 171).

STOP: Trochu

(See page 170)

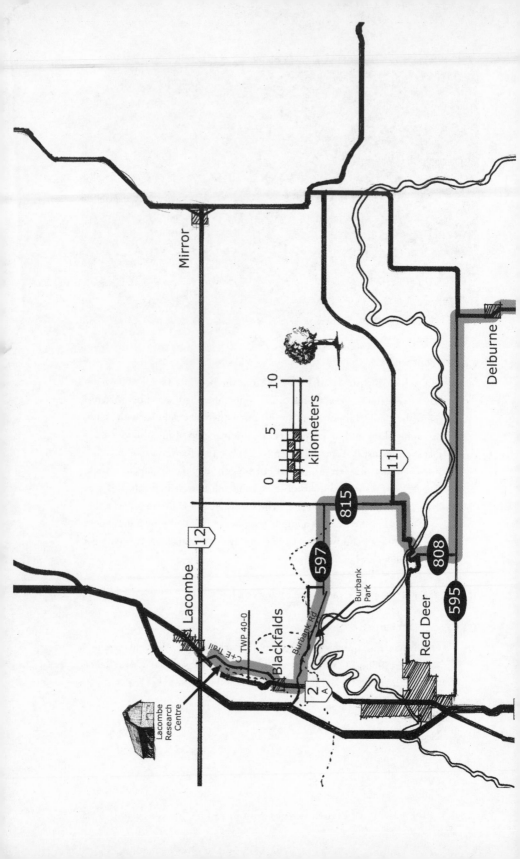

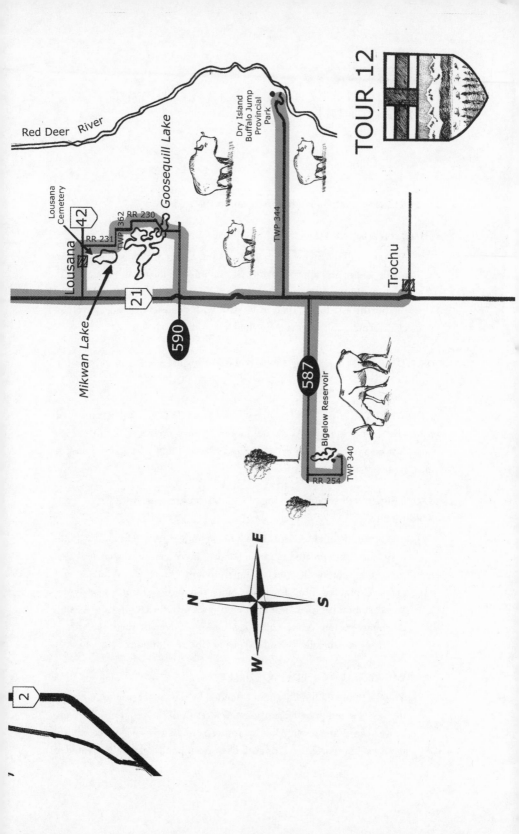

TOUR 12

Red Deer River

Goosequill Lake

Lousana Cemetery

Lousana

RR 231

RR 230

TWP 362

42

21

590

Mikwan Lake

Dry Island Buffalo Jump Provincial Park

TWP 344

Trochu

587

Bigelow Reservoir

RR 254

TWP 340

2

N E S W

Trochu to Lacombe, via Lousana and Blackfalds

DIRECTIONS: Travel north from Trochu on HWY 21.

ALONG THE WAY: **Esker**

> As you travel the highway north of Trochu, a long, winding ridge, running north–south, and approximately five kilometres long, can be seen to the west. A stream flowing underneath a massive glacier as it melted toward the northwest slowly filled in its path with deposits of sand, gravel, and clay, forming this long ridge, called an esker.

OPTION: Excursion to Bigelow Reservoir Provincial Recreation Area for bird watching.

DIRECTIONS: From HWY 21 turn west on HWY 587. After 16 KM the road passes between two lakes. At the next intersection, turn south onto RR 254. Turn east on TWP 340, then drive past the "Gravel Ends" sign and turn north into the Bigelow Reservoir site.

STOP: **Bigelow Reservoir Provincial Recreation Area—A Buck for Wildlife Site**

> The damming of Three Hills Creek to encourage growth of local wildlife populations has created these wetlands. The reservoir was created as a partnership between Alberta Environment, Buck for Wildlife, and Ducks Unlimited. Waterfowl, pheasants, songbirds, pelicans, shorebirds, and cormorants either nest here or use the site for feeding and resting during migration. White-tailed deer and mule deer frequent the area.
>
> Facilities include pit toilets, picnic table, and firepits.

WHAT IS BUCK FOR WILDLIFE?

The Buck for Wildlife Program is funded by the sale of fishing and hunting licenses and private donations. As a result of the program, there are more than 200 sites in Alberta. You can fish at streams where critical trout habitat is protected, or at stocked trout ponds, generally created in areas that have few natural fishing opportunities. At these sites you can also view habitat enhancement techniques such as nesting islands and shelter belts. In areas lacking natural nesting sites, platforms have been built for hawks and ospreys to nest.

FEATURED **WILDLIFE:** Ring-necked Pheasant

Keep on the lookout for a chicken-sized bird with a shiny green head and bright red patches around the eyes. The colourful head is set off from the rest of the body with a thick white collar and most other feathers are richly bronzed, mottled with dark markings. This bird looks more suited to a game farm of exotic species, so its origins will not surprise you. The ring-necked pheasant was first introduced to Alberta from southern China in 1908. Since then, the bird has fared quite well, although its popularity with hunters, and our cold winters, limits the

Ring-necked pheasant.
PETER LLEWELLYN / SPLIT SECONDS

population. Wild birds are supplemented with pheasants released from hatcheries.

Bigelow Reservoir is a popular release site for the pheasant, where hunting for males is normally allowed from October 15 to November 15.

DIRECTIONS: Retrace your route to HWY 21 and turn north.

DIRECTIONS: Turn east on Buffalo Jump Canyon Road (TWP 344).

I SPY: Feedlot

Here the topography of the land alternates between rolling hills and wide expanses of farmland. On the south side of the road you will pass a feedlot belonging to the Huxley Hutterite Colony.

DIGGING *DEEPER*: Hutterite Colonies

Hutterites remain a visible minority in rural Alberta—the men wear short beards, black clothing, and hats or caps, and the women wear polka-dot kerchiefs and long print dresses with aprons. The Hutterian Brethren have their origins in the European Protestant reformation. Ancestors of Alberta's Hutterites settled in the USA in the nineteenth century, and came to Canada in 1899. More followed after WWI. They live a religious, pacifist, communal agricultural life where all things are held in common and adult baptism confirms adherence to the strict discipline and hierarchy of colony life. Despite a resistance to modernization of dress, the Hutterites have adopted large modern machinery and technology as central to their efficient farming operations that support them. Many colonies welcome visitors and sell their produce at local farmer's markets and at the farm gate. Here at the Huxley colony, you can purchase honey.

I SPY: Outcropping of Sand

Have you noticed what looks like beach-quality sand exposed along the roadsides? If you take a close look you will notice that most of the grains are the same size. This means they were sorted by flowing water. Flowing water sorts particles by dropping them in the order of their weight: pebbles, sand, silt, and finally clay (very small, light particles). These almost pure layers of sand were once at the bottom or on the shores of ancient lakes. In various locations, you will see these deposits being mined for commercial uses.

ALONG THE WAY: The Prairie Opens Up

As you approach the Red Deer River Valley, all you can see is the gentle prairie landscape. Without warning, the earth opens up, as if in one of those IMAX films where the aircraft-encased camera glides out over a cliff and your stomach lurches as the land drops away. The river valley, cavernous and breathtaking, lies 210 metres below.

STOP: Dry Island Buffalo Jump Provincial Park

The park is open May to September but the gate is locked during bad weather when the road can be unsafe. There are picnic tables, fire pits, and pit toilets by the river.

INTERPRETIVE TRAIL

At the edge of the valley a short interpretive trail explains the history and geology of the site.

The Blackfoot chased herds of buffalo over the edge of this valley wall toward the south. A slight rise near the edge masked the deadly drop. As the buffalo fell in a tangled heap below, waiting hunters pounced on them with knives and spears to finish them off. This is close to the northern limit for buffalo jumps, since the forest and parkland geography north of here provided cover for hunting with arrows and spears.

Native people camped and hunted in this bountiful valley. They made use of clay deposits present within the valley floor for shaping ceramic vessels. Archaeologists have retrieved numerous artifacts in the area

Dry Island is named after the flat-topped hill stranded in the valley. This type of hill is called a mesa, which is capped by rock more resistant to erosion than the material eroded away from its steep sides. Look to the left as you enter the park.

including pottery fragments, arrow and spear heads, scrapers, and bison teeth, skulls, and ribs. It is estimated that people have used this site for the past 3,000 years.

Although the uplands are totally cultivated, the river valley has been disturbed very little, displaying typical badland landforms, plants, and animals. As you drive down the steep slope to the river, notice how the dry prairie plants cling with determination to the parched soil: long-leafed sage, prickly pear cactus, juniper, cinquefoil, hawthorn, and thorny buffaloberry.

EXPLORING THE SITE

From the parking area at the river, walk to the river's edge. Here the vegetation changes completely. Plains cottonwood, a variety of poplar commonly found along rivers in southern Alberta (see page 182), grows among balsam poplar and dense shrubbery including saskatoon, dogwood, wolf willow, and snowberry. You can follow informal trails for miles along the riverside.

HOW DO BADLANDS DEVELOP?

Badlands develop in places where sedimentary bedrock has lost its cover of plants and soil. The bedrock in this area is composed mostly of shale and sandstone, which are the compressed mud and sand deposited millions of years ago. They are easily eroded by wind, water, and ice—but unevenly, since some layers are softer than others. Thus we get the deeply etched folds called rills, hoodoo caps, and pillars of rock left like sentinels on a barren hillside.

FOSSIL HUNTERS

In 1910 well-known paleontologist Barnum Brown came from New York to search for dinosaur bones in the Red Deer River valley. He travelled downstream from Red Deer on a flat boat loaded with provisions and plaster for encasing bones. He searched out areas where the bank had slid into the water due to erosion. In one of those slides he found "small mammal jaws and teeth not known before from Canada, associated with fossil clam shells of Eocene age." Brown returned the following summer and published his findings in 1911. Canadians became alarmed at the rate at which specimens were leaving the country, so the Canadian Geological Survey hired another American collector, Charles Sternberg, to dig for Canada. In 1912 Sternberg came to Alberta to begin many years of exciting discoveries, which formed the basis of the dinosaur bone collection in the National Museum of Canada. Today Drumheller boasts the internationally acclaimed Tyrell Museum of Paleontology. If you should find a fossil, leave it; it is protected under the Alberta Historical Resources Act.

At some point in time old wire was replaced with new during a farmer's
never-ending labour to maintain his fences. This small rusty roll has been left behind for
emergency repairs when a moose breaks the wires or cattle push a section over.

DIRECTIONS: Retrace your route to HWY 21 and continue north 27.4 KM
toward Delburne.

OPTION: The Prairie Pothole Loop around Goosequill Lake.

DIRECTIONS: From HWY 21 turn east onto HWY 590. You are driving
along a ridge overlooking Goosequill Lake. Once over the railway crossing,
take the next gravel road, RR 230, north.

ALONG THE WAY: Prairie Potholes

(See page 83) Since evaporation exceeds precipitation in this part of
Alberta, the prairie potholes you see along this route are prone to drying
up, and so also fit into the category of the slough.

Sloughs are shallow bodies of water that vary tremendously in
depth and may disappear completely during dry years. Along the edges
of the sloughs grow common slough grass, wild barley, awned sedge,
and smartweed. They are collectively referred to as slough hay, and are
harvested by farmers when a slough dries up. Moving into deeper
water, cattails, bulrushes, and spiked rushes are evident, and deeper yet

duckweed, pondweed, white-flowered crowfoot, bladderwort, and burrweed. Slough bottoms are rich in both plants and invertebrates—ideal nesting and feeding habitat for waterfowl.

FEATURED *PLANT*: White Water Crowfoot (Buttercup Family)

Plants that grow in shallow water do not need the sturdy stems of their dryland cousins. If you took the crowfoot out of its water environment, it would fall into a shapeless heap! The stems contain air pockets that buoy the white buttercup flowers to the surface.

FEATURED WILDLIFE: Muskrat

The muskrat is the aquatic version of the mouse in its ability to flourish in just about every corner of Alberta. If there is a pond, lake, or stream, you can bet on the presence of this beaver-like rodent. Their preference for accommodation is to dig an underwater entrance into the banks of the pond, digging tunnels to dry chambers where they are relatively safe from harm. However, predators such as the slender mink will follow the muskrat directly into its home quarters.

DIRECTIONS: As you leave the northeast end of Goosequill lake you begin to climb uphill. Turn west onto TWP 362. Follow this winding road with sloughs on either side. At the T junction turn north on RR 231. At Lousana cemetery turn west onto HWY 42.

I *SPY*: Mikwan Lake

Mikwan Lake lies to the south of Lousana.

DIRECTIONS: Cross the railway with caution and continue west to HWY 21. Turn north toward Delburne to rejoin the main tour.

I *SPY*: Historic Point of Interest Sign

The Content/Buffalo Lake Trail was an early route for the Métis south to the Hand Hills.

STOP: Delburne

THE ANTHONY HENDAY MUSEUM

Housed in the 1913 Grand Trunk Pacific Railway Station, this museum is well-worth a visit, not least to see its relocated railway water tower, built in 1930. Railway water towers, built every twenty or thirty miles along the track, were a familiar part of the prairie landscape only forty years ago. They housed the water necessary for the operation of coal- or oil-fired steam locomotives. The introduction of diesel locomotives in the 1950s made the water towers obsolete. Relentless demolition has left only four water towers still standing in Alberta. The interior of the water tower at Delburne has been modified. Two new floors host additional museum gallery space for exhibits, including blacksmithing, and harness and shoe repair.

Open June Wednesday–Sunday

July–Labour Day daily

DIGGING *DEEPER*: Railway Water Towers

Railway water towers were octagonal wood frame structures over forty feet high, capped by an octagonal pyramidal cedar-shingled roof. The water indicator, a large galvanized metal ball on a metal rod through the apex of the roof, was visible for miles. The ball was connected by two rods on either side of the mast to a float inside the tank or tub. On the trackside wall was the delivery system, with a galvanized goose-necked spout.

Inside the tower, twelve vertical cedar posts, set in cement footings, provided the support for the tank above. The cedar stave tanks were approximately twenty-five feet in diameter, and were caulked. If the seams dried out the tub would leak. When the tank eventually became water-

The water tower at the Anthony Henday Museum.

logged it had to be replaced. Water was pumped up through the intake pipe, and a gate valve at the base of the tank prevented backflow. Water towers had to be heated in winter to prevent the water from freezing.

The imposing height of the tower allowed the locomotive to be filled by gravity. The fireman on the tender reached out for the chain under the sway spout to pull it down and secure it in position over the tender car, which was coupled behind the locomotive to carry water and fuel. He then pulled on a rope attached to the spout, which lifted a rod attached to a valve on the floor of the tank. The water rushed through the open valve, and out through the spout. Letting go of the rope, which snapped the quadrant lever down and shut the valve, shut off the water flow. The spout was then released, and returned to its upright position against the wall.

HERITAGE MURALS

Two of our favourite heritage murals in central Alberta are in Delburne. Watch for the Delburne Creamery mural as you come into town from the west, as well as the calf-roping mural on the main street. Sadly, as the fabric of our small-town built heritage is disappearing we are left with only memories. Many communities in Alberta have tried to recapture the past through the painting of large murals on buildings. Look out for murals in Wetaskiwin (page 46), Sylvan Lake (page 201), Bashaw (page 79), Millet (page 48), Three Hills (page 170), and Innisfail (page 211).

DIRECTIONS: Continue north on HWY 21. At HWY 595 turn west for 23.8 KM.

DIGGING DEEPER: In the Heart of Llama Country?

You may have noticed signs for llama farms on this and other tour routes in this book. Central Alberta is not much like the Andes, but both llamas and alpacas are increasingly familiar farm breeding animals. Both these animals belong to the genus *lama* and to the camelid family. And believe it or not, they originated right here on the plains of North America about 40 million years ago, dispersing to South America much later. The last ice age left them extinct in North America. Recently they have been reintroduced from Andean domesticated animals that serve as beasts of burden as well as providers of meat and wool. Alpaca wool in particular—grease-free and light, yet remarkably warm and strong—is popular with knitters and weavers. Solid, spotted, or in a variety of patterns, the wool can be black or white along with lovely shades of beige, brown, red, and roan. The llama is larger and taller than the alpaca. Both produce a baby called a *cria*, chew their cud like cows, and both are gentle, shy and intelligent animals that are sometimes trained to be guard animals. They sometimes spit when annoyed, or to establish who will get dinner first at feeding time!

DIRECTIONS: At HWY 808 turn north.

I *SPY*: Cliffs

Look north as the road curves downhill to spot the cliffs of the Red Deer River Valley.

DIRECTIONS: At HWY 11 turn east downhill into the Red Deer River Valley and over the bridge. Continue east 6 KM and turn north on HWY 815, with the chemical plant to the west.

ALONG THE WAY: Joffre Chemical Plant

You cannot miss the industrial side of rural Alberta on this road. The NOVA Chemicals Joffre manufacturing facility is one of North America's largest petrochemical complexes and is a major employer for residents in the area. The facility has about 640 full-time employees and over 150 contract employees. The facility produces ethylene and polyethylene and is currently the second-largest ethylene production site in North America.

DIGGING *DEEPER*: What is Natural Gas Used for Besides Heat?

Ethane, a component of natural gas, is the feedstock for ethylene production at Joffre. The ethane used at Joffre is extracted from Alberta natural gas and transported to the site via pipeline. The site produces 3.4 billion pounds (1,540 kilotonnes) of ethylene per year. Thirty per cent of the ethylene produced at Joffre is used on site in the manufacture of polyethylene. Polyethylene is shipped via rail and road to North American customers, and by ship to offshore destinations. These customers manufacture consumer end products such as grocery sacks and garbage bags, stretch film, milk pouches, and wire and cable coatings. The Joffre site also produces hydrogen, carbon dioxide, propylene, butadiene and benzene, sold locally or shipped by rail across North American to be used in a variety of industrial applications.

DIRECTIONS: After 7.3 KM turn west on HWY 597 for Blackfalds.

I *SPY*: Scenic Views

Watch for scenic views of the Red Deer River as you leave the industrial development behind you.

The NOVA Chemicals plant at Joffre.

DIRECTIONS: After 14.4 KM, turn left onto Burbank Road for Burbank Park.

I SPY: Woodpecker Cavity

The slough in the dip in the road before the park has become home to woodpeckers—notice the nest cavities in the dead trees.

DIRECTIONS: Turn left at the sign for Burbank Park immediately before the railway line.

I SPY: Trestle Bridge

Watch for a glimpse of the large railway trestle bridge over the Red Deer River to the west as you drive down into the park.

STOP: Burbank Park

Trails from the campground and picnic areas lead you down to the canyon where, depending on the water levels, you can easily spend an hour exploring the river environment. If you have children, be cautious around the water since the current can be quite strong when water levels are high.

At the confluence of the Blindman River with the Red Deer River, the waters have eroded a deep canyon into the surrounding sandstone,

Burbank Park is situated where the Blindman River feeds into the Red Deer River.

creating a sheltered environment for wildlife. Eagles, herons, and pelicans are often seen here as they migrate to their favourite lakes in central and northern Alberta. Close to the water, the wet-loving balsam poplar grows rapidly. On drier spots, colourful blooms of goldenrod, sweet clover, and purple aster decorate the shoreline.

The canyon walls are much older than you might think. These sands were originally eroded from the Rocky Mountains and deposited here by ancient rivers about 65 million years ago. These are the same sandstones that in other locations were quarried and used for building many government buildings and churches throughout Alberta, the best-known being the Legislature Building in Edmonton. Paskapoo sandstone is soft enough to carve into building blocks yet hard enough to serve as a building material, and it comes in colours from buff to yellow and grey. Sandstone quarrying only lasted until 1915, after which limestone became the preferred building material.

Facilities: day use area, picnic shelter and tables, playground and ball diamond.

FEATURED WILDLIFE: Bald Eagles

During the migrating seasons of spring and fall, you have a good chance of seeing bald eagles as they move from their winter homes on the BC coast,

Bald eagle.

PETER LLEYWELLYN / SPLIT SECONDS

California, and Mexico to their summer nesting grounds along the shores of Alberta lakes. Bald eagles are continuously searching for food by scanning the ground below. To make flying easier, they use thermals: upward-moving pockets of air created when the ground, particularly a field of black soil, warms the air. Since thermals not only rise but drift, the eagle can glide along at a good clip while barely moving a muscle. Keep in mind that bald eagles do not grow those beautiful white head feathers until they are four or five years old. Young birds are often mistaken for golden eagles or hawks.

DIRECTIONS: Return to Burbank Road. Turn left and continue over the railway. Caution: railway line is in use. Rejoin HWY 597 and turn west. At the traffic lights, the junction with HWY 2A, turn north. Just past the housing and strip mall east of Blackfalds town, 2.2 KM north, take the first turn right and follow the winding road east and north. You are now on the Calgary–Edmonton Trail. (See pages 51). Cross TWP 40-0 and continue north. Cross the rail line with caution—this is a main line. Cross HWY 2A and continue on the Calgary–Edmonton Trail past the Lacombe Research Centre.

ALONG **THE WAY: Lacombe Research Centre** (formerly the Dominion Experimental Farm)

> This is the home of the famous Lacombe pig, the only breed of pig to originate in Canada. It appeared on the swine scene in 1957. The Lacombe Dominion Experimental Farm was established as part of a system of experimental farms across Canada in 1907, and grew a huge variety of grains, fruits, vegetables, and fodder crops to determine hardiness and productivity for the district. Shrubs, trees, and flowers beautified the grounds, which soon had a barn, boarding house, and superintendent's residence.
>
> The Lacombe Fairground, currently administered by the Central Alberta Agricultural Society, was established in 1907 on the north end of

the experimental farm. In 1908 a cereal building was constructed to store grain, and provide workspace as well as hold a farm museum. By 1912 the farm had expanded and moved into animal husbandry. The Central Alberta Livestock Pavilion is still used for livestock sales.

You are welcome to explore the grounds at the Research Centre. Take the main entrance by the spruce trees. The left fork will take you to the Administration Building where there is parking and a site map. The right fork will take you to another parking area where you can take a walking trail through the arboretum.

For further information telephone (403) 782–8126 during working hours.

STOP: Lacombe

(See page 94)

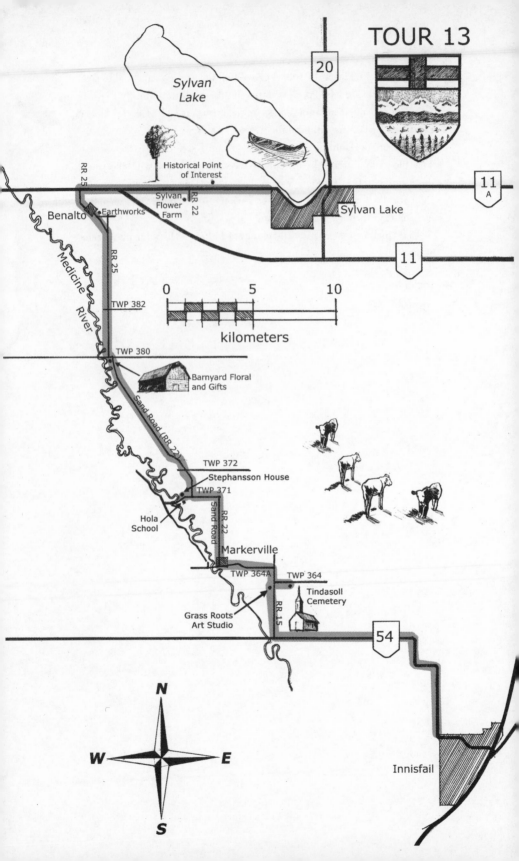

TOUR 13

Sylvan Lake

20

11 A

Historical Point of Interest

RR 25

Benalto · Earthworks

Sylvan Flower Farm

RR 22

Sylvan Lake

11

Medicine River

RR 25

TWP 382

0   5   10

kilometers

TWP 380

Barnyard Floral and Gifts

Sand Road (RR 22)

TWP 372

Stephansson House

TWP 371

Hola School

Sand Road

RR 22

Markerville

TWP 364A   TWP 364

Grass Roots Art Studio

RR 15

Tindasoll Cemetery

54

Innisfail

N
W   E
S

Sylvan Lake to Markerville

DIRECTIONS: This tour begins at Sylvan Lake. Follow the shoreline west on HWY 11A through Sylvan Lake town.

ALONG THE WAY: **Sylvan Lake**

The first settlers here called the lake "Snake Lake" because of the large number of garter snakes found here. Soon the snakes disappeared and the name Sylvan Lake, deemed more suitable for the burgeoning resort, was bestowed in 1909. By 1900 a small hotel had been built and ex-North West Mounted Police officer William Jarvis was the first to build a summer house. In 1911 Alex Loiselle built the fine Alex Hotel, located on the site of the parking lot of the present golf course. It was linked to the railway station by a mile of wooden sidewalk.

Sylvan Lake was fast becoming popular with wealthier citizens, and in the years before WWI many of the prominent families of Red Deer took summer homes at the lake. By 1913, the first pier served as a dock for Joe McClusky's motor launch cruises. Sailboats and regattas became popular during the 1920s. Sylvan Lake became a venue for dances and well-known orchestras entertained holiday makers and the many day trippers who came by excursion train from as far as Edmonton through the 1920s and 1930s. The lake has remained a popular destination and the town has grown to a community of over 6,000. The beach waterfront rocks

Genteel boating on Sylvan Lake, when hats rather than life jackets were the order of the day.
PROVINCIAL ARCHIVES OF ALBERTA: IR. 312

with summer crowds, attracted by the cool, clean waters of the lake.

DIRECTIONS: Continue past the marina heading west of town.

I SPY: Historic Point of Interest (north side of the road)

Learn about early Finnish settlers in the area.

STOP: Sylvan Flower Farm (South on Kuusamo Road [RR 22] at sign)

Rick and Shelia Davison invite you to wander through acres of flowers in hundred-metre rows—waves of larkspur, Queen Anne's lace, poppies, and peonies, to name but a few. Browse through the cozy drying barn where the cats love to curl up. You can buy specialty grasses, natural wreaths, and dried flowers by the bunch.

> Open daily June 1–August 31 12:00 PM–9:00 PM
> September 1–May 31 Wednesday–Sunday 9:00 AM–5:00 PM
> Tel: (403) 887-2808

DIRECTIONS: Continue west on HWY 11A. Turn west at the junction of HWY 11A and HWY 11. 1.7 KM after the junction, turn south on RR 25 at the sign for Benalto.

ALONG THE WAY: Benalto

The name Benalto has a Gaelic and Latin origin, *ben* meaning hill and *alto* meaning high. The "Benalto Booster Club" championed the fortunes of this village established in 1912 on the Central Alberta Railway. One of its campaigns during the 1930s was "Better Roads to Benalto!" In summers during the 1940s you could have gone to the annual stampede—complete with boxing match, dance and fireworks. Today Benalto is a quiet spot, and has become a haven for artists.

EARTHWORKS (200 metres left from the fork into Benalto)

Studio potter, weaver, and artisan, Betty Nielsen, welcomes visitors while she works.

> Open by chance or appointment.
> Tel: (403) 746-3104

DIRECTIONS: Here is where you leave the beaten track. Turn left from Earthworks Studio and take the next right fork to continue south for Markerville on a winding gravel road—the scenic route through the Medicine River Valley. At the T junction veer right and continue due south on RR 25.

ALONG THE WAY: Medicine River Valley

The vista opens up here in the fertile fields of the Medicine River valley. After 5.7 KM, as you reach TWP 382, look west; you are bypassing Evarts. Evarts has been slighted before—in 1913 when the route of the Central Alberta Railway did not run as far south as had been hoped. If you are curious, take a detour west on TWP 382—a cairn on the north side of the road will tell you more about this locality, which had a post office until 1969, and takes its name from Louis P. Evarts, an early settler.

DIRECTIONS: Continue south on RR 25.

ALONG THE WAY: Shelterbelts

Look for a long line of tall aspen mixed with spruce trees on the east side of the road. Shelterbelts are often the only clue that a farmstead once existed at a certain spot. Aside from sheltering buildings, they serve a greater purpose. Shelterbelts add beauty and variety to the landscape—but that is not all. Wildlife depend on them for shelter, nesting, and a source of food. Soils and crops are sheltered from wind damage for a distance of twenty times the height of these trees— about 400 metres! Trees increase moisture in the field by trapping and shading snow. To make the most of a good thing, some farmers use shelterbelts to supplement their income with the sale of berries and selective cuts of firewood.

Look for cedar waxwings by picking out dogwood berries growing in shelter belts. Snowshoe hares clip twigs in the undergrowth and the eastern kingbird waits high in a tree for an unsuspecting insect to appear.

PETER LLEWELLYN / SPLIT SECONDS

DIGGING DEEPER: The Development of Farm Sites

Farm sites were usually developed over time as money and energy allowed. Small one-and-a-half-storey houses with gable roofs were replaced as soon as possible with more sizable dwellings in as ornate a design as circumstance allowed. Many of these houses were demolished during the 1950s and 1960s in favour of modern bungalows with wiring for electricity and indoor plumbing. Old houses converted into granaries are still found today.

Outbuildings such as barns, implement sheds, and machine shops were built, along with granaries to hold threshed grain. A number of types of early barns are to be found in central Alberta, including the gambrel-roofed, and the arched- or Gothic-roofed barn. They are now often proudly maintained and painted a characteristic "barn red" by their owner. Implement sheds have largely been replaced by metal Quonsets that look like airplane hangars. And the permanent wooden granary of the past has been almost completely replaced on farmyards by large steel cylindrical bins, but you can still see examples of the portable small wooden grana-ries, which could be moved to the fields on skids for temporary storage during harvest, along the treelines of fields in central Alberta.

The layout of farmsteads in central Alberta varies considerably, and is sometimes shaped by ethnic background and place of origin of the origi-nal landowner. Separate driveways from the road to the house and yard are quite common. A well, often the first thing on a farmstead, was generally located between house and outbuildings. Hand pumps were gradually replaced with pump jacks and electric or gas motors for bringing water to cattle. Eventually, pressurized systems were installed, often not until the 1960s, for a direct water supply to the house.

The farm garden was, and still is, an important part of the layout of farmyards in central Alberta. Many rural women continue the tradition of canning fruit and vegetables. Other garden and driveway windbreaks of willows and caragana hedge, which were largely established in 1920s

Rural mailboxes come in a variety of shapes and designs! See how many unusual ones you can find on your road trips in central Alberta.

through shelterbelt programmes of the Dominion Experimental Farms, have outlived the life of the farmstead.

***STOP*: Barnyard Floral and Gifts** (located at the T junction of RR 25 and TWP 380)

Jaye Hillman has tasteful fresh and dried arrangements, along with western-style wall decorations for sale at her shady barnyard. The farm is home to a fourth generation of the Icelandic settlers who made their home through the Medicine River at the beginning of the twentieth century.

Open Tuesday–Saturday 10:00 AM–4:00 PM
Tel: (403) 746-3592

DIRECTIONS: At the T junction turn east onto TWP 380 and then immediately south onto Sand Road (RR 22), a scenic winding gravel road to Markerville along the east side of the Medicine River, which follows the route of an early trail.

I *SPY*: Bird watching

After 7.7 KM look for a slough on the west side of the road. Park safely at the intersection of RR 22 (Sand Road) and TWP 372. This is great spot for bird watching. There is a second slough to the south of TWP 372, west of Sand Road. On the east side of Sand Road, look for a cattail marsh.

FEATURED *PLANT*: Cattails

The cattail rootstalk can be boiled, and tastes much like a potato. The young green seed head makes a decent substitute for corn, and even the pollen from the developing male flower, which spires above the "corndog," can be shaken into a bag and used to flavour and provide extra nutrition to pancake batter or bread dough. The leaves are commonly woven into baskets and furniture, having an impressive fibrous strength, and they are, of course, waterproof.

Cattails are often confused with bulrushes. Both plants grow

The cattail is one of the most versatile wild plants.
PETER LLEWELLYN / SPLIT SECONDS

in shallow waters and to heights of about two metres, but that is where the similarity ends. The bulrush has perfectly round, thick stems, with few leaves at the base of the plant. The flowers are quite unremarkable, consisting of a sparse, drooping cluster of tiny seeds.

Cattails are much showier. They have stems with long flat leaves with a flower that is one of the most recognized symbols of the marsh. It is a corndog-shaped, tight cluster of brown seeds. In the fall, the "corndogs" burst into masses of silken fluff, which ride the winds to other potential marsh sites.

FEATURED WILDLIFE: American Bittern

The American bittern likes to hunt for frogs and other marsh prey within the cover of these dense cattail forests. When threatened by approaching humans or predators, it freezes, pointing its long spear-like beak directly upward. Its slender build, swaying stance, and striped colouring are an amazing mimic of the cattail plant. So effective is its camouflage that most people have never spotted one. However, its call is often heard in the evening. The bird was nicknamed "slough pumper" because its call sounds like an old wooden water pump, making a sound similar to "pumperlunk."

DIRECTIONS: Continue south for 1.8 KM. At the T junction turn west onto TWP 371 at the sign for Stephansson House (0.6 KM west).

STOP: Stephansson House Provincial Historic Site

The visitor orientation display will give you the background to Icelandic settlement in the area and to the story of Stephan Stephansson (1853–1927), the renowned Icelandic-Canadian poet, who homesteaded at this spot. Stephansson's home, restored to its 1927 appearance, gives you a glimpse into the life of this remarkable writer. Here he lived with his wife and family of eight children, farming alongside his neighbours by day and writing in his study by night. Tapes of Stephansson's poetry in translation, among other publications, are available at the house.

Open daily May 15–Labour Day 10:00 AM–6:00 PM
Admission fee.

I SPY: Hola School

Continue another 0.5 KM west. Just before the bridge, now closed, is Hola School. Markerville was quite a distance for the children who lived at the north edge of the Icelandic settlement, so this school was built on a parcel of land donated by Stephansson. It opened in 1904 to great celebrations, and students later planted the spruce trees around the building. Today it is used for student programs from Stephansson House.

DIRECTIONS: Retrace your route to the junction with Sand Road. Head east on TWP 371. Turn south on RR 21 and follow for 3.7 KM into Markerville.

STOP: Markerville

The first twelve Icelandic families arrived in this area in 1888, from their first North American home in Dakota. They were followed by another group in 1899, among them Stephan Stephansson. The name first bestowed on the community was Tindasoll. As they had done in Iceland, the settlers raised sheep and spun their own wool for knitted gar- ments, and dried the fish they caught in the Medicine River where they

As you enter the front door framed by climbing hop plants at Stephansson House, you will catch the aroma of freshly baked *Astarbollar.*

watered their dairy cows. Three small cheese factories were established during the 1890s, bought out by the creamery in 1899. In that year the name of the community was changed to Markerville for C. P. Marker, Dairy Commissioner for the North West Territories, who had encouraged the establishment of the government-supported creamery. Monday was cream day and library day—the settlers had established a library that sub- scribed to two major Icelandic-Canadian newspapers long before a church was built.

Rev. Pjetur Hjalmson delivered his legendary fiery sermons from the pulpit of Markerville Lutheran Church, which opened in May 1907. Hjalmson, in a community where contemporary theological differences within the Icelandic Lutheran Church ran deep, soon ran into trouble as he eagerly engaged the free thinkers in heated arguments on the street. He was soon released from his duties by the Church board, who never found a replacement. So Hjalmson continued as a part-time minister until the late 1930s. Today the church is used on special occasions and is open dur- ing the summer months to visitors.

MARKERVILLE CREAMERY

Do you know what a tamper is used for? At the creamery museum you will find out—and a good deal more about butter making, and how it has changed since the late 1890s. The creamery was built in 1908 to replace an earlier building. First Dan Mokeberg, then his son Carl, ran the business until Carl retired in 1972. In 1978 the creamery was designated a Provincial Historic Resource, and in 1984 the Stephan G. Stephansson Icelandic Society of Markerville, with assistance from the federal and provincial governments, restored the building. You can take a self-guided tour through the creamery or go with an interpretive guide.

The *Kaffistofa* offers typical Icelandic food including *vinarterta*, and the gift shop has local crafts and artwork.

The second Sunday in August is Cream Day at Markerville with entertainment for everyone and the best homemade ice cream you can find anywhere!

Open May 15–Labour Day Monday–Saturday 10:00 AM–5:30 PM; Sunday 12:00 PM–5:30 PM

Small admission charge. Wheelchair accessible.

Tel. (403) 728-3006

WALKING TOUR OF THE VILLAGE

Pick up a map for the walking tour at the creamery and follow the history of Markerville through the interpretive signs through the community. Markerville has become a popular place in the last number of years, not least because you can walk around this peaceful, immaculately kept community and experience a different pace of life. During the summer the gardens in Markerville are a blaze of colour.

FENSALA HALL

Named after the Gods in Icelandic mythology, the Fensala Hall was constructed in 1903, due to the efforts of *Vonin*, the ladies aid society for women of Icelandic descent. The hall has hosted numerous bands over the years including the Markerville Brass band, speakers from the Icelandic community across Canada, and as an annual bazaar known as *Toombolaö*. You can picnic and use the playground in the grounds.

CHRISTMAS IN MARKERVILLE

This festival is held annually on the first weekend of November, Friday to Sunday. Local artists and crafts people go all-out to offer an opportunity to do Christmas shopping early at this popular community event.

LINGER AWHILE

Before you leave Markerville you may want to sit on a bench or picnic by the river.

DIRECTIONS: Follow the main street east onto TWP 364A. After 3.3 KM turn south onto RR 15. After 0.8 KM turn east immediately after the bridge onto TWP 364 for the Tindasoll Cemetery located in the spruce trees on the south side of the road.

STOP: Tindasoll Cemetery

Here are buried some of the early Icelandic settlers, including Asmundur and Kristin Christianson and Bjorn and his wife Margaret Bjornson.

DIRECTIONS: Return to RR 15 and continue south.

ALONG THE WAY: Grass Roots Arts Studio

The work of well-known Alberta artist Marie Sveinson, who features local scenes, includes oriental brushwork on rice paper.
Open by appointment.
Tel: 728-3577

DIRECTIONS: At HWY 54 you can turn west to join Tour 14: Innisfail to Sundre (page 211).

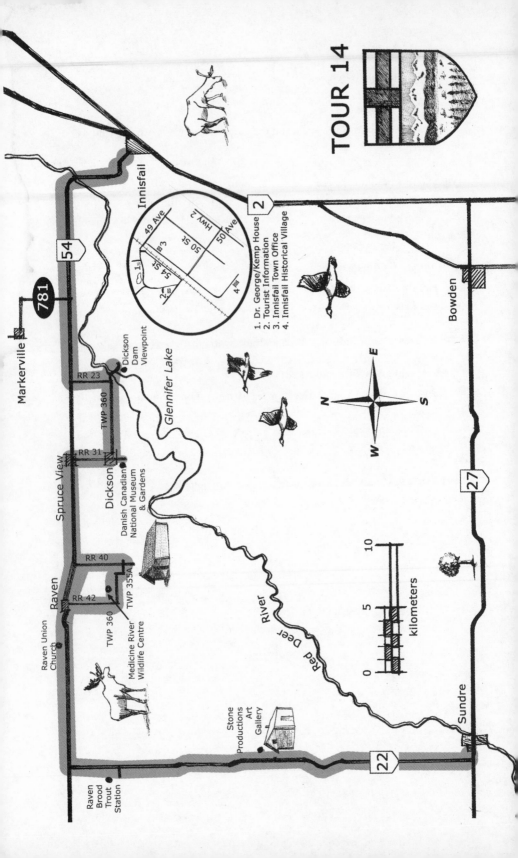

TOUR 14

Innisfail

1. Dr. George/Kemp House
2. Tourist Information
3. Innisfail Town Office
4. Innisfail Historical Village

49 Ave
50 St
Hwy 2
50 Ave
54 St
1
3
2
4

54

781

Markerville

Dickson Dam Viewpoint

RR 23

Glennifer Lake

TWP 360

RR 31

Spruce View

Dickson

Danish Canadian National Museum & Gardens

RR 40

Raven

RR 42

TWP 355A

TWP 360

Medicine River Wildlife Centre

Raven Union Church

Red Deer River

Stone Productions Art Gallery

Raven Brood Trout Station

2

Bowden

27

N
E
S
W

Sundre

22

0   5   10
kilometers

Innisfail to Sundre, via Dickson, Raven, and James River

DIRECTIONS: If you just reached HWY 54 at the end of Tour 13, skip to page 214, Dickson Dam viewpoint.

STOP: Innisfail

The Northwest Mounted Police noted in 1888 that Poplar Grove was a good camping spot with plenty of water, wood, and pasture, on the Calgary–Edmonton trail. When the railway came through, the hamlet became Innisfail. It sounds as though it may have its origin in an Irish place name, but there is no Innisfail in Ireland. It may, however, come from the Irish *Innis Fáil*—that translates as the Island of Destiny, a reference to Ireland.

Innisfail boasts several murals depicting the history of the town. Their locations are marked on a map, which also shows the location of twenty historical information plaques. Pick up the map at the town office (4943 53rd Street) or the Tourist Information / Chamber of Commerce building (HWY 54 and 50th Street) and design your own stroll through Innisfail as you learn the history of its important events and personalities.

The town also has a trail system providing over twenty kilometres of interesting walks. One of these trails will lead you through the Napoleon Lake Natural Area on the northwest side of town—named for Napoleon Remillard, who ran a stopping house. Nearby is Dodd's Lake, where John Dodd took out a homestead in the mid-1890s. It is a pleasant underused picnic spot, with a covered sitting area. Stroll along the boardwalk into the trees and out onto the pontoon to sit by the water's edge to watch ducks and Canada Geese sun themselves. Pick up a trail map along with an historical map.

INNISFAIL HISTORICAL VILLAGE (42nd Street and 52nd Avenue) Here you will find thirteen buildings and many of the artifacts have a story of their own. Look for the trunk in the 1904 Canadian Pacific Railway Station house. It's an Alberta Titanic story! Albertan David Marshall and his English bride, Gertrude, along with the trunk, could well have per-ished in April 1912 on the Titanic. The newlyweds were booked on the ill-fated ship so David could return home quickly to help with the Spring seeding, but he decided to linger in Britain.

Some of our favourite artifact picks include the wooden water pipes for the town from the 1930s, the Eaton's horse-drawn furniture wagon, and the sousaphone owned by Isidore Tedeschini, a local band leader.

Open mid-May–Labour Day, Tuesday–Sunday 11:00 AM–5:30 PM

Friday evenings and statutory holidays 7:00 PM–9:00 PM

Tea served Fridays June–first Friday in September 2:00 PM–4:00 PM

Small admission fee.

The mobile bunkhouse for a threshing crew gets a new coat of paint.

THE SPRUCES STOPPING HOUSE

This stopping house, now located at the Innisfail Historical Village, originally served travellers on the Calgary–Edmonton Trail. Here John and Edward Millar opened a stopping house in a little sod-roofed shack, built by one James Brown circa 1883. As the North West Mounted Police noted in 1887, it had good wood and water. The cabin was soon found to be too small. Chris White, an experienced carpenter, built a sixteen-foot by twenty-four-foot log house in 1884. A second log building, along with stables and a corral, according to the *Calgary Tribune* of June 21, 1884, were also constructed. Millar, however, planned to be a veterinary surgeon and in October 1886 he returned to Toronto to complete his studies.

In 1887 the business was taken over by Mr. Charles Ross, who was also a farming instructor. The stopping house was popular because Ross could sing, play the banjo and fiddle, and call off dances. Soon after the railway was through, business fell off. Ross moved to Innisfail and the days of the stopping house were over. In 1900 the property was purchased by Countess de Bouteyre from Paris. Later the Daines family lived in the house. By 1940, when the W. K. Gibson family moved into the house, it had deteriorated. They gradually returned it to its turn-of-the-century appearance and donated it to the Innisfail Historical Village.

DR. GEORGE/KEMP HOUSE MUSEUM (Corner of 56th Street and 51st Avenue)

Physician Dr. Henry George came to Innisfail with his wife Barbara in 1893. He served an area east to Pine Lake and west to Markerville, and was often away from home. An avid collector of natural history specimens, rocks, insects, birds, and mammals, Dr. George soon turned the front rooms of his house over to this collection. It was one of the first museums in Alberta. Henry George founded the Territorial Natural History Society in 1899, which became the Alberta Natural History Society in 1905.

The Georges set out to recreate their cultural background on the Canadian frontier. A recently discovered photograph of a house of the same name owned by Dr. George's grandfather in England shows a building of very similar design. When the George family moved to Red Deer in 1907, local businessman William Kemp bought the house. On her husband's death in 1920, Katy Jane Kemp supported her family by running a boarding house.

Saved from the wrecking ball in 1989, the house was restored by the Dr. George Preservation Society, and is today owned by the town of Innisfail, which has offices upstairs. Interpretive panels, natural history specimens, and memorabilia tell the story of the George House.

Open year-round daily 8:30 AM–4:30 PM, when Innisfail town staff are working in the building. To avoid disappointment call ahead.

Tel: (403) 227-7744

DIGGING *DEEPER*: Barbara George

Barbara George (née Bernard) was born in Dublin, Ireland, in 1867. At the age of twenty she fell for a young English doctor, Henry George. By the time the Georges arrived in Alberta in 1889, Barbara's family had immigrated to Calgary where her father established a law practice.

Lindum Lodge was the name the Georges gave to the new two-storey house built with locally manufactured brick. Unfortunately, the tea room is no longer open.

Mother to ten children, seven of whom were born in Innisfail, Barbara George was an energetic woman. She found time to pursue her Victorian passion for collecting, preserving, and painting the flowers and plants around her home. Several of her watercolour botanical sketches are on display in the house, along with her paint box and easel. Barbara George has also been credited with designing the Alberta Provincial Crest, now featured in the stained glass fanlight over the front door to the Innisfail home.

DIRECTIONS: Take HWY 54 west for 24.1 KM. Turn south at sign for Dickson Dam onto RR 23 for 3.2 KM.

STOP: Dickson Dam Viewpoint

Pull in for a good view of the dam and the drop below it. The Red Deer River begins in the Rocky Mountains and flows southeast through central Alberta. When Alberta's population was small, there was little concern for an adequate water flow through the Red Deer River valley. However, by the 1980s, the communities along the river had increased many-fold, along with requirements for good quality water. Not everyone supported the construction of the dam—farmers and environmentalists marched on the legislature in protest against the destruction of farmland and habitat.

Dickson Dam, however, ensures a good supply of water by storing water in its reservoir, called Glennifer Lake, and helps to control flooding. This reservoir is eleven kilometres long, two kilometres wide and 948 metres deep—that is 203 million cubic metres of water! The reservoir is filled in the spring and summer when glacier and snowmelt from the mountains and precipitation is high. During other times of the year, when natural levels would normally drop, the reservoir is used to maintain adequate flow in the river. Glennifer Lake is an on-stream reservoir, releasing water at all times to maintain flow of the river. The water flows through giant turbines in the dam, creating small-scale hydroelectric power. During high-water days, water cascades over a spillway to the river below.

DIRECTIONS: Continue south and follow the road over the top of the dam to the Dickson Dam Visitor Centre.

DICKSON DAM VISITOR CENTRE

Displays and film footage capture the massive job of building this structure, which needed 3.6 million cubic metres of landfill. Short walks from the centre offer outstanding views of the dam, both upstream and downstream. Recreational use of the lake increases every year. Picnic and camping areas, and a trout pond will tempt you to stay and relax for a while. The main lake holds a good supply of walleye and brown trout.

Open Tuesday, Friday 8:00 AM–4:00 PM

Tours can be arranged by appointment.

Tel: (403) 227-1106

Dickson Dam.

DIRECTIONS: Retrace your route back over the dam and turn west onto TWP 360 for the village of Dickson.

I _SPY_: Transmission Towers

These transmission towers are vital to Alberta's electrical grid distribution system. The transmission lines carry power that is steam–generated at Wabamun, south via the Benalto substation and on to the city of Calgary. The Benalto substation also acts as a gathering point for water-generated power coming from the reservoir at Abraham Lake west of Nordegg. This power, released more quickly than steam-generated power, then feeds into the grid system to provide enough power for peak hours.

DIGGING _DEEPER_: Rural Electrification

You may think power lines ugly, but when power lines first ran along the side of the road they were a welcome sight. This part of central Alberta, unlike southern Alberta, did not get electric power until the 1950s. Farmers formed cooperatives to erect power lines and service farms with electricity; most subsequently sold out to large provincial power companies. Electricity transformed country life with household appliances, and furnaces. It relieved farm families of the drudgery of pumping water by hand for livestock. Dangerous lanterns were replaced by electric lights, and plug-in block heaters allowed cars and trucks to be driven in winter.

STOP: Dickson

In July 1903, seventeen Danish migrants from Nebraska arrived in this area, their hopes pinned on reports of good farming land from Canadian Dominion Land agents. A chinook made their first Christmas a memorable one, and a group photograph taken outside with a box camera amazed family and friends in Nebraska who thought of Canada as a cold northern land. The area was in fact swampy, and drainage ditches had to be built before the land was productive. Dickson, as the district was known, became the largest Danish settlement in western Canada as they were joined by an influx of other Danes in 1905–06. The present Lutheran Bethany Church was built in 1968 and has an unusual modern design for a rural area. If you would like to visit, ask for the key at the Dickson Store Museum.

DICKSON STORE MUSEUM (Dickson crossroads)

Owners Carl and Laura Christaensen kept the Dickson store well-stocked with a host of items from flour to oyster shells for chickens, hardware to candy. Eggs were bought and sold here, mail picked up, business deals struck, and local gossip circulated.

Dickson store is typical of the type of community store that was common in central Alberta until after WWII. Carpenter Axel Lundgren finished it with locally milled drop siding. Exterior stairs led to the upper floor where the family lived. The store soon needed to expand, and in 1919 a northern addition enlarged both the store and the living quarters. By 1922 the area had 600 inhabitants and was connected with Innisfail by a stage route. Then in the 1930s the post office was enlarged with a new western addition. The store has been restored to its 1930s appearance by the Danish Heritage Society of Dickson and was officially opened in fall 1991 by Queen Margarethe II of Denmark.

This unique museum store was the commercial hub of Dickson from 1909–80.

Relive shopping in the 1930s! Many of the brand names are familiar, but the packaging is different. Find the cheese wheel and the original coffee grinder. Meet earlier customers, including the Larsen, Jensen, and Pedersen families, through exhibits and photographs. See how the Christaensens lived over the store and see if you know what all the domestic tools are! If you wish to tarry awhile, ask one of the interpreters about the video library of oral history interviews. And yes, foothills ice cream and old-fashioned candy is for sale! The gift store features books by local authors, including Dickson's well-known Irene Morck, and the work of local craftspeople.

Open mid-May–Labour Day Monday–Saturday 10:00 AM–5:30 PM; Sunday 12:30 PM–5:30 PM

Admission by donation.

Tel: (403) 728-3355

THE GAMMEL HOUSE GALLERY & POTTERY STUDIO

(Two doors north of the Dickson Store Museum)

Enter this charming old (*gammel* in Danish) house and you are transported into another world. Anna Rasmussen has turned it into a exhibit space with dark wood panelling that sets off her wonderful functional stoneware in alluring blue, green, and purple hues, produced in her large studio.

Open mid-May–mid-September Wednesday–Saturday 10:00 AM–5:00 PM

Call ahead at other times.

Tel: (403) 728-3764

Enjoy browsing for fine handcrafted pottery.

DANISH CANADIAN NATIONAL MUSEUM & GARDENS

(0.8 KM south of Dickson on RR 31)

A seven-acre site is home to the Danish Canadian National Museum and Archives. The museum, which aims to preserve and promote an interest in Danish culture in Canada, is in its first phase of development. "Give our past a future" is the theme of the AV exhibit which tells the story of this endeavour. Presently situated in the old girls' dormitory building that served the Dickson high school boarders of the area from 1933–62, the museum is collecting artifacts and documents from across Canada. Landscaping with walking trails already includes a Danish perennial garden, a pioneer garden, and a lake with replica of the Little Mermaid in Copenhagen sitting on an Alberta rock. The miniature church and the Children's Garden of Imagination will delight children with storytelling hour from the fairy tales of Hans Christian Andersen.

Sample some traditional Danish delights in the Dormitory Coffee House.

Open May–September Monday–Saturday 10:00 AM–5:00 PM; Sunday 12:00 PM–5:00 PM

Tel: 1-888-443-4114 or (403) 728-0019

DIRECTIONS: Retrace your route and continue north on RR 31 from Dickson Store 3.3 KM to Spruceview. At HWY 54, turn west. At Raven, turn south off HWY 54 onto RR 42 for 3.9 KM. Turn east at the T junction onto TWP 360 at the Watchable Wildlife sign. It is a further 1.6 KM to Medicine River Wildlife Centre.

STOP: Medicine River Wildlife Centre

Have you ever seen an eagle with a sling? This is an extraordinary hospital for injured or orphaned wildlife, where emergency admissions are twenty-four hours around the clock. Carole Kelly and her staff, which includes many dedicated volunteers, treat hundreds of casualties a year. There are many man-made hazards, such as electrical wires, that can injure birds. Patients at the centre can expect surgery, intensive care, and then convalescence with physiotherapy, hunting, and flight training before being released into the wild.

You will find displays, a children's activity area, a research corner, and a video booth. Watch recovering water birds, and see songbirds practicing their flight skills. Closed-circuit TV monitors bring you into the hospital area to watch treatments and feedings.

Open daily April 1–October 15 10:00 AM–5:00 PM

Admission by donation. Open 24 hours for patients.

Tel: (403) 728-3467

A short interpretive trail begins outside the centre. It winds through a mixed-wood forest to the observation tower. The reward is a great view of the Sandhill Slough. If you add up the tremendous variety of animals, insects, and plants that make their home or feed in this open water and marsh habitat, you will discover that it is one of the most productive habitats in our region.

FEATURED WILDLIFE: Great Horned Owl

Owls hunt primarily at night, using their formidable eyesight. But even more important for finding their prey is their sense of hearing. Can you see Hoover's ears? If you are looking at the two prominent tufts of feathers adorning his head, you have been fooled! Those are simply features that help owls to identify each other. The ears are located on either side of the facial disk, covered by feathers. The recessed feathers of the facial disk serve to amplify sounds into the ears. Also, one ear is placed lower on the face, allowing the owl to better pinpoint the location of sounds.

DIRECTIONS: Continue east on TWP 360 from the Medicine River Wildlife Centre.

I SPY: Threshing Machine

Watch for the old abandoned threshing machine parked in a field on the south side of the road.

DIGGING *DEEPER*: Threshing Machines

For about fifty years threshing machines were at the heart of the harvest operation on many farms. The ripe grain was first cut and tied into bundles with a binder. The farmer then stooked the bundles in neat rows throughout the field and left them to dry. The thresher was set up in a convenient location in the field. A gasoline engine or a steam traction engine powered it, using a long flat belt that ran from the tractor belt pulley to the large pulley on the thresher. A crew of men and horses drawing bundle racks—a type of wagon built to hold the bundles—were needed to haul the bundles to the thresher. The men forked the bundles onto the self-feeder jutting out from the front of the machine. The threshing machine separated the grain from the straw and chaff. The grain was then conveyed into a wagon, or portable granary, while the straw and chaff were blown onto a huge stack. The last threshing machines used in central Alberta were built in the 1940s and used through the 1950s until combines superseded them. A few remain parked where they built their last straw stack.

DIRECTIONS: The road takes two curves, south and east, and then heads over a Texas gate, coming to a T intersection at TWP 355A and RR 40. Turn north for 4 KM to HWY 54 and turn west once again retracing your route past Raven.

I SPY: Raven Union Church

Built in 1926, this log structure, a non-denominational community church, is still used. The tombstones in the cemetery reflect the nature of people who have lived here. One has an etching of mountains with a house—cowboy country. Another speaks of a cowboy and his horse, and yet another shows an angler casting his beloved line while a moose looks on silently.

Look for Raven Union Church on the north side of the road.

DIRECTIONS: Continue west on HWY 54. Take HWY 22 south for 4 KM from the junction with HWY 54. Watch for sign for Raven Brood Trout Station.

DIRECTIONS: Turn west at the sign. After 1.2 KM you come to the Raven Brood Trout Station.

STOP: Raven Brood Trout Station

Nature cannot keep up with the demands of Alberta's fishermen. That is why close to 300 of our lakes are stocked with rainbow trout every year. The Raven Brood Trout Station does not actually raise the fish. It nurtures a population of about 5,000 trout for brood stock. These fish are stripped of millions of eggs, which are then fertilized with milt from the males. The fertilized eggs are placed in incubation jars and held inside the buildings until they are "eyed"—meaning the eyes of the fish are well developed. At this stage, they are placed in containers for transport to hatcheries.

The Trout Station set up shop in this remote location to take advantage of the series of natural springs that flow from the surrounding watershed.

It is a short walk from the parking and picnic area to the Information Board, which explains the activities at the Station. The public is not allowed inside the facility, because disease may be easily spread to the fish population. Staff members regularly rinse their rubber boots in chlorine solution whenever they re-enter the buildings. A short trail leads past the fenced-off buildings to viewing ponds, where specimens of rainbow and wild brook trout can be viewed in shallow ponds. Fish pellets are available for feeding. Bridges and trails lead past a small waterfall where clear spring water is piped into the station.

Facilities include educational signs, trout pond, picnic shelters, pit toilets, and fire pits.

The grounds are open to visitors year-round.

Tel: (403) 722-2180

FEATURED WILDLIFE: Rainbow Trout

Originally, the rainbow trout was found only in the northern part of the province. It is used to stock other Alberta lakes because it is a hardy and active sport fish that is easy to raise in hatcheries. The colouring of the rainbow has a silvery sheen: olive-green with black spotting over most of the body and a red-coloured stripe along the sides. Although wild rainbow trout spawn in the spring, fish culturists have developed fall-spawning fish that allow hatcheries to raise young fish over the winter so they can be released at a cacheable size in the spring.

DIRECTIONS: Continue south on HWY 22.

ALONG THE WAY: Tamarack

The golden-leaved conifer seen mixed with spruce along this route, is the tamarack—which is an American larch. This needle-leaved tree is not ever-green as you might assume. In fact, it is a deciduous tree. In fall the trees turn a brilliant gold before they drop their needles annually at the same time as their broad-leaved cousins. Close up, the needles of the tamarack are unmistakable, growing in clusters of ten to twenty. Tamarack is quite common along the foothills terrain. See if you can spot clumps of them along the way, keeping in mind that they prefer the wet soil of muskeg.

Tamarack at the lake located 6 kilometres south of turnoff for Raven Brood Trout Station.

STOP: Stone Productions Art Gallery

Renowned wildlife artist John Stone has a studio-gallery tucked away up on the hill overlooking the James River Valley. Here he is surrounded by the wildlife that he has a special eye for, developed from years in the saddle in the Alberta foothills. His extraordinary work is realist, almost pho-

John Stone points out some of the intricate detail in one of his paintings.

tographic. Stare into the eye of a bighorn sheep and you are out there on the mountain. Stone's work has received many awards and sponsor prints have raised considerable funds for Ducks Unlimited in Alberta and British Columbia. You may recognize his paintings from wildlife magazine covers. You are always welcome to browse in his gallery that displays originals and limited prints of his work.

Open April–November Monday–Friday 9:00 AM–6:00 PM; Saturday, Sunday 2:00 PM–6:00 PM

December–March Saturday, Sunday 2:00 PM–6:00 PM

Tel: (403) 638-2116

DIRECTIONS: Continue south 16 KM on HWY 22. At the junction with HWY 584, turn east to bring you to the main street of Sundre.

STOP: Sundre

(See page 130)

Digging Deeper: The Farmer's Seasonal Round

1. The parkland of central Alberta is a region of aspen bluffs and rolling meadows. Most of the land is privately owned and used for agricultural purposes. Mixed farming predominates. Wherever the topography allows the fields to be tilled, the soil and climate is ideal for small grains, hay, and alfalfa. The remaining areas are fenced and used as pasture for cattle.

2. In January and February farmers care for their cattle during the short daylight hours. If you are out for a drive you will see farmers using their tractors, often equipped with special hydraulic round bale handlers, to haul the huge round bales to their cattle. Cattle survive outside despite the cold. When the farmer has checked the water supply for his or her herd, the cattle are left to fend for themselves until the next day.

3. March is calving time for many farmers. Expectant cows must be monitored carefully as they give birth. Much depends on the weather. If the weather is good a cow may calve outside, but a storm or spring blizzard can be fatal to an hour-old calf. Farmers are often up the entire night ensuring the safe delivery of calves, bringing them into warmth and shelter when necessary. By the month's end, if all goes well, most of the cows should have a hundred-pound calf bounding at their sides.

4. In April the pace of activity in the country picks up. Grain farmers are busy preparing their machinery, and planning crop acreage for seeding time. When it is dry enough you can see the ranchers out riding along the fencelines checking their summer pastures. Then comes the difficult work of replacing rotted-out posts with new ones—heavy work with a post pounder—and the rolling out of new rolls of barbed wire.

Late in April the ground is usually dry enough to start preparing the soil for seeding. This involves the spreading of manure by some farmers, with what is generally called a honey wagon. You cannot miss it! Farmers press their largest tractor into service to pull a large deep-tillage cultivator or tandem disc to loosen up the soil, and disperse the straw left from the previous year's crop. Nitrogen deficiency is a problem with the soils of central Alberta, so farmers spread anhydrous ammonia, often at the same time as cultivating. The fertilizer is injected into the soil as a gas, and any vapour escaping from the large tank or surfacing behind the cultivator smells vile. Always stay upwind if you are outside.

5. May is seeding time. Farmers work on the land from dawn to long past dusk, cultivating, fertilizing, harrowing, and disking. Finally, the fields are ready to be seeded. Many farmers use air-seeders. A large tank is pulled around the fields in conjunction with a cultivator. A large fan, mounted with tank, is used to blow the seed out of the distributor, through the tubes and into the ground. Granular fertilizer is injected into the ground in the same way. Other farmers prefer to cultivate the fields first, and then seed with traditional seed drills. A seed drill has a long narrow box mounted over a row of disc openers or hoes. By the end of May, seeding is nearly complete; farmers harrow the fields smooth and wait for the crops to germinate. Very little land is left fallow; it is all seeded or growing a perennial crop such as hay or alfalfa.

6. In June the greening of central Alberta is underway. The pastures and hay fields begin to grow and the grain crops emerge in spaced rows. Farmers, however, have plenty to do during the long days. June is the month for cattle drives as cattle are herded to summer pastures, often miles from the paddocks where they spent the winter. Meanwhile crop spraying begins. Farmers, often in the company of agrologists from the local farm supply centre, walk the fields of emerging crops looking for problem weed infestations. Most often herbicides are necessary to ensure the crop will not be choked out. A weed sprayer, often with booms up to eighty-feet wide, is used to spread herbicide on the fields. No one should walk on the field for a couple of days afterwards until the chemical has dissipated. Towards the end of June, hay and alfalfa fields are ready for their first cut.

7. Farmers use a haybine, either tractor drawn or self-propelled, to cut the hay. It is left lying on the ground in long green windrows. These are either allowed to dry and then rolled up into large round bales or ensilaged. To make silage, the farmer uses a forage harvester to pick up the hay, chop it, and blow it into a truck or wagon behind. The chopped hay, still wet, is hauled to the farmyard where it is packed into a pit to ferment. Alternatively, it is blown into tall silos to store for winter. Throughout the summer farmers continue to cut hay, check on the growing calves, and monitor the stretching crops. The grain fields become a checkerboard of yellow, white, and green as the pea and canola crops burst into flower alongside the still green but swelling grain heads. If you happen to see a blue field, it is a flax crop, rare in central Alberta.

8. As August unfolds, farmers swarm into the grain fields to begin the age-old race to save the crops before winter comes. Depending on the weather, the earliest-maturing crops are often ready to cut by the middle of the month. The grain falls in long swaths, where it stays until it is dry. After a few days without rain it is ready to combine. The combine harvester picks up the grain lying in the

swath. The grain kernels are threshed out of the heads, and conveyed into a hopper on the combine. The chaff is blown out the back of the combine. Combining is slow and a team job. Trucks to collect the threshed grain work in tandem with the combine or combines. The trucks bring the grain into the yard at intervals to be dumped and augered into storage bins. The combine harvesters lumber their way around the fields by day, by night looking like so many ships at sea, for weeks on end until the job is done. Periods of wet weather delay the process. If all is not done by mid-October the farmers are getting anxious. Who wants to combine in spring?

9. After harvest, the fields are covered in round bales as farmers gather the straw from the crop for cattle feed or bedding. The end of September and October is once more a time for spotting cattle drives. Calves are rounded up and brought into pastures nearer the farm site. If you hear a good deal of mooing and bawling while you are out it is a sure sign some calves have been weaned from their mothers. By November all is peaceful as the breeding herds settle down to a long winter on a diet of hay and straw. The calves are sold off or put in a feedlot, either on the farm or at a custom feedlot, to be fattened up for slaughter. At the year's end, farmers assess the year's crop, settle crop insurance claims, and yes, find time to go curling!

A Note on Sources

Research for this book was based on a wide variety of sources. Archival documents and old newspapers; unpublished reports for central Alberta museums and historic sites; research files of the Cultural Facilities and Historical Resources Division at Alberta Community Development; and files at the Red Deer and District Archives, provided most of the historical information. Useful also were the numerous local histories of communities in central Alberta. Natural history information was based not only on published works, but also on a variety of government research reports and environmental assessments. The authors consulted with colleagues and a range of experts including farmers, ranchers, horticulturalists, fisheries specialists, bird watchers, gardeners, archaeologists, and geologists.

The quote from Bessie Goodhand on pages 39–40 is taken from *Pioneer Pathways*, Vol. 1. Wetaskiwin, Circle 8 Historical Society, 1981.

The source for the story of the Pepper family is *Hoofprints to Highways: Leslieville and Districts Commemorate Alberta's Seventy-fifth Anniversary*. Leslieville and District Historical Society, 1980. pp. 834-37.

Further Reading
Alberta Forestry, Lands and Wildlife. *Alberta Wildlife Viewing Guide*. Edmonton: Lone Pine Publishing, 1990.

Belliveau, Anne McMullen. *Small Moments in Time: The Story of Alberta's Big West Country: Upper North Saskatchewan River Corridor, Shunda Basin, Brazeau Colleries, and Nordegg*. Calgary: Detselig Enterprises, 1999.

Buziak, Kelly. *Taking to the Road: Early Auto Touring and Camping in Alberta*. Wetaskiwin: Friends of the Reynolds-Alberta Museum Society, 1992.

Buziak, Kelly. *Toiling in the Woods, Aspects of the Lumber Business in Alberta to 1930*. Wetaskiwin: Friends of the Reynolds-Alberta Museum Society, 1992.

Dawe, Michael. *Red Deer: An Illustrated History*. Red Deer: Red Deer and District Museum Society, 1996.

Fisher, Chris & John Acorn. *Birds of Alberta*. Edmonton: Lone Pine Publishing, 1998.

Forsyth, Adrian. *Mammals of the Canadian Wild*. Camden House Publishing, 1985.

Goa, David and David Ridley. *Aspenland, 1998: Local Knowledge and a Sense of Place*. Red Deer: Central Alberta Regional Museums Network, 1998.

Hardy, W. G., ed. *Alberta—A Natural History*. Edmonton: Hurtig Publishers, 1967.

Hooks, Gwen. *The Keystone Legacy: Reflections of a Black Pioneer*. Edmonton: Brightest Pebble, 1997.

Hubschmid, Charles. *Of Trails, Trains, and Tepees*. Bowden: Bowden Pioneer Museum, 2000.

Johnson, D., L. Kershaw, A. MacKinnon, and J. Pojar. *Plants of the Western Boreal Forest & Aspen Parkland*. Edmonton: Lone Pine Publishing / Canadian Forest Service, 1995.

Lahring, Heinjo. *The Water and Wetland Plants of the Prairie Provinces*. Regina: Canadian Plains Research University / University of Regina, 2003.

Larmour, Judy. *Making Hay While the Sun Shone: Haying in Alberta Before 1955*. Wetaskiwin: Friends of the Reynolds-Alberta Museum Society, 1992.

_____. *Judge William Brigham Gray of Stettler*. Stettler: Stettler Town and Country Museum, 1999.

Mussieux Ron, and Marilyn Nelson. *A Traveller's Guide to Geological Wonders in Alberta*. Edmonton: Provincial Museum of Alberta, 1998.

Myers, Patricia. *Facing the Land: Homesteading in Alberta*. Wetaskiwin: Friends of the Reynolds-Alberta Museum Society, 1992.

_____. *When the Whistle Blows: Steam Threshing in Alberta*. Wetaskiwin: Friends of the Reynolds-Alberta Museum Society, 1992.

Palmer, Howard and Tamara Palmer. *Alberta: A New History*. Edmonton: Hurtig Publishers, 1990.

_____, eds. *Peoples of Alberta: Portraits of Cultural Diversity*. Saskatoon: Western Producer Prairie Books, 1985.

Pearman, Myrna. *Naturescapes Alberta*. Edmonton: Federation of Alberta Naturalists, 2002.

Place Names of Alberta, vol. 3: Central Alberta. Calgary: Friends of Geographical Names of Alberta, Alberta Community Development, and University of Calgary Press, 1994.

Saley, Henry. *Nature Walks and Sunday Drives 'Round Edmonton*. Edmonton: Edmonton Natural History Club, 1995.

Salt, W. Ray & Jim R. Salt. *Birds of Alberta*. Edmonton: Hurtig Publishers, 1976.

Tingley, Kenneth. *Steel and Steam: Aspects of Breaking Land in Alberta*. Wetaskiwin: Friends of the Reynolds-Alberta Museum Society, 1992.

Touring the Circuit. Pigeon Lake: Rundle's Mission Society, 2002. Available at the office at Rundle's mission or at stores around the Lake. It explores trails and tales around Pigeon Lake complete with maps for hikers, bikers and drivers.

Wetherell, Donald G. and Irene Kmet. *Useful Pleasures. The Shaping of Leisure in Alberta, 1896–1945*. Edmonton: Alberta Culture and Multiculturalism/ Canadian Plains Research Centre, 1990.

Wilkinson, Kathleen. *Trees and Shrubs of Alberta*. Edmonton: Lone Pine Publishing, 1990.

Web sites
The following web sites may help you to choose your route on a particular day when farmer's markets are open, or when there are fairs, exhibitions, and rodeos taking place in towns along the route.

www.agric.gov.ab.ca/store/farmersmarket/index.html
www.agric.gov.ab.ca/general/fairexhs.nsf

Also: see www.boomtowntrail.com for more information on communities along Highways 21 and 56.

ACKNOWLEDGEMENTS

The authors, along with Olds College, thank the many organizations and individuals who contributed information and advice for our tours. Derry Armstrong, Alberta Environment; Michael Payne, Pat Myers, Merrily Aubrey, Dean Wetzel, Joan Dankjar, Dorothy Field, and Heinz Pyszczyk, Cultural Facilities and Historical Resources Division, Alberta Community Development; Ron Bjorge, Buck for Wildlife Program; Tom Daniels, Sunpine Forest Products; Mark Fenton and John Pawlowicz, Alberta Geological Survey, Alberta Energy and Utilities Board; Carol Kelly, Medicine River Wildlife Centre; Myrna Pearman, Ellis Bird Farm; Doug Taylor, Burnstick Lake Management Plan. Thanks also to everyone at numerous museums and parks in central Alberta who helped to locate materials and pointed out items of interest. Not least, a special thank you to all those individuals, including artists, potters, farmers, horticulturists, and others, who received us so warmly while on our adventures, and who shared our vision of guiding you to the best of what central Alberta offers.

JUDY LARMOUR is a heritage consultant specializing in social, agricultural and architectural history. For the last twenty years she has been involved with research for many projects in Alberta, including the Provincial Historic Site at Dunvegan, the John Walter Museum in Edmonton, and the restored NWMP Detachment Building in Canmore. Judy's publications include *Hay Making in Alberta before 1955*, *How to do Oral History*, and *North Red Deer Historical Walking Tour*. She is a regular contributor to *Legacy* magazine. Judy lives on a farm at the foot of the Medicine Lodge Hills, west of Bentley.

HENRY SALEY is a writer, educator, and publisher based in Rimbey. For eleven years he worked as a Nature Interpreter for Alberta Parks, and consulted on the development of environmental education programs, exhibits and educational trail signs, including those at the Alberta 4-H Centre, Dinosaur Provincial Park, and the Sherwood Park Natural Area. He is the author of *Nature Walks and Sunday Drives 'Round Edmonton* and writes for Central Alberta newspapers and magazines. He publishes visitor guides for lakeside communities, an annual Health & Senior's Guide, and a monthly newspaper.

Celebrate Alberta!

The bestselling *Food Lover's Trail Guide to Alberta* will make
even the armchair traveller hungry for the road. This is the
motherlode of appetizing information —a must for
every glove box, briefcase and bookshelf.

WHERE TO FIND:

• the cafés, bistros, diners and neighbourhood joints
• the best home-grown ingredients
• the most exotic and hard-to-find pantry items
• the culinary shops and cooking schools
• great restaurants for big nights, splurges and celebrations
• harvest festivals, farmers' markets, U-picks

**Plus the tastemakers, the food artisans, the chefs,
the sausage king and the giant pyrohy!**

THE FOOD LOVER'S TRAIL GUIDE TO ALBERTA
BY MARY BAILEY & JUDY SCHULTZ
AVAILABLE IN BOOKSTORES • WWW.BLUECOUCHBOOKS.COM
6 X 9 PAPERBACK • 256 PAGES • $22.95 CDN • $16.95 US